PERSONALITY
IN MIDDLE
AND LATE LIFE

This is a volume in the
Arno Press collection

GROWING OLD

Advisory Editor
Leon Stein

See last pages of this volume
for a complete list of titles

PERSONALITY
IN MIDDLE
AND LATE LIFE

Bernice L. Neugarten, et al.

ARNO PRESS

A New York Times Company
New York • 1980

Editorial Supervision: BRIAN QUINN

———

Reprint Edition 1980 by Arno Press Inc.

GROWING OLD
ISBN for complete set: 0-405-12813-4
See last pages of this volume for titles.

Manufactured in the United States of America

———

Library of Congress Cataloging in Publication Data

Neugarten, Bernice Levin, 1916-
    Personality in middle and late life.

    (Growing old)
    Reprint of the ed. published by Atherton Press,
New York, in series: Atherton Press behavioral science
series.
    Bibliography: p.
    Includes index.
    1. Middle age--Psychological aspects. 2. Aged--
Psychology. 3. Personality. I. Title. II. Series.
[BF724.6.N42 1980]   155.6   79-8677
ISBN 0-405-12794-4

PERSONALITY IN MIDDLE AND LATE LIFE

PERSONALITY IN MIDDLE AND LATE LIFE
Empirical Studies

Bernice L. Neugarten

in collaboration with
Howard Berkowitz
William J. Crotty
Walter Gruen
David L. Gutmann
Marc I. Lubin
David L. Miller
Robert F. Peck
Jacqueline L. Rosen
Alexey Shukin
Sheldon S. Tobin

and with the
editorial assistance of
Jacqueline M. Falk

Atherton Press
70 Fifth Avenue
New York 10011
1964

PERSONALITY IN MIDDLE AND LATE LIFE
Empirical Studies
Bernice L. Neugarten & Associates

Copyright © 1964 by Prentice-Hall, Inc.
Atherton Press, New York, New York

Atherton Press, A Division of Prentice-Hall, Inc.
70 Fifth Avenue, New York, New York 10011

Printed in the United States of America 65769

THE ATHERTON PRESS
BEHAVIORAL SCIENCE SERIES

William E. Henry, General Editor

The University of Chicago

PREFACE

This volume consists of a series of studies of personality based on psychological data gathered in connection with the Kansas City Studies of Adult Life. The studies constituted large-scale investigations of the social and psychological aspects of middle age and aging carried out under the sponsorship of The Committee on Human Development of The University of Chicago in the years 1952 to 1962.

During the first years of the project, a large field staff in Kansas City gathered cross-sectional data on more than seven hundred men and women aged forty to seventy from all social-status levels. The primary focus was on middle age and the variations that occur in life styles and in social-psychological patterns of behavior with age, sex, and social status. This first set of studies was financed by a grant from the Carnegie Corporation and was conducted by a research

committee of which Robert J. Havighurst was chairman and which
included for varying intervals Ernest W. Burgess, Richard A. Cole-
man, Walter Gruen, William E. Henry, Everett C. Hughes, Martin
B. Loeb, Bernice L. Neugarten, Robert F. Peck, Warren A. Peterson,
David Riesman, John Scott, Ethel Shanas, and W. Lloyd Warner.

The second group of studies focused on changes that occur over
time in middle-aged and older persons. A panel of men and women
aged forty-nine to sixty-nine and a group of older persons between
seventy and ninety, nearly three hundred subjects in all, were interviewed at intervals over a six-year period. This group of studies was
financed by a grant from the Professional Services Branch, National
Institute of Mental Health (#M-9082), with William E. Henry as
principal investigator, with Robert J. Havighurst and Bernice L.
Neugarten as co-principal investigators, and with the collaboration
and support of Richard H. Williams.

Kansas City was chosen as the site for the studies of adult life for
several reasons. Adult behavior was to be viewed in an urban setting, and, in order to understand that setting, it was planned from
the outset to carry out certain investigations of the community itself,
in particular, studies of the social-status structure. These plans made
it necessary to select a site that, although urban in character, would
not be so large that its inhabitants would have lost the sense of living in a community. Neither could the city be so large or so complex
as to preclude the possibility of completing the descriptions of the
community setting as one of the first phases of the research. Most
important in choosing a city was the fact that a cooperative arrange-
ment was made with Community Studies, Inc., a local social science
research organization then under the direction of William D. Bryant,
which had already gathered much of the basic data needed for a
project of this scope. Members of Dr. Bryant's staff were of particular assistance in planning the sampling designs and carrying out the
field work. In Appendix A methods of sampling are described for
both sets of the Kansas City Studies.

A large number of publications based on these studies have already appeared, dealing with social role performance, leisure patterns, age status, social status and social mobility, adjustment patterns, the disengagement theory of aging, and related topics. The

present volume brings together the series of investigations that dealt with personality and which, with a few exceptions, have not been reported elsewhere. The contributors to the present book were affiliated with The Committee on Human Development as members of the research team or field staff or as graduate students in the years in which the Kansas City Studies were in progress.

CONTENTS

COLLABORATORS

Howard Berkowitz, Ph.D.
*Professor of Psychology, State University College
Oneonta, New York*

William J. Crotty, Ph.D.
*Administrator, Northwest Cooperative
Community Mental Health Clinic,
Arlington Heights, Illinois*

Walter Gruen, Ph.D.
*Psychologist, Veterans Administration Hospital
Canandaigua, New York*

David L. Gutmann, Ph.D.
*Assistant Professor, Department of Psychology
University of Michigan, Ann Arbor*

Marc I. Lubin, M.A.
*The Committee on Human Development
The University of Chicago*

David L. Miller, Ph.D.
Staff Psychologist
Illinois State Psychiatric Institute, Chicago

Bernice L. Neugarten, Ph.D.
Associate Professor, The Committee on Human Development
The University of Chicago

Robert F. Peck, Ph.D.
Professor of Educational Psychology
University of Texas, Austin

Jacqueline L. Rosen, Ph.D.
Research Psychologist, Beth Israel Hospital, Boston
Instructor in Psychology, Department of Psychiatry
Harvard University Medical School, Cambridge, Massachusetts

Alexey Shukin, Ph.D.
Assistant Professor of Psychology
George Williams College, Chicago

Sheldon S. Tobin, Ph.D.
Instructor, The Committee on Human Development
The University of Chicago

INTRODUCTION

Bernice L. Neugarten

Knowledge of personality changes in the second half of life is meager. Relatively few empirical studies are available from which findings can be generalized, nor is there an integrated body of developmental theory that encompasses the total life span and that provides impetus for research in this field. As a consequence, the eight studies presented in this volume should be viewed as exploratory. A variety of research strategies have been utilized, one after another, with regard both to theory and to method. As a group the studies illustrate the usefulness and the limitations of various research instruments and a number of theoretical and conceptual approaches to the topic. An underlying aim common to all the studies has been to operationalize theoretical constructs and, by moving from theory to data and back again, to help shape both to the research question: What are the changes in personality that are associated with chronological age in the second half of life?

The context in which these studies were undertaken should be briefly described. The paucity of developmental studies of adulthood may be traced to various factors, not least, perhaps, to the intellectual climate which in the past has encouraged psychologists to focus attention on the child rather than the adult. Thus far the developmental psychologist has been particularly handicapped by lack of theory. Although attention to developmental issues is growing, as witnessed by the present *rapprochements* between learning theorists and psychoanalytic theorists and between developmental theory and research in cognitive processes (for example, Bruner, 1964), attention has been focused primarily on the first part of life, and the issues have not yet been projected into adulthood. Dynamic theories of personality, on the other hand, with the notable exception of Erikson's formulation of the eight stages of ego development (Erikson, 1950; elaborated in Erikson, 1953; Erikson, 1956; Erikson, 1959), have not been concerned with the problem of change in adulthood, and there still is widespread and uncritical acceptance of the view that the personality is stabilized, if not fixed, by the time early adulthood is reached.

These obstacles have been compounded by problems of sampling and method. Sampling becomes increasingly difficult as investigators move up the age range from childhood to young adulthood to old age. The captive research groups available in nurseries, schools, and colleges are lost; adults have different, sometimes suspect, motives for participating in research projects; and investigators become aware that, as the age of their subjects increases, they must be increasingly wary about generalizing to normal groups from what may be deviant samples (such as generalizing from volunteers to nonvolunteers or from the institutionalized to the noninstitutionalized aged).

From a developmental point of view, there is also difficulty in the fact that the rhythm of change in adulthood differs from that in childhood. A year, which is so long an interval in the early stages of life, is a very short interval in later stages. Long intervals must therefore be used as units. Yet there is the difficulty that, the longer the intervals or the more the samples are separated by chronological age in the attempt to highlight age differences, the more other characteristics will operate to confound the age variable itself. For instance, if a group of young persons are to be equated with a group of middle-aged with regard to educational level, systematic bias with regard to socioeconomic level is likely to be introduced. This distortion grows in geometric proportion as the age interval between groups is enlarged. Nor can the effects of survival bias be evaluated; that is, what types of people have died, and what types have survived. Yet the effects of this selectivity become greater and greater at advanced ages. If, furthermore, investigators are cautious about drawing inferences with regard to developmental changes from studies based on cross-sectional data, they face the added difficulties inherent in carrying out longitudinal research over the long intervals required to produce meaningful findings for adult subjects.

This is to say nothing of the difficulty involved in disentangling the effects of historical and social changes in the society from the effects of increasing age per se. This problem also occurs in studies of children and adolescents, but it is particularly salient in studies of adults. It is true that longitudinal approaches, as compared with cross-sectional, provide some measure of control over the latter factors; yet investigators of adult phenomena are becoming increasingly aware (Kuhlen, 1963) that both cross-sectional and longitudinal approaches are vulnerable on this score. The effects of social change and historical influences are not easily separable from developmental changes, even when the data have been obtained from repeated observations of the same individuals. Nor is it often possible to control at least partially for these factors—to design a meaningful study in which observations are made, for instance, on one group of persons when they are forty and again when they are fifty; on a second group who are forty when the first group reaches fifty; and in which comparisons are then drawn between Time 1-Time 2 and Group 1-Group 2 differences.

Another problem related to choice of method is that of generalizing from behavior in the experimentally controlled situation or from test performance to behavior in the real-life situation. The difficulty is not unknown to child psychologists, but it appears likely that it weighs even more heavily in studies of adult personality. A recent example is provided in a study of a group of healthy aged men (Birren, Butler, Greenhouse, Sokoloff, & Yarrow, 1963) where relative autonomy was found, on the one hand, between a set of measures based on psychological test performance (including projective tests of personality) and, on the other hand, evaluations of purposive-adaptational behavior in everyday activities in the community. The gap between presently available methods of studying personality and the usefulness of these methods in differentiating among normal adults—a gap that is not always given the consideration it merits—has also probably operated to discourage research on adulthood. In somewhat different words, the problems of studying adult personality are confounded by questions regarding the selection of suitable methods in an area in which suitable criteria have yet to be defined.

This situation was even more true in the 1950's, when the present series of investigations was initiated. Previous studies of personality had been based on small samples of volunteers, on psychiatric patients, or on groups of institutionalized older people. That which was known about normal adult personality had been extrapolated for the most part from studies of clinical groups and represented, in general, the presumed absence of pathological phenomena found in these groups. Psychological terminologies were often inappropriate for describing normal patterns of behavior and for characterizing personality processes in the mature rather than the immature individual.

The eight studies presented here should be viewed in the context just described. All these studies share one important characteristic—they are all based on relatively large study populations drawn from the same pool of over seven hundred cases on whom psychological data had been gathered in connection with the Kansas City Studies of Adult Life. This pool was built up from probability samples of adults aged forty and over, all of whom were living in their own homes and participating in the usual round of activities characteristic of functioning members of the community. None of these persons were volunteers, but were men and women who, following various degrees of persuasion by members of the field staff, had agreed to be interviewed one or more times. (A more detailed description of the samples is given in Appendix A).

Although the eight studies reported here are self-contained units and may be read as such, they constitute a related set of inquiries, as can be seen in the following brief account.

In the first study, Erikson's theory of ego development provided the frame of reference. As already implied, this theory stands not only as a landmark in the field of psychoanalytic ego psychology, but, at the time this series of studies was begun, provided the solitary example of a developmental theory of personality which specifically encompassed adulthood as well as childhood and adolescence. In this instance, an attempt was made to operationalize the theory by conceiving Erikson's eight stages of ego development as personality variables and by devising rating scales by which to measure the variables. The ratings were then analyzed for age, sex, and social-class, differences.

In the second study, a different framework was utilized. The investigators began by defining the major crises faced by persons in the middle and later years of life and then defined the personality characteristics required to master such crises. A set of personality variables that were regarded as the most relevant for good adjustment was formulated, and a set of rating scales by which to study individuals of various age, sex, and social-status backgrounds was devised.

In neither of the first two studies were consistent age differences discovered. In the third, the focus was turned away from interview data to projective test data that could be coded, analyzed without awareness of the subject's age, then decoded. A specially devised TAT picture was used to elicit images of adult age-sex roles, and these images were then analyzed with regard to underlying personality processes in the respondents. This was the first in this series of studies to demonstrate consistent age differences in personality processes in the years from forty to seventy. As such, it provided a major impetus for the subsequent investigations.

Building on the preceding study but drawing from the writings of other ego psychologists, the investigators in the fourth study formulated a construct of "ego energy" and operationalized the construct in terms of variables measurable from TAT protocols. Although this study, like the preceding one, was based on projective data, it provides a contrast in method. In the former, the method was essentially inductive, with descriptive categories emerging from the data. Here, with hypotheses formulated in advance and tested statistically by analysis of variance, the design was a more rigorous one. The findings from both studies were congruent in supporting the interpretation that certain ego qualities in the personality become more constricted with age in the period from the forties to the seventies.

In the fifth study in this series, the set of TAT protocols used in the preceding study was reanalyzed, this time utilizing a set of variables that had proved useful in clinical practice. This study had been planned as a replication—one in which a second system of measurement was to be applied to the same set of data, rather than the more typical replication in which the same system of measurement is applied to a second set of data—with the anticipation that the age differences demonstrated in the third and fourth studies would be verified and extended. The findings were surprising, however, for age differences did not appear. This provided somewhat serendipitous evidence that personality constructs useful in clinical settings, and measures derived from them, may be quite unsuccessful in developmental studies of adults.

In the sixth study, the investigator followed another of the leads from the findings described in Chapter 3—that, with advancing age, there is increased difficulty in dealing with impulse life. Using a more elaborate set of projective protocols and again working inductively, the researcher developed a typology of "mastery" styles that refer to covert ego-coping and ego-defense processes. The styles were then elaborated in terms of other sets of data on the same individuals. In interpreting his findings, the author has presented his views that personality change in aging males follows a different course from that in aging females.

The seventh study represents another conceptual approach. Here the investigators followed a lead provided by the disengagement theory (Cumming & Henry, 1961) to the effect that certain changes in personality can be expected to accompany decreased social interaction as individuals grow old. A set of personality variables that presumably reflected psychological disengagement was formulated. The ratings on these variables were found to correlate with age but not with the extent of social interaction.

The final study in this series is one in which, using a model of personality based upon psychoanalytic and ego concepts, the investigators defined a large set of variables and then used techniques of factor analysis and obverse factor analysis to establish one set of personality types for men and one set for women. The types that emerged were then studied in relation to age and to independent ratings of adjustment.

The studies are presented here in the order in which they were undertaken, but they fall into two groups—those which demonstrate significant age change (chapters 3, 4, 6, 7) and those which do not (chapters 1, 2, 8). The difference between the two groups is discussed in the final chapter, which is a summary of the eight studies and a statement of the implications for future research. The reader may prefer, however, to begin with Chapter 8, in which the descriptions of the types may serve to communicate something of the quality and the variety of personalities which constituted the subject matter of these investigations.

Although chronological age has been a major variable throughout the series, all these studies, with the exception of the addendum to Chapter 4, are cross-sectional. Inferences regarding changes with age are, therefore, based on observed differences among age groups and should be interpreted cautiously with regard to processes of change over time.

PERSONALITY
IN MIDDLE AND
LATE LIFE

1

ADULT PERSONALITY: AN EMPIRICAL STUDY OF ERIKSON'S THEORY OF EGO DEVELOPMENT

Walter Gruen

In most personality theories adulthood is viewed as the period of relative stability. It is presumed that, once adolescence is over, the personality structure no longer undergoes major changes and that the behavior of adults can be ascribed to underlying patterns laid down in childhood. A few investigators, on the other hand, have indicated that profound changes which may systematically affect the consistency and organization of behavior may occur in adulthood. There are, for example, Jung's concept of individuation in the older adult, Maslow's discussion of self-esteem and self-actualization needs as important focuses of developing adult personality, and Fromm's concepts of "productivity" (Fromm, 1941; Jung, 1933; Maslow, 1954). For a more systematic formulation of personality variables that would be relevant to a study of age differences in samples of middle-aged people, however, we turned to Erik H. Erikson's formulations of ego development.

Erikson's observations have been drawn not only from his long experience as a practicing psychoanalyst, but also from his field-work studies of personality development in two American Indian societies. His observations have been systematized into a develop-mental theory in which there are postulated eight stages of ego de-velopment from infancy to old age, each stage related to the increasing complexity of function in the maturing organism (Erik-son, 1950).

Each of the eight so-called nuclear stages of ego development represents a choice for the expanding ego at successive chronolog-ical periods of life. The resolutions of ego crises and their expression in behavior determine for Erikson the future development of the personality and the individual's reactions to people and to objects, his success in adapting both to external and internal demands, and his perception and evaluation of self. Erikson's theory represents a systematic formulation of the effects of maturation, experience, and social institutions on the growing individual, hence on personality organization. Growth is seen as a continuous process, neither sta-bilized nor completed when the individual reaches physical maturity.

The eight basic stages of ego development are (1) in early in-fancy, development of a sense of basic trust versus a sense of dis-trust; (2) in later infancy, when anal-muscular maturation has occurred, a growing sense of autonomy versus a sense of shame and doubt; (3) in early childhood, the period of greatest locomotor de-velopment, a developing sense of initiative versus a sense of guilt; (4) in the middle years of childhood, the latency period, a sense of industry versus a sense of inferiority; (5) in adolescence, a sense of ego identity (certainty and a sense of belonging regarding career, sex role, and system of values) versus role diffusion; (6) in early adulthood, the development of intimacy (mutuality with a loved partner of the opposite sex with whom one is able to regulate the cycles of work, procreation, and recreation) versus a sense of ego isolation; (7) in middle adulthood, the development of generativity (expansion of ego interests and libidinal cathexes and a sense of having contributed to the future) versus a sense of ego stagnation;

and (8) in late adulthood, a sense of ego integrity (a basic acceptance of one's life as having been inevitable, appropriate, and meaningful) versus a sense of despair (fear of death).

When the present investigation was undertaken, Erikson's theory had not yet been used in research in nonclinical settings. Not only did the theory need to be operationalized, but also, in this instance, procedures had to be devised whereby it could be used with cross-sectional rather than with longitudinal data and with data obtainable through field-work interviewing. Certain adaptations and translations of the theory were necessary, therefore, to make it applicable to the present purposes.

The eight stages of ego development were accordingly defined as personality dimensions, each operating as a predisposing tendency within a relatively wide range of behavior. The two extremes of each dimension were defined by Erikson's descriptions of the consequences for personality that emerge when the ego conflict is resolved in one or the other direction. Thus, for example, the resolution of the trust issue in early infancy provided the basis for a personality dimension used here that was called "trust-mistrust" and that was assumed to be operating in the adult personality. This approach is in keeping with Erikson's statement that, although a particular issue constitutes the nuclear conflict for the ego at each developmental stage, the same issue is also present in preceding and later stages. For instance, problems of ego identity are predominant in adolescence, but the issue of ego identity is also present during childhood, although in embryonic form, and adulthood, although in a form modified by the individual's increased complexity and experience. Similarly, a rudimentary solution of the integrity-despair conflict influences behavior at earlier ages, but in less perceivable ways than in old age.

With the eight stages of ego development conceived as eight dimensions of personality, rating scales were then devised for assessing these dimensions. Erikson has described in some detail the behavior that accompanies alternative solutions of ego conflicts at early stages of development, but he has dealt only summarily with adult behavior and with the last three stages—intimacy, generativity, and integrity. The task for the investigator was, therefore, to signify the behavior and the attitudes that illustrated each of the eight dimensions in a middle-aged adult. The eight dimensions were defined in relatively narrow terms. The investigator took what he interpreted as the essence of the dimension and did not, in those cases where the opportunity existed, attempt to deal with the several corollary manifestations described by Erikson. The definitions of the personality dimensions appear below.

After deciding to use the eight stages of ego development as scalable dimensions of personality, the investigator decided to view them as independent. It was recognized that, in doing so, the study was departing from Erikson's theory that a solution at any one stage of ego development affects all subsequent solutions and that, for instance, an individual cannot successfully resolve issues of intimacy if he has not first successfully resolved issues of ego identity. Treating the dimensions as if they were independent, however, made it possible to explore this aspect of the theory.

After several pretrials, a ten-point rating scale was adopted for each dimension, with the expectation that the use of a refined scale would provide greater spread of the ratings and would thus prove advantageous in correlational analysis of the data. As results subsequently showed, however, these scales required somewhat finer discriminations between respondents than raters could comfortably achieve, and the use of such refined scales undoubtedly lowered the reliabilities of raters' judgments. The high and low points of the scales were defined as follows:

1. "Trust versus distrust"

   a) Makes statements about liking and trusting his work associates, friends, relatives. Feels essentially optimistic about people and their motives. Confides in someone.
   b) Makes statements of distrust about people, about associates. Prefers to be alone because the cultivating of friends "gets you into trouble." Dislikes confiding in anyone.

2. "Autonomy versus doubt and shame"

a) Shows and emphasizes that his attitudes and his ways of doing things are his own and not necessarily followed because others expect it of him. Not afraid to hold opinions of his own or to insist on doing what he likes. Enjoys having his own opinions and carrying out his own ideas.

b) Shows a good deal of self-consciousness about his ideas and his ways of doing things. Prefers to stay within the tried and trusted ways and avoids asserting himself against his group. Will emphasize how much like others he acts and feels.

3. "Initiative versus guilt"

a) The emphasis here is on planning and taking pleasure in the initiation of action. Not so much self-assertion as in autonomy, but in the enjoyment of activity that stems from one's own incentives. Likes to plan ahead and design his schedule. Takes initiative in arranging his day, his work, his life, his environment.

b) Lets others initiate for him. Feels defeated about his efforts, about his own attempts to plan his day, his work, his life. Plays down any success or accomplishment.

4. "Industry versus inferiority" (referring to skill mastery, not achievement mastery)

a) Likes to make things and carry them out to completion. Skill mastery. Enjoys seeing things done. Has some hobby and feels capable in it. Takes a good deal of pride in what he has made and produced as far as activities, hobbies, and products are concerned.

b) Shows passivity. Leaves things undone or does not get to things or tasks. Feels inadequate about his abilities to do things, produce work.

5. "Ego identity versus role diffusion"

a) Has rather strongly defined social roles—feels at home in his work, his family, his affiliations, his sex role, and so on, by indicating that he enjoys carrying out role behavior. There is a sense of belonging to groups, a sense of comfort with his style of life and his daily activities. Is very definite about himself and who he is. Feeling of continuity with past and present self.

b) Is rather ill at ease in the roles he has to play. Feels lost in his groups, affiliations, and so on. Does not enter into required role behavior with much conviction. May have history of radical switches in work, residence, and so on, especially in sequences that seem devoid of meaning or purpose.

6. "Intimacy versus isolation"

a) Has a close intimate relationship with spouse and with one, two, or more friends (shares thoughts, spends time with, expresses warm feelings for). Depends on and confides in them and provides mutuality in the relationship. Strong and mutual emotional attachments.

b) Lives relatively isolated from friends, spouse, children. Avoids contact with others on intimate basis. Either absorbed in self or indiscriminately sociable. Relations with people are stereotyped and/or formalized.

7. "Generativity versus ego stagnation"

a) Has plans for the future that require sustained application and the utilization of skills and abilities. Implies continuity of his life with the future by investing energy and ideas into something new; not merely passive adaptation to what is given. If he has children, he takes an active interest in their development and a part in their education. A sense of continuity with the future generation. Attempts at immortality by directing his efforts toward activities and products that will leave memories and traces.

b) Seems to be vegetating. Does nothing more than the routines of work and necessary daily activities. Is not active with children, home, outside activities, or projects. Preoccupied with himself.

8. "Integrity versus despair"

    a) Respondent feels satisfied and happy with his life, his work, his accomplishments. Accepts responsibility for his life. Maximizes his successes.

    b) Feels depressed and unhappy about his life, emphasizes failures. Would change his life, career, and so on if he had another chance. Does not accept his present age and mode of life. Emphasis is on the past. Fear of getting older. Fear of death.

The Sample and the Data

Following the general design of sampling described in Appendix A, this study population consisted of 108 cases distributed by age, sex, and social class as shown in Table 1.1.

TABLE 1.1

THE SAMPLE

Age	Social class				Total
	Upper middle	Lower middle	Working	Lower	
MEN					
40–45	4	6	6	5	21
50–55	5	6	4	4	19
60–65	4	5	3	4	16
Total	13	17	13	13	56
WOMEN					
40–45	5	6	5	4	20
50–55	4	6	2	6	18
60–65	2	5	4	3	14
Total	11	17	11	13	52

The ratings were made on the basis of interview data. The interview schedule, carefully designed and pretested and requiring approximately two hours of the respondent's time, contained fifty-five open-ended questions covering a variety of topics in roughly the following order: attitudes about job and social status; retirement and plans for the future; use of leisure time; health (and, for women, the menopause) ; attitudes toward present age and aging; marriage and the marriage partner; attitudes toward and plans for children; religion; concepts of God, death, and afterlife; friendship patterns; the expression of various emotional states (anxiety, loneliness, anger) ; general evaluation of life (including major successes and failures) ; comparison of the present with the past; awareness of changes in the self over the years; accounts of best and worst years.

The interviewers, with one exception, were graduate students in psychology who had had experience in clinical settings or who had had considerable interviewing experience. Interviewers were carefully trained to take notes as verbatim as possible during the interview and to fill in more details from memory immediately afterward. The interviewer also filled out a check list describing the dress, appearance, and behavior of the respondent and wrote a thumbnail sketch of the way in which the respondent handled the interviewing situation and the relationship established between respondent and interviewer.

Findings

Reliability of Ratings

Two judges independently rated forty-eight randomly selected records on the eight personality dimensions. Correlations between the two sets of ratings were .51, .51, .59, .62, .71, .73, .72, and .79 for the eight dimensions respectively. Reliabilities for the first four dimensions are much lower than for the last four, perhaps because of greater difficulty in defining behavioral correlates in adulthood for those personality dimensions that are most pertinent to childhood developmental stages.

Relations between Dimensions

Table 1.2 shows that the correlations between the eight dimensions were consistently positive, varying from .34 to .74 (with a mean of .57), all of them statistically reliable. The highest correlations were generally those occurring between adjacent dimensions, that is, those assumed by Erikson to be chronologically adjacent in the development of the ego.

TABLE 1.2

CORRELATIONS BETWEEN THE EIGHT PERSONALITY DIMENSIONS

	1	2	3	4	5	6	7	8
1. Trust	—	.48	.40	.39	.48	.56	.42	.34
2. Autonomy		—	.66	.57	.61	.44	.53	.44
3. Initiative			—	.70	.65	.54	.66	.64
4. Industry				—	.70	.57	.68	.62
5. Ego identity					—	.70	.74	.61
6. Intimacy						—	.71	.57
7. Generativity							—	.66
8. Integrity								—

These results tend to bear out to some extent Erikson's assumptions of stages in development and of the influence of earlier ego solutions on subsequent ones. On the other hand, these data are by no means so clear nor so consistent as the theory might lead one to anticipate. The difficulty may lie, of course, with the methods used here. The investigator may not have succeeded in defining behaviorally the dimensions of personality that Erikson had in mind; the data may have been too scant and too superficial; there may have been a halo effect in making the ratings. Whatever the importance of these factors, the findings may be interpreted to support this aspect of Erikson's theory.

Age, Sex, and Social-Class Differences

In order to determine the relationships between the personality ratings and age, sex, and social class, an analysis of variance design was undertaken. If all cells had contained an equal number of cases, an analysis of variance design of triple classification with N cases per cell could have been used. Because, however, the number of cases varied from one cell to the next, a compromise was reached by calculating means for each cell and treating these means as single entries for an analysis based on triple classification, with the three sources of variation being age, sex, and social class. This method introduced the possibility that, in the four cells with only two or three cases, one deviant case would greatly influence the mean rating. This method, however, enforced a very stringent criterion for testing F ratios, since the ratios had to be referred to a distribution based on only twenty-four cases (twenty-four cell entries) rather than to one based on 108 cases. Although this method may have obscured a number of significant trends, it made it possible to reject more confidently the null hypothesis for any F ratios found to be significantly different from chance.

For the first four personality dimensions, none of the sources of variance contributed significantly to the total variance. The data on these four dimensions have been omitted from tables 1.3 and 1.4 not only because no significant group differences were found, but also because, as already indicated, the judges' agreement in rating these dimensions was relatively low, indicating that the definitions of those variables were not altogether communicable.

Examination of tables 1.3 and 1.4 shows relatively few statistically significant results with regard to ego identity, intimacy, generativity, or integrity. With due regard to the absence of systematic sex or social-class differences, it was the absence of age differences which was most unexpected—especially on the last two dimensions, which, according to Erikson, are embryonic in the personality organization of the young adult but become focal at later ages. It is possible that, in our adaptation of Erikson's theories, we have gone a step further than he himself would find warranted. To say that generativity is the focal problem for ego development in the middle years of life is not synonymous with saying that middle-aged persons should rate higher on generativity than young adults. To face a problem is not necessarily to solve it successfully. It was anticipated, nevertheless, that, given our nonclinical sample of normally functioning adults, there would be higher scores with age on at least the dimensions of generativity and integrity. (It is possible that the age range forty to sixty-five is not sufficient to reveal major age differ-

TABLE 1.3

MEAN RATINGS ON EGO IDENTITY, INTIMACY, GENERATIVITY, AND INTEGRITY

Dimensions	Social class			Lower	Age group			Total
	Upper middle	Lower middle	Work-ing		40–45	50–55	60–65	
			MEN					
Ego identity	6.03	6.65	6.06	5.45	6.24	5.69	6.21	6.05
Intimacy	4.32	5.48	5.36	3.27	5.10	4.53	4.19	4.61
Generativity	4.77	5.73	5.00	4.25	5.15	4.49	5.18	4.94
Integrity	4.52	4.93	5.19	4.43	5.01	3.72	5.58	4.77
			WOMEN					
Ego identity	5.36	6.03	6.15	6.17	5.79	5.94	6.05	5.93
Intimacy	5.55	6.68	5.47	5.17	5.20	5.90	6.05	5.72
Generativity	4.47	5.53	5.43	5.89	5.01	5.59	5.40	5.33
Integrity	3.63	4.81	4.08	3.83	3.98	4.63	3.67	4.09

ences. It would be useful, in this connection, to compare these ratings with similar ratings of younger and older samples.)

On the dimension of ego identity, none of the three sources of variation had systematic influence on the total variance observed. According to Erikson, the issue of ego identity is focal during adolescence. It may well be, as our findings seem to indicate, that, once a person has moved far beyond adolescence and into middle age, his manner of dealing with this issue is based on idiosyncratic adjustment patterns.

On intimacy women had significantly higher ratings than did

TABLE 1.4

VARIANCE ESTIMATES FROM THE ANALYSIS OF VARIANCE OF RATINGS
ON EGO IDENTITY, INTIMACY, GENERATIVITY, AND INTEGRITY

Source of variance	Degrees of freedom	Variance estimates			
		Ego identity	Inti-macy	Gener-ativity	Integ-rity
Sex	1	.09	7.37*	.93	2.77†
Social class	3	.51	3.70*	1.06	.90
Age	2	.20	.02	.15	.43
Sex–social-class interaction	3	.65	.83	1.19	.27
Sex-age interaction	2	.24	1.64	.80	4.14*
Age–social-class interaction	6	.80	.88	.63	.83
Triple interaction	6	.35	.76	.60	.65

* The F ratio is significant beyond the .05 level. Although it is possible that this finding occurred by chance, it should also be kept in mind that the F ratio is based on only twenty-four observations (the means of twenty-four cells), rather than on 108, and hence reflects a much more stringent criterion of significance.

† The F ratio is significant at the .07 level.

men, especially in the fifty- and sixty-year age groups. Perhaps this is because of the greater preoccupation with work and loss of work in men who are facing retirement. The issue of retirement may produce increasing feelings of inadequacy and greater preoccupation with self-feelings which, in turn, might make men less able to be intimately involved with others. Women, on the other hand, may maintain close affective ties with children and grandchildren and may experience less discontinuity in personal relationships. Whatever the correct explanation, these findings with regard to intimacy seem to be in agreement with Neugarten and Gutmann's findings based on projective data (see Chapter 3). There, in a similar sample of forty- to seventy-year-olds, older men were seen, in the stories of older respondents, more and more as isolated and as ineffectual members of the family. The higher ratings on intimacy for lower-middle- and working-class groups may be a reflection of the intensive emphasis on social mobility and achievement that is presumably characteristic of the upper-middle class, on the one hand, and of the relatively unstable and shifting life patterns characteristic of the lower class, on the other hand, neither of which is conducive to the development of close relationships or a firm sense of intimacy.

No significant group differences were apparent on the generativity dimension (although the difference between average ratings for men and women as shown in Table 1.4 was significant at the .01 level).

On integrity, there was a significant age-sex interaction, with the fifty- to fifty-five-year-old women rating higher than the other groups of women and with the fifty- to fifty-five year-old men rating lower than the other groups of men. The factors that might underlie this reversal in trend for the two sexes at age fifty–fifty-five are not readily apparent.

Summary

A review of these results suggests, first, that the utilization of Erikson's model of personality in assessing adult personality was relatively successful in this pilot study. The proposed stages of ego development were translated into personality dimensions which could be rated from interview data. These ratings proved to be reliable above the level usually required for group comparisons. If the scales can be further refined, they may prove useful also in individual case analysis.

Second, the translation of the theory into empirical measuring devices has made possible at least an initial step in testing some of the assumptions of that theory. This initial step is represented in this study by the correlations obtained between the dimensions. Although the possibility of rater bias or halo effect was not completely con-

trolled here, the correlations suggest that the hypothesized inter-
dependence of ego dimensions and their proposed hierarchical order
has some validity.

Third, the dimensions that, according to the theory, were seen as
most salient in adult personality development did not yield many
significant group differences. Notwithstanding the need for caution
because of the small number of cases and the exploratory nature of
the methods, the indication is that within the age range of the
present sample there are no major group differences by age, sex, or
social class. This finding tends to put the major emphasis of personality dynamics, at least as expressed in the last four of Erikson's ego
dimensions, on individual factors in development.

2

PERSONALITY AND ADJUSTMENT IN MIDDLE AGE

Robert F. Peck

Howard Berkowitz

In this study, two general questions were posed: (1) What attributes of personality are required to adjust to life successfully during middle age? (2) What effects does age have on the individual's adaptive powers and on personal adjustment?[1]

Erikson (1950) has described eight stages of man and certain key psychological characteristics which are essential to successful adaptation. His first seven stages cover childhood, adolescence, and young adulthood. The rest of the life cycle is given to the eighth stage, ego integrity versus despair. Many major changes occur, however, through the long years of the second half of life—decline in physical vigor, menopause in the female, departure of children from

[1] Some of the data presented in this chapter were reported in *Geriatrics,* 1960, **15,** 124–130, and are included here with the permission of *Geriatrics.*

the home, retirement from work, grandparenthood, and widowhood. These biological and social changes pose very different psychological challenges to the aging individual. An effort was made earlier to identify several crisis stages (Peck, 1956). It was proposed that particular adaptive capacities become salient, one after another, as the adult attempts to resolve successfully the psychological crisis that accompanies each stage of development. It was suggested that this developmental theory would provide an appropriate frame of reference and that the capacities or psychological attributes that follow from the theory would provide a set of meaningful variables for studies of personality and adjustment in the second half of life.

In the present study, because only cross-sectional data were available, it was not possible to study individuals as they moved through middle and old age; thus certain aspects of the developmental theory could not be directly investigated. Seven psychological attributes were, however, conceptualized as variables that could be measured empirically.

1. "Cathectic flexibility" is the capacity to invest strong, meaningful emotion in new activities, new relationships, new experiences. The individual does not cling to old psychological attachments which are no longer possible to maintain, nor does he feel that life is meaningless when a psychological loss occurs. This quality might equally well be called "emotional flexibility"—the capacity to shift emotional investments from one person to another and from one activity to another. In some ways, this capacity cuts across all adjustive shifts that are made throughout life. It becomes more crucial in middle age than at earlier ages, perhaps, because middle age is the period when parents die, children grow up and leave home, and the individual's circle of friends and relatives begins to be broken by death.

Some people suffer an increasingly impoverished emotional life through the middle and later years because, as their cathexis objects disappear, they are unable to reinvest their emotions in other people or in other pursuits. For others it is in the middle years that they have the greatest range of potential cathexis objects, when they have the widest circle of acquaintances, when they have achieved informal and formal status as experienced people to whom others turn, and when they have contacts with the widest range of people, from young to old. It may be that experience with a greater variety of people and roles can lead to a more complex set of relationships in middle age than is possible at younger ages.

Hence middle age is a developmental stage where positive adaptation requires new learning—not only of new cathexes, but of a generalized set toward forming new cathexes (or redefining existing relationships, as in the case with one's grown-up children). The death of parents and the departure of children are new experiences. Because primary ties with parents and children are so important to most people, the adaptive problems posed when these ties are broken or changed become crucial.

2. "Mental flexibility" is the capacity to use, in the solution of new problems, experience and prior mental sets as provisional guides rather than as fixed, inflexible rules. It implies open-mindedness, as opposed to dogmatic, opinionated, or passive closed-mindedness.

There is a widespread assumption that people, as they go through the middle years, tend to grow increasingly inflexible in their opinions and actions and close-minded to new ideas. Middle rather than old age is probably the time when mental flexibility becomes a critical issue, for it is in the middle years that most people have attained their peak status, when they feel they have worked out a set of answers to life, and when, at least in some ways, they may forgo strenuous effort to envision new or different patterns of thought and action.

3. "Ego differentiation" is the capacity to pursue and to enjoy a varied set of major activities in life and to value oneself for a number of personal attributes, not to rely entirely on one or two life roles (for example, worker or parent) for a sense of self-worth or for enjoyment and meaning in life.

A major crisis, particularly for men in our society, is created by the impact of retirement. Retirement may call forth a general shift in the value system by which the individual can reappraise and redefine his worth and can take satisfaction in a range of role activities broader than the work role. Although the process of ego differentiation begins in early childhood, it becomes a central issue at the time of retirement. For many men, the ability to find a sense of self-worth in activities other than work seems to make a major difference between a despairing loss of meaning in life and a continued, vital interest in living. For many women, this stage may arrive when their role as mother is drastically diminished by the departure of grown children. Thus the crisis that accompanies loss of work role may well come earlier for women than for men.

There is an even broader issue at stake, however. For many, retirement means a sharp reduction in income, usually bringing with it a reduced standard of living. Many retired people, furthermore, must adjust to a new state of dependence on others, in sharp contrast to their long experience of self-sufficiency and self-support. If this change is to be met successfully, it requires ego differentiation not only among varied role activities, but among various attribtues of personality and interpersonal relationships. The person who has built his self-respect primarily on the value of rugged independence may face a major crisis when he loses his independence. On the other hand, a man or woman who finds satisfaction in friendships, in leisure activities, may welcome retirement as an opportunity to develop other aspects of life more fully. Thus one requisite for successful adaptation to old age may be the establishment of a varied set of valued activities and valued self-attributes, so that any one of several alternatives can be pursued with a sense of satisfaction.

4. "Body transcendence" is the capacity to feel whole, worthwhile, and happy because of one's social and mental powers and activities, whether or not physical health is good, and to avoid preoccupation with health, physique, or bodily comfort. For persons to whom comfort means predominantly physical well-being, illness and declining vigor may be the gravest insult of aging. There are many people whose middle and later years seem to move in a decreasing spiral, centered around their growing preoccupation with the state of their bodies. There are other people who, despite illness and pain, continue to maintain satisfying human relationships and creative activities and for whom social and mental sources of pleasure and self-respect transcend physical comfort. The latter attitude should be an important factor in good adjustment.

5. "Ego transcendence" is the capacity to engage in a direct, ac-

tive, emotionally gratifying manner with the people and the events of daily life, with a strong concern for others' well-being; not to be mainly preoccupied with private, self-centered desires, but to find satisfaction in fulfilling the needs of others.

One of the facts of later life is the new awareness of the certainty of death. The individual who is high on ego transcendence is one who feels he has achieved enduring significance and to whom the prospect of personal death—the night of the ego, it might be called—seems less important than the secure knowledge that he has built for the future through his children, his contributions to the culture, and his friendships. Such a person is likely to experience a gratifying absorption in life.

6. "Body satisfaction" is the degree of satisfaction one subjectively feels with one's body. This variable may or may not directly reflect the actual state of health, vigor, or physical attractiveness, but the extent to which the individual feels contented or unhappy about his body. Many people who have real physical impairments manage to minimize them. Others suffer from a deep sense of physical inadequacy or malaise.

7. "Sexual integration" is the capacity to mesh one's sexual desires with other aspects of life, among them, affection for the sex-partner, a sense of responsibility for children born of the couple, and an integration of sexual and other motivations in social relationships. At the high end of the scale, all these elements are integrated into a harmonious pattern. At the low end there may be either free indulgence of sexual impulse without regard for other aspects of the relationship or, on the other hand, intense repression. In the latter case, sexuality may become either unacceptable or so guilt-ridden that sexual behavior is emotionally dissociated from the self-concept as well as from the affectional aspects of human relationships.

This characteristic seems crucial to adjustment in middle age because of the occurrence of the biological climacteric in this period. There is the obvious experience of the menopause for women, but for both men and women there is an awareness of change in patterns of sexual expression. (In response to our interviewers, for instance, some men as well as women calmly described a "change of life" that occurred in middle age.) This change, although often described in terms of loss, is sometimes seen as an opportunity for a certain type of gain, in which people come to be valued more on the basis of their personalities than on the basis of their attractiveness as sexual objects. It is possible, indeed, that it is only the individual who is trying to work out unfulfilled needs from an earlier period in his life who feels particularly frustrated about lessened sexual potency.

In addition to these seven personality characteristics, a measure of over-all adjustment was used in the present study.

8. "Adjustment" is an estimate of the net effectiveness and satisfaction with which the individual is adapting to his present situation. This is obviously a very generalized measure, and there are various patterns of good, average, and poor adjustment. The investigator, in making his adjustments, attempted to weigh both the subject's inner adjustment, or satisfaction with life, and the degree of effectiveness the subject demonstrated in dealing with the world around him.

The Sample and the Data

The study population consisted of 118 persons drawn from Sample I (see Appendix A), distributed in twenty-four cells according to age, sex, and social class. There were three age groups—forty–forty-five, fifty–fifty-five, and sixty–sixty-five—and four social-class groups—upper-middle, lower-middle, working, and lower class. In order to carry out an analysis of variance based on equal numbers of cases in each cell, two hypothetical cases were added to one cell (the upper-middle-class women aged sixty–sixty-five). The analysis was then based on 120 cases, with five cases in each cell and forty cases in each age range.

The basic data consisted of a structured interview that took from one to three hours of the respondent's time and projective stories told in response to cards 1, 2, 4, 6BM, 7BM, and 17BM from the Murray Thematic Apperception Test (Murray, 1943) and the family-scene card (see Chapter 3). Areas covered in the interview included experiences and attitudes regarding work, health, family, sex, religion, friendships, leisure activities, and the over-all pattern of the person's life as he viewed it in retrospect.

A seven-point scale was constructed for each of the eight variables. After randomizing the cases with regard to age, sex, and social class and then removing the explicitly identifying data about age and class, the investigators read all the data on each case and made independent ratings. Since the sample was presumably a normal cross-section of the population, in making the ratings, it was kept in mind that the distribution of scores on each variable should approximate a normal curve.

The agreement between the two raters was high, as measured by the intraclass correlation technique (Haggard, 1958). For all ratings on all cases, $r = .78$. The coefficients ranged from .68 for body transcendence to .86 for adjustment. Since there were no significant differences in the rating patterns of the two investigators, the two sets of ratings were pooled, and the average of the two ratings was used in the subsequent analyses.

Personality Characteristics and Adjustment

As shown in Table 2.1, there is a considerable amount of communality among all eight variables. When the influences of age, sex, social status, and rater differences are removed, the "pure" (intraclass) correlation among the eight scales is .57.

Correlations of this size have been reported in many other studies of personality and adjustment. In the present case, the sizable correlations could be attributed to one or all of three factors: a strong halo effect in the raters' judgments, some degree of overlap in the definitions of the variables, and a factual relation among these characteristics in the personalities of the people studied. The first of these factors cannot be accurately evaluated. With regard to the second, it is logical that there should be a certain amount of overlap. Ego differentiation, for example, logically implies a considerable degree of mental and emotional flexibility. Similarly, ego transcendence implies, even requires, the quality of body transcendence. With regard to the third factor, it was the considered judgment of the investigators that the interview and TAT data most often gave strong evidence for a general level of personality integration and adaptability in any individual case and that, to a significant degree, personal integration and adaptability is a generalized quality. On the whole, the well-adjusted people in this sample tended to show high degrees of flexibility, ego differentiation, and—to somewhat lesser

TABLE 2.1

CORRELATIONS AMONG THE PERSONALITY CHARACTERISTICS
AND ADJUSTMENT

	2	3	4	5	6	7	8
1. Cathectic flexibility	.73	.82	.57	.73	.35	.62	.82
2. Mental flexibility		.68	.45	.68	.26	.60	.73
3. Ego differentiation			.62	.72	.36	.61	.77
4. Body transcendence				.67	.29	.40	.67
5. Ego transcendence					.35	.60	.62
6. Body satisfaction						.32	.54
7. Sexual integration							.62
8. Adjustment							

extent—ego transcendence, body transcendence, and sexual integration. Body satisfaction seemed relatively independent of the other traits. In terms of psychodynamic processes, it is no discovery to find that conflict or incapacity in one area of life tends to incapacitate the individual in other areas or that clarity and effectiveness in one aspect of behavior are more often than not accompanied by a similar degree of effectiveness in other areas.

As indicated in the last column of Table 2.1, the personality characteristics are significantly related to adjustment and support the hypothesis that adjustment in middle age is a function of these seven adaptive and integrative qualities. (Additional evidence for the validity of the adjustment ratings was obtained from independent objective analysis of sentence-completion data on the same subjects [Peck, 1959].)

Cathectic flexibility is most closely related to adjustment, with ego differentiation and mental flexibility next. These are all related qualities, yet the coefficients of correlation are not so high as to indicate that they measure only one underlying characteristic.

The same feature is evident with regard to adjustment. Although most of the variance can be attributed to the seven personality characteristics, there remains considerable variance that must be attributed to other factors. (For instance, one lower-class woman had had her home and all her belongings swept away in a flood, only to have her husband die the next year. When interviewed two years later, she was deeply depressed. Whatever her personality resources —even if they had always been limited, as the data suggested—her general adjustment was inevitably affected by the external catastrophes that had deprived her of her main sources of economic and emotional security.)

Age, Sex, and Social Class as Factors in Personality and Adjustment

Tables 2.2 and 2.3 summarize the data and the results of an analysis of variance undertaken to assess the significance of age, sex, and social class.[2]

Age Differences

The most unexpected and, perhaps, the most important finding was that there were no consistent age differences on any of the seven personality characteristics. Contrary to the folklore and the initial expectations of the investigators, the sixty-year-old subjects

---

[2] We are greatly indebted to Professor Carson McGuire of the University of Texas for his assistance in the analyses of variance, particularly for some refinements he developed in applying this method to our data.

TABLE 2.2

MEANS AND STANDARD DEVIATIONS OF POOLED RATINGS ON PERSONALITY AND ADJUSTMENT ($N = 120$)

Age Group and Social status	Cathectic flex.		Mental flex.		Ego diff.		Body trans.		Ego trans.		Body satis.		Sexual integ.		Adj.	
	M	Σ	M	Σ	M	Σ	M	Σ	M	Σ	M	Σ	M	Σ	M	Σ
WOMEN																
40–45 Years																
Upper middle	7.6	1.82	9.4	3.33	8.4	1.14	7.6	0.90	8.8	1.64	7.4	1.14	7.8	2.48	9.2	1.92
Lower middle	7.2	1.78	6.2	1.64	7.4	2.73	7.8	1.92	6.8	2.58	8.2	1.92	6.8	1.92	7.8	1.78
Working	7.4	2.88	8.2	1.92	6.8	2.77	5.8	1.30	8.0	2.12	10.0	3.46	8.6	3.49	8.8	2.86
Lower	7.2	3.11	7.0	3.16	5.6	2.30	7.0	2.00	8.2	3.11	8.4	2.40	8.0	3.82	8.0	4.18
50–55 years																
Upper middle	8.4	1.14	9.4	2.73	8.6	1.82	9.6	1.51	9.4	2.30	10.0	2.91	9.6	2.73	9.4	2.30
Lower middle	6.8	1.30	7.6	2.73	6.8	2.38	7.8	2.38	7.6	2.50	8.8	2.86	6.4	2.88	8.2	2.59
Working	3.8	0.84	4.8	2.38	4.2	0.84	7.0	2.91	5.2	1.95	6.4	2.73	6.2	3.27	5.0	1.73
Lower	6.8	2.77	7.2	2.28	5.8	2.59	7.0	1.58	8.4	2.59	8.0	0.71	7.6	0.55	7.0	2.23
60–65 Years																
Upper middle	8.0	1.58	9.0	0.71	8.2	2.59	7.8	1.48	8.6	2.61	6.8	2.49	8.8	1.78	8.0	1.87
Lower middle	7.4	2.70	7.2	1.30	8.4	2.63	8.2	2.19	8.0	1.22	9.2	2.59	7.6	3.50	8.0	2.92
Working	9.2	3.27	7.6	2.97	8.0	2.91	8.6	3.21	8.0	2.91	9.2	3.42	6.8	1.92	8.4	3.44
Lower	7.2	3.15	6.6	2.70	6.8	3.42	7.8	3.63	7.8	2.59	8.6	3.51	6.2	2.28	7.6	3.13
MEN																
40–45 Years																
Upper middle	9.0	2.91	9.4	2.74	9.4	2.70	8.2	2.77	8.2	1.30	10.0	2.51	8.6	0.90	10.0	2.19
Lower middle	8.2	1.64	8.6	1.34	7.8	1.92	7.6	1.82	7.4	1.95	10.0	1.58	7.8	1.95	8.8	1.78
Working	7.6	1.51	8.8	1.30	8.0	1.41	7.6	1.78	8.2	1.48	9.6	2.70	9.8	1.48	9.6	2.74
Lower	7.4	3.85	7.2	2.95	5.8	2.17	5.0	1.58	5.6	1.14	8.0	1.41	8.0	2.92	7.8	3.42
50–55 years																
Upper middle	9.2	3.42	9.0	2.35	8.6	2.88	8.0	1.22	7.6	1.95	8.8	2.39	9.6	2.79	9.2	2.59
Lower middle	6.2	2.59	7.2	0.84	6.2	2.17	5.8	1.48	5.8	1.64	6.4	4.98	7.0	1.87	5.4	2.30
Working	7.2	2.59	6.6	2.19	6.6	2.88	6.4	0.55	6.8	2.49	9.6	2.41	7.4	3.50	7.8	2.17
Lower	5.6	1.51	5.2	0.84	6.6	1.34	5.0	2.35	5.0	2.35	8.6	3.85	5.4	1.82	5.6	1.34
60–65 Years																
Upper middle	7.6	3.36	9.0	3.54	9.0	1.87	8.6	2.41	8.2	2.59	10.0	2.74	8.2	2.49	9.4	3.65
Lower middle	8.6	2.97	7.8	2.49	8.2	2.86	8.0	2.55	8.2	3.09	9.4	2.19	7.8	1.92	8.6	3.13
Working	7.4	3.51	6.2	1.30	7.6	2.30	7.6	2.74	6.6	3.50	9.0	2.65	10.0	2.28	8.4	3.44
Lower	4.8	0.84	4.6	1.51	4.0	0.00	5.8	2.59	4.8	2.39	8.0	3.06	6.4	1.14	5.4	2.51

TABLE 2.3

SOURCES OF VARIATION IN ADULT PERSONALITY

Source of variation	Significant influence
Individual variation	
Age	No
Sex	No
Social class	Yes
Interactions of these	No
Variations between scales	
Scales	Yes
Sex and scale interaction	Yes
Class and scale interaction	Yes
Other interactions	No
Variations between raters	

A weak interaction effect (.05 level) occurred for the sex-class-rater interactions. No other inter-rater variation occurred for age, sex, or social class, over-all.

were, on the average, no more or less flexible, mentally or emotionally, than the fifty- or forty-year-olds. In the same way, ego differentiation and ego transcendence showed no consistent changes with age.

More surprising, perhaps, was the finding that age was not consistently related to body satisfaction, body transcendence, or sexual integration. On rereading the interview data, keeping in mind the definition of body satisfaction, this finding appeared to be an accurate reflection of the facts. More people in their sixties than in their forties had arthritic, cardiac, or other chronic disabilities, as might be expected. However, for every older subject who had complained about an ailment, there was another who, seemingly in a similar physical condition, said: "Oh, my joints bother me some, but I have better health than most people my age, I'd say. Yes, I feel I'm in good shape." For the latter persons, what evidence the TAT provided usually confirmed their sense of physical integrity and their lack of any marked anxiety or unhappiness about the general state of their bodily well-being.

Only in adjustment was there a significant difference with age (.05 level of confidence). This was not a steady, downward trend; instead, the respondents in their fifties averaged significantly lower on adjustment than either the forty-year-olds or the sixty-year-olds.

It is possible that, for a majority of men and women in our society, a crisis occurs in the early fifties, when a new dissatisfaction with life and oneself seems to arise. The trend in these data looks like the somewhat vaguely identified syndrome known to some psychologists and psychiatrists as "middle-age depression." Specific reasons for this slump are not yet understood, but it has been observed in clinical and industrial consulting practice that this period of distress, or of poor adjustment, appears to be temporary and that by the sixties there is spontaneous recovery. Because the present data are cross-sectional, they do not, it is true, permit the conclusion that particular individuals go through this slump-and-recovery phase as they move from forty through fifty to sixty, but the age differences shown here are congruent with such an interpretation.

There were also age differences with regard to variability on several of the dimensions. On ego transcendence, body transcendence, and adjustment the dispersion of scores in the sixty-year-olds was significantly greater than in the forty-year-olds. On body satisfaction and sexual integration, on the other hand, significantly more extreme scores appeared in the fifties than in either the forties or sixties.

Sex Differences

With one exception, there were no significant sex differences in these data. The one exception was that women averaged higher than men on ego transcendence (.05 level of significance). Although this single sex difference must be interpreted with caution, it is possible that it reflects the greater personal interest and self-sacrifice for one's children that are said to distinguish women from men in our society.

Social-Class Differences

There were very significant social-class differences in the data, reflecting differences in people with different styles of life. The pattern is best illustrated by the adjustment ratings, which showed differences between social classes that were significant at the .01 level. The upper-middle-class people, on the average, were best adjusted; the lower-middle- and working-class people were about average; and the lower-class people, in most cases, showed distinctly poor adjustment. The same pattern was found on mental flexibility, ego differentiation, ego transcendence, and body transcendence; there was a trend in the same direction on cathectic flexibility.

There were two exceptions to this general pattern. Ratings on body satisfaction showed no significant social-class differences. This variable appears to be a more superficial characteristic than the others, more related, perhaps, to the actual state of the subjects' physical well-being than to personality. (As mentioned earlier, ratings on this variable were not closely related to the other personality dimensions, although they were significantly related to adjustment, as shown in Table 2.1.)

On sexual integration, the social-class variance was significant (.01), but here the upper-middle and working groups had almost equal, relatively high ratings whereas the lower-middle and lower-class groups were equally low. The lower-middle-class respondents frequently showed a tendency to repress and disassociate sex from other parts of their lives and from their self-images and to have deep feelings of shame and guilt. This was evident in such comments as these: "My husband and I are more like sister and brother than man and wife. I come from a family of women who are cold by nature." "Oh, I don't think that [sex] was a main issue at all. (Importance?) Oh, I don't remember that we ever. . . . It wasn't so important. (You could have gotten along without sex?) I think so."

Some people were rated low on sexual integration for the opposite reason. In some of the interviews it was clear that sexual activities were indulged in with abandon and with little concern about other kinds of mutual interests or responsibilities toward the sex partner. Although these cases were infrequent, they occurred only in the lower class. The majority of lower-class people who were rated low on sexual integration, on the other hand, evidenced a severe, guilt-laden repression of sexuality, like those in the lower-middle class.

Although these differences between social classes on sexual integration are of interest, more noteworthy is the pattern earlier described as characteristic of six of the eight variables, a pattern in which, the higher the social class, the more favorable the average ratings. If this pattern occurred only on adjustment, it might merely be a reflection of the more secure external resources of upper-status people and of the deprived circumstances of lower-class life. Although it is also recognized that there might have been bias on the part of both raters in favor of middle-class life styles, there is abundant evidence from the interviews and the TAT's that there is a genuine difference in the personality integration and adaptability of the different social-class groups. Variations in personality and in life styles at different social levels are illustrated in four examples that follow.

Case 1959F. A fifty-three-year-old woman, described by the interviewer as very warm and friendly, "a gracious and charming woman," living in an attractively furnished, very well-ordered house that had a homey, lived-in feeling. During the interview, Mrs. Q made these statements, among others:

> (Best years of your life?) I would have to say right now [laughs]. I guess I'm reaping the harvest of all the years of working and sending my daughter through school. I'm really enjoying being a housewife. [She held a supervisory position in business until two years ago.] (The most important thing today?) My husband, home, daughter and my family. Yes [I've changed in past ten

years]; I'm not as tired as I used to be, and really I'm happier.

[Early in the interview, she explained that she had re-married three years before. Her first husband had gone into the Navy and had come out a "mental case." About five years before he had committed suicide. She said that she didn't go out for a long time, but after a while she began going out at the insistence of her friends. She married her present husband about a year after they met.]

I married first at eighteen. I liked being married and having a home of my own. Oh, yes, I liked the responsi-bility. . . . I have Mother here part time now—five months of the year. [She visits other children, too.] I think the second marriage was hardest to adjust to. My second husband is quite different. He is always teasing me and laughing. My first husband was the serious type. I was pretty set in my ways, and it was hard to change. Of course, another thing is sexual adjustment. My second husband thinks it is very important; my first didn't; so I have had to make quite an adjustment there. You know, if you want to keep your husband happy, you'd better adjust [smiles].

(Did you think husband sexually attractive? Impor-tant?) Yes, both my present husband and the first. I think it is essential in marriage. . . . We are not too old to enjoy it. Of course, I think sex has to be spontaneous, that is the way it is around here. (?) Oh, no set time, just when you feel like it [smiles]. (Choose same hus-band?) Yes, I am very happy. He provides home and good companionship. He is a very thoughtful husband.

I always go to visit my daughter once a year, if she doesn't come here. It just is understood. We write and talk things over in our letters. . . . She has a lovely home, two fine children, and is happily married. I be-lieve that's all any mother could ask for.

[She named five people as very close friends, when asked.] I think I could talk over anything with any of the friends I've told you about. (Prefer a few or a lot of people?) Well, if I have people in, I like to have quite a few. I really enjoy talking and meeting new people when I'm in the entertaining mood.

No [I'm not unhappy to be alone]. Oh, no, I like to stay home. I really enjoy being here in the house doing things I like to do.

(Feel closest to ———?) My husband; because I'm happily married to him. . . . (Have you had the breaks in life?) I think I've had some. One of the biggest, as far as I'm concerned, was meeting my husband, who—well—is just wonderful.

(Sometimes feel no one cares about you?) I used to, when my first husband died, but not since I've remarried. I think that is a state of mind. (What do you do when you get mad at somebody?) Freeze them. (?) I hold my temper. I just don't talk to them. They say you shouldn't do that, but I just don't let it get out. (When?) When people are talking about character, saying untrue things. I usually like everyone, but, if they do that, I get mad. (Sorry?) Yes, maybe I was wrong, I think; then I get over it pretty fast.

(Health?) Excellent. Haven't been to a doctor in two years. (Past illness?) Partial hysterectomy, ulcer, for about ten years—duodenal—that was about twenty years ago. I can eat anything now [laughs]. (Compared with others your age?) Better, because most women don't feel as good as I do. . . . My health is better than it was twenty years ago. I don't worry; enjoy life. Keep busy all day long, and really I never feel very tired [smiles].

I go to church. I try to lead a better life. (Has religion given peace of mind?) Oh, yes. I think you realize as you get older how important it is to lead a decent life.

(As you look back, what do you like most about yourself?) I have a good personality [laughs].

Case 400M. A sixty-four-year-old man who has built, in his own
lifetime, a highly successful business of his own. He was seen in
what the interviewer described as "a truly beautiful private office"
in a modern building which Mr. Y had designed himself. In the
course of the interview, Mr. Y said:

(What do you like most about your work?) Well, I'd
have to go back to give you a little background. . . . I
started about thirty-five years ago. I had very little
money. Now I have a successful business. I have five
hundred employees. Not only do I feel great responsibility to my stockholders and to myself, but I am also
making a living for all our employees and their families.
And the responsibility you feel as you go along if you
have employees twenty-five, thirty, and some thirty-three
years. You feel like you have been able to make a living
for all these people through your steering and management efforts, and that puts quite a substantial responsibility on you.

(And you enjoy having this?) Yes, I think you do,
just like the ways of the child. There's the suffering you
have done, and the prestige you have built on the company and on the personnel, and the prestige of being
part of the managerial group. There is a great deal of
satisfaction in building it, and I am very fortunate. I
have my three sons here with me, and they are in key
positions and have earned the right to those positions
through their own efforts. It gives me a great deal of
satisfaction to have my three sons ready to take over
when I am ready to check out. I am getting older, you
know [chuckle], but there is a great deal of satisfaction
in building this.

My son said to me in his junior year at college that he

didn't like this business because there is no romance to
it. I told him that it made no difference whether you
made peanuts or locomotives, but it is the business side
of it itself. Of course, he went to Harvard Business
School and found out that this was true. (And it has
been a romance to you?) Oh, yes, very much so—for
instance, all the civic activities I have had. That makes
you feel like one of the community leaders—and the
right to earn them, like being in the Chamber of Com-
merce and the Boy Scouts and the Girl Scouts and other
activities. And the prestige you earn as a result of having
established a business. For instance, bankers and others
respect you; and being known as a leader in most activities I've been into, it's been a great deal of satisfaction
to me.

(What do you expect to be doing after retirement?)
Oh, I wouldn't retire. It will probably be like the last
three years. I have traveled over one hundred thousand
miles. I was twice in Europe and all over the North
American continent. I am going on another trip now.
All over South America.

(Then you've not thought about retirement?) No, my
sons had three five-year plans. (?) To get me out, but they
did not succeed [merry laugh]. No, I have no desire to
retire. I walk more slowly and take more leisure time—
and if I want to, I get away two or three months every
so often. But my job is now more or less to lay down the
policies of the company. To steer, as you might say,
the younger generation. I have always been very successful, but I am open-minded on the progression as long as
we expand. Not one of these fellows feels wholly responsible for the success of the company. It is the people you
gather around you. If you don't have good people
around you, you don't get very far.

(What do you do just for fun?) Well, I enjoy as-
sociating with people, playing cards; and my principal
hobby is taking pictures, when I'm on trips. I never had

too much time for play. I have never been a fisherman. I like to travel and see new things. For instance, the pictures I take are not just pictures, but a subject I can talk about . . . [talks earnestly]. For instance, they can lead to a discussion, and there was some reason for taking the picture.

(Do you get more pleasure from your work or from the things you do in your spare time?) Oh, I think it is about a fifty-fifty deal. I also enjoy my home and family. I spend a great deal of time with the family.

(What do you do when you find you have time on your hands? Does it make you restless?) I never plan to have it [laughs happily]. I don't have time on my hands. There never was any time that there was not something I like to do. At my age there are a number of things I like to do but can't, such as golf. I enjoy football and basketball. I am not so crazy about baseball. I am interested in athletics; for instance, I have played tennis all my life—until I was fifty-five, I played with the kids. My daughter used to beat me. Now all four beat me at golf. Therefore I don't play any more [twinkle and jolly laugh].

(How is your health at the present time?) As far as I know, I believe I would pass a physical for any reasonable amount of life insurance. I have no heart condition as far as I know; I'll grow older gracefully. I have checkups occasionally.

(What major operations or illnesses did you have?) I never had an operation. I was ill . . . twenty-eight years ago for about three years, caused from infected teeth. I had them all taken out—a toxic poisoning. It made me very nervous, but, since I have been over that, about 1930, I don't think I have been away a full day on account of sickness.

(Do you think your health is as good as that of most people your age?) Yes, I think so; probably even a little better.

(Was it easy or hard for you to get used to being a husband?) I think it was fun [spontaneous laughter] in all ways. Fun and pleasure. I was very much in love. We have never been in financial straits. We also had a little money in the bank, because we both came from families without much income [sic].

(How do you and your wife get along these days?) [Shrugs shoulders as if to brush away question.] Wonderful [as though to say how else should it be?]. We take trips, and we don't care to have anyone else with us. We thoroughly enjoy each other's company, and I very seldom take trips when she is not with me. We have a great big house—of fourteen rooms—and our life is built around this home and all these years.

(What part do you think sex has played in your marriage?) I think I married her for her money. She had thirty-five dollars [laughs]. No, it was not too important —I don't think it's ever been of outstanding importance —but the ability to live with and make each other happy, those were the most important things.

(Would you be satisfied if your children did as well as you did?) I think they will all do better [laughs]. (?) Well, they will carry this business to bigger heights. They are very active. Building of schools and churches . . . [talks more about children]. They had a better life than I had, and they will do better. They had good surroundings, a good religious life, and good education.

(How do your children treat you now?) Well . . . I think with a great deal of respect and admiration for what I have done, and they are willing to follow in my footsteps. Of course, we have discussions and arguments, and sometimes I win and sometimes they win. As with all employees, experience is the teacher.

(Whom do you feel closest to of all the people in your life?) (Long pause) Oh . . . [frowns] I would say my family. (Who?) I would include everybody.

(Do you have as many friends now as you had ten

years ago?) Well, I think it's . . . I think I have more
because I have been so active in community activities
until four years ago. Lots of people know me because of
this. But I enjoy my associations. For instance, I have
been on the board of all of my banks here. A fine group
of men. I have an amazing variety. My friends vary
from a taxi driver to a multimillionaire. I treat them all
the same.

(What do you do when you get good and mad at
somebody?) Oh, I haven't for twenty-five years. (On
occasion?) Not too often. A doctor cured me of that.
I used to fly off the handle, but the doctor suggested
one day I was taking advantage of my employees, who
have to take it because you are the boss. I never looked
at it that way, so I changed. (Mad at your equals?) I
never had any arguments. For instance, some competitors have given me a chance to get mad, but, as long as
it concerns facts, why should I get mad? If it is due to
an untruth, I just consider the source and just forget it
[mischievous laugh]. Why get mad? It takes years off
your life. (So you have not done that for twenty-five
years?) Yes, life is too short. I never carry a grudge.

(As you look back over it all, what do you like most
about yourself?) Oh, that I am friendly, have a smile
for everybody. I am congenial, open-minded, always
trying to be what I think is fair. With a record of
thirty-five years in business it proves that my policies
have always been fairly good. Of course, without this
"live and let live," I couldn't have been a success.

By contrast, the interview data frequently depict dismal physical
and social circumstances in the lower classes. Moreover, the interview and TAT data show inner barrenness, unhappiness, and confused, vague ego resources in a disproportionate number of middle-
aged people at the lowest social level. These people not only have
to work hard for a bare subsistence, but they also tend to have few
meaningful associations with people outside their immediate fam-

ilies. They do not know how to find or invent significant leisure activities for themselves. When at home, if not doing household chores, they tend to watch television endlessly, "putter around" aimlessly and without satisfaction, or sit and do nothing. Questions indicate that, even when they watch television, many of them do not pay any real attention to it. Two illustrations follow.

Case 2048M. A sixty-two-year-old man who lives alone in one room, which the interviewer described as extremely dirty, jumbled up, and "depressing." During the interview, Mr. X said:

> My life has been mostly rough. I've had bad marriages, hard jobs, hard work when I had jobs. [Life has been] pretty much what I've made it, but it seems, if you try to be good to some people, they try to misuse you or do you no good. . . . [I used to have what I wanted in life], but I don't have it now—a home, plenty of clothes. Now I can't get it. No money, can't get money; no jobs. . . . What do I like about my work? Don't like nothing about work. I like the paydays. . . . No, I don't belong to any [organizations]. I'm just too tired at night to do much. [He does yard work.] I ain't got no spare time. All I do is work. It keeps me going.
>
> (Health?) I feel pretty good most of the time. I ain't had no sickness. I get tired and sore from digging, but that doesn't last long. (Major illnesses in past?) Well, I think I had a little stomach trouble here a few years ago, but it don't hurt now. (Go to doctor?) No. I have stomach ulcers, and I've had some bad colds, that's all. [He was drinking whiskey out of a cup during the interview.] My health is as good as most people's my age. I can work just as hard as some young ones I know.
>
> (Change of life yet?) No [smiles]. I get some [intercourse] every three or four weeks.
>
> (Age?) Well, I feel old. Wish I was younger, but I can't do nothing about it, so I'm just gonna try and live as long as I can.

I was fifteen or sixteen when I left home. Ran away to get a job working for a man. We had no money at home, so I wanted to get out and get some of my own.

I was married twice, both times by a judge. Both women were no good—ran around with other men. Yes [I thought my first wife was sexually attractive]. Big and nice built, good looking. I like big women. (Place of sex in marriage?) Yes, I enjoyed it. Yes, sir, a major part of life. . . . My two wives were a world of grief. Because of my wife being no good, caused me to kill a man and go to the pen. (Why?) I caught him with my wife in bed. . . . Since then, I lived with a couple other women. [Didn't marry them.]

(What do you do when you get good and mad at somebody?) I get mad—I hurt them, if I don't kill them. Killed one man, tried to get intimate with my wife. I was sentenced to twenty years. I served eleven years and then was pardoned by the state governor. (When do you usually get mad?) When a person does me a dirty deed or lies to me. (Sorry afterward?) Not if I'm right about it.

(Do you drink much?) Not since a year ago. I used to drink heavy. Now I'm a church member.

(Is your life better now, or not, than when you were younger?) Better. I'm living a Christian life now. When younger, I'd cut, then; now I'd walk away from an argument. . . . My church life has helped me to do better. I don't go out any more with a wild bunch or gangs—the bunch that drinks and would do most anything.

Yes [I sometimes feel no one cares what happens to me]. It's more true now; less people care for, seems that way. (Often lonely and blue?) Yes. Seems like I haven't a friend in the world at times. I go to church and talk with church people and feel relieved.

I like to have company. It makes me lonely to be alone. (Prefer a few friends or a lot?) One or two. I do not like crowds. It ain't good, causes trouble a lot of times; too much talking, and do things that causes you to do them. (What kind?) Mostly bad things. . . . I don't go out or associate much. I haven't got much money now. Friends leave you when you're broke.

Case 1534F. A forty-four-year-old married woman, mother of ten children aged three to twenty-five (two dead). The interviewer described her small house as "plain, impoverished—no chairs; had to sit on bed—disordered. The dirt, although she had made an attempt to clean up, was oppressive. With the children and men constantly coming and going, she could hardly help the mud. The whole yard was either liquid or frozen mud." The circumstances of the interview were of some significance. In the interviewer's words:

> I had been to Mrs. R's house the day before the interview, and she agreed very readily for me to come back the next day. She was washing and couldn't talk that day. When I got there the second time, she was expecting me, and *so* was her husband! The moment I was inside the door, Mrs. R informed me that her husband did not want her to talk with me, that he was very angry that she had agreed for me to come back. . . . She assured me that he was "funny," that he just didn't like anyone coming around asking questions, and that he had a terrible temper. Then she told me that someone was threatening to sue them for a bill (which she says she paid) and that he thought that was why I was there. Mr. R came in about then. I tried to explain who I was, but he walked out without even speaking. Mrs. R told me she felt badly, but there was nothing she could do; he would be mad at her for six months if she went ahead. I picked my way through the junk yard until I came to where he was. He was loading junk on a truck which his son was driving and would not even look my way, even though I was right beside him. I waited un-

til he finished loading. I told him I did not wish to talk with his wife unless he felt that it was all right. He invited me back into the house. "It's cold out here." So back we went. He went into a long discussion of why should they help anyone. No one helped them. After the flood, Red Cross wouldn't help them. No one ever helped him. I sympathized. . . . I told him that, if I talked with his wife, I'd like for him to be present and help her answer. So we began. He answered more than she did. After five or six questions, he was laughing and joking, in fine humor. Mrs. R was very cautious in answering any questions except the ones about her health. She was afraid to open her mouth unless he told her to. When I got ready to leave, Mrs. R invited me to come back and visit with her. I thanked her, and she said, "Yeah, come back, and we'll jaw together *any* time."

Mrs. R made these statements during the interview:

(Did you ever work outside the home?) Just worked out cutting corn. That's all I've ever done. (Miss?) Now I got my hands full here at home with these kids. [Discussion of kids; she sent them off to the show so they wouldn't be underfoot when I came. Tells me about her six-year-old. How mean he is—always hitting at the girls, pretending he's a cowboy.] (Ask if he's in school this year.) She said he was and doing fine. She was afraid he'd give the teacher trouble, but he was doing fine. Hadn't missed but two half-days. Once he fell in the mud and got his jeans dirty so couldn't go, and the other time he was sick. Mrs. R's husband asked her if she had a pair of his jeans so I could see how big he was, but she said no, they were all in the wash. Both obviously very proud of him. Then she told me that her oldest boy had "got whipped" the night before. She said that's what came of his going to the beer joints and not staying home with his wife and kid. The police took him home. She hadn't seen him but they said he was a sight. He had to go to the doctor.

(What do you do just for fun?) [Husband] Argue! That's about all. [Wife] Going to hear cowboy musicians tomorrow night. They are going to be at the auditorium. [Discussion of how much she likes that kind of music.] (How is your health at the present time?) Not any good. Spells with stomach. [Discussion of how bad she feels. Ask her what the doctor says is wrong, and she said he told her she had too much fat around the heart. She needed to reduce so he gave her some pills. She took them a week but got so nervous she couldn't stand it. Threw pills away. Mrs. R said she had smothering feeling so much at night had to get up and walk floor. Her husband laughed and said he guessed he'd better go and get her a wheel chair right away. She laughed with him but didn't seem to think it was funny.]

(How do you feel about being forty-four years old?) Don't feel very good about it [laughs]. Ain't that a question, though! [Husband says he doesn't see why she minds; he doesn't.] (Do you wish you were some other age instead?) Twenty years. (Why?) Think might live much longer. [Husband says he'd hate to think he'd have to go back and live the same thing all over. She agreed with him that she wouldn't want to have to live over her past life.] (When you think ahead, how do you feel about getting older?) I kind of dread it. Would like to stay age I am.

(What part do you think sex has played in your marriage?) [Asked this at very end when husband was out. Mrs. R looked surprised and said she wouldn't know how to answer that. There were lots of things she didn't understand, possibly because she was not able to read and write.] (How do your children treat you now?) Boys sassy. [Discussion of how the teen-age boys are girl-crazy. Have their own cars.] (What do you do about religion?) Pray; not went to church none this winter. All children go. Young one too mean to take. (Do you believe in life after death?) Yes, shore do. [Husband says he does, too.] (What do you think it will be like?) Lord, I don't know. I expect it'll be all right there.

(Do you have any close friends with whom you can talk over anything at all?) [Husband] She don't *tell* me what's bothering her—she just lets it fly all over me. [Mrs. R. laughs.] I guess I'd tell husband or my mother or sister. (Do you sometimes get the feeling that no one cares much what happens to you?) I shore do. I get to thinking husband or none of them care. [He laughs.] (Is that truer now than ten years ago?) I guess so. (Are you often lonely and blue?) I shore do. Think it's nervousness. (What do you do about it?) Just walk. I just walk and walk and take Alka Seltzers. Husband bought me a big bottle up at the store yesterday.

(What do you do when mad at somebody?) Lord, I don't know. Get so mad some times can't see. [Husband] Why don't you tell her you pack up your clothes and leave? (Do you do that?) Well, I used to more than I do now. (What do now?) Just argue. Or, if it's the kids, I just spank them. (When does this usually happen?) Kids arguing and aggravating me. (Feel sorry afterward?) Yes, I get so I can't sleep after I whip B. Lay awake and think about it.

(What do you think your life has been like, on the whole?) An awful hard life. Been sick a long time seems like. [Husband] The way you talk, you'll be pushing up daisies before your ten years is up [laughs]. (Have you gotten out of life what you wanted?) Yeah, I guess. (What were the best years of your life, the happiest times?) God, I don't know. When first married, I guess. (Eighteen years old) We had fun. (As you look back on it all, what do you like best about yourself?) I don't know what to say about that. What do you say? [to husband, who doesn't answer; she looked a little downcast and said she didn't know].

Implications for Mental Health

In summary, utilizing a set of personality variables that were derived from a developmental theory, it appears that persons in the age range forty to sixty-five vary consistently by social class but not by age or sex. The lack of age differences—especially the lack of a steady downward trend in adaptability with increasing age—suggests that aging per se, at least between forty and sixty-five, does not result in decreasing mental or emotional flexibility. In fact, many of the old assumptions about age-linked decline in general personality integration and adaptability may be untrue. Some middle-aged people cannot or will not learn much that is new, but many can and do continue to adopt new ideas and new behaviors.

This finding strongly suggests that personality patterns are firmly established long before middle age and that they tend to continue throughout adult life. The implication is that measures designed to maximize general adaptability and personal integration in the interests of successful aging need to be taken early in life, in the formative years of personality development. Although extraordinary measures, such as intensive emotional re-education, may effect change in the adult years, personality characteristics laid down earlier in life do not show much change under ordinary circumstances. It seems correct, therefore, to emphasize the importance of good mental health in the first ten to twenty years of life. If good adjustment in middle age and old age is largely the product of emotional health and sound development during youth, then the promotion of optimum personality development in children is not only a measure for child welfare, but also a measure for successful aging.

The social-class differences in adaptability to aging have several important implications. There is now abundant evidence that emotional stability and social effectiveness tend to be positively related to social class. In this connection the present findings confirm the results of the New Haven study (Hollingshead & Redlich, 1958). Whatever the causes—and the causes are undoubtedly complex —a majority of the upper-middle-class people have the best integrated, most adaptable personality systems. The lower-middle- and working-class people come next, at an adequate but not entirely satisfying level of personal effectiveness. Lower-class people, on the average, show unintegrated, undifferentiated, unresourceful personalities.

Adjustment to the aging process comes most easily, it would appear, to upper-status people, but not primarily because they are economically advantaged. Lower-class people suffer genuine economic and social deprivations which handicap them as they grow old. At the same time, their ill-developed personalities also interfere with good adjustment at least as early as early middle age. The social-class differences in adaptability and adjustment, thus, are not only a matter of financial resources, but also of inner psychological resources.

3

AGE-SEX ROLES AND PERSONALITY
IN MIDDLE AGE:
A THEMATIC APPERCEPTION STUDY

Bernice L. Neugarten

David L. Gutmann

The original purpose of this investigation was to explore the use of projective techniques in studying adult age-sex roles in the family.[1] At least two considerations prompted the choice of the Thematic Apperception Test technique. The first was that the responses would be relatively uncensored, more closely related to the respondent's personal values and experiences than those he might feel constrained to give in answer to more direct questions. Second, fantasy material, although presenting certain difficulties of analysis as compared with questionnaire data, would have a decided

---

[1] This study was first published in *Psychol. Monogr.*, 1958, 72, No. 17 (Whole No. 470). It has been condensed and is reprinted with permission of the American Psychological Association.

advantage for exploratory research. The richness and unstructured nature of projective data enable the investigator to follow an inductive process; he can follow up clues as they appear in the data rather than check dimensions and hypotheses defined in advance.

The Thematic Apperception Test and adaptations thereof emerged from the field of clinical psychology and have been used mainly in the study of individual personality. They have also been used, however, to study groups of people, as, for instance, in studies of personality patterns common to persons of different ages or different cultures (Henry, 1947; Schaw & Henry, 1956).

The primary concern of the study was with the collective role images of husbands, wives, sons, and daughters, as those images emerged from the projections of different respondents. After the role images had been delineated, the investigators turned to implications in the data regarding the personalities of the respondents. Thus, this investigation broadened in scope as the research progressed, and, as will become clearer in following sections, this report deals not only with familial roles but also with the relations between role image and personality in middle age.

The Sample

The study population consisted of 131 men and women, all drawn from Sample I (see Appendix A), distributed by age, sex, and social class, as shown in Table 3.1. The middle-class men were well-to-do business executives and professionals, none of whom were retired. All but seven considered their present positions to be the top positions of their careers. The working-class men were stable blue-collar workers, of whom three had retired. Only nine reported that they held better jobs in the past than in the present. Of both groups of women, the large majority were married housewives, only a few of whom held part-time or full-time jobs outside the home. With only a few exceptions, all the people in the study population were native-born of north European ethnic backgrounds. The large majority grew up in Kansas, Missouri, or neighboring Midwest states. Almost all were Protestant. With regard to family status, of the total 131 cases, only four women had never married; only eight of the men and six of the women were childless. One-half of the women and one-third of the men were grandparents.

TABLE 3.1

THE SAMPLE

Social status	40–54		55–70	
	Men	Women	Men	Women
Middle class	18	22	14	13
Working class	21	12	15	16
Total = 131				

The Data and Methods of Analysis

The standard TAT has no single picture appropriate to the purpose of studying age-sex roles in the intergenerational family setting. Although it is possible to explore these roles through the standard TAT, the investigators sought a more economical research tool. A specially drawn picture was therefore used, one designed specifically to evoke the sentiments and preoccupations of middle-aged respondents in relation to family roles (Fig. 3.1).

The picture was pretested in two different ways. First, it was tried with men and women of various ages. The responses proved to be greatly varied in tone and content, thus indicating that the picture was successful as a projective technique insofar as it elicited wide individual differences in response. Second, a check was made against the possibility that the picture presents the respondent with too limited a stimulus to yield data appropriate to the problem. This picture was accordingly administered along with cards 2, 6BM, and 7BM from the standard TAT to thirty-six middle-aged men and women. Analysis was made, on the one hand, of the respondent's descriptions of a young man, a young woman, an older man, and an older woman, as these descriptions emerged from responses to

FIG. 3.1

ADULT FAMILY SCENE

cards 2, 6BM, and 7BM and, on the other hand, of the descriptions
that emerged from responses to the specially drawn picture. The
two sets of descriptions for each respondent were then compared.
Using different methods of judging consistency and of quantifying
judgments, two independent analysts made these comparisons, and
both concluded that there was a generally high degree of consistency.
It was concluded, therefore, that this picture was providing data
that were consistent, but not synonymous, with data obtainable from
the standard TAT, but that, for the purpose of studying adult age-
sex roles, the special picture had marked advantages over the standard TAT.

Administration

The picture was presented to the respondent at the end of a long
interview that covered various aspects of his life, his views of the
life periods that constitute adulthood, and his attitudes toward
aging. The interviews were conducted for the most part in the
respondent's own home; occasionally, in his place of business.

Three levels of inquiry were employed in using the picture. The
person was asked, first, to tell a story about the picture—a story
with a beginning, a middle, and an end. Then the interviewer, moving clockwise around the picture and beginning with the figure of
the young man, asked the respondent to assign an age and to give a
general description of each of the four figures. Again moving clockwise, the respondent was finally asked to describe what he thought
each figure in the picture was feeling about the others.

Stimulus Value of the Picture

Almost without exception, all respondents saw the picture as
representing a two-generation family. One of the younger figures,
most often the young man, was frequently seen as being outside the
primary group, usually in the role of suitor or fiancée, son-in-law or
daughter-in-law. Although always structured as a family situation,
the stories varied widely. It might be a story of a young man coming to ask for the daughter's hand in marriage and being opposed

by the older woman; it might be a mother, father, daughter, and son-in-law having a casual conversation before dinner; it might be a young couple asking for financial help from parents; or it might be an older couple coming to visit the younger.

It is within the setting of the two-generation family, then, that the role images of the young man, young woman, old man, and old woman emerged.

General Approach to Role Analysis

Having used the three levels of inquiry, the data for each figure can be regarded as a set of expectations as to how that category of person (YM, YW, OM, OW) relates to the social environment and to other categories of persons in the family in terms of action and affect. It is this set of expectations which were regarded operationally as the role description. The following assumption was made: granted that the different attributes ascribed by the respondent to the four figures in the picture have their roots in intrapsychic determinants, the respondent's expectations, based on his experiences with real people, will still have a highly determining effect on which aspects of the self he chooses to ascribe to each figure in the picture. In other words, the investigators took the respondent's perceptions as projections, mindful of the fact that what was given was intrapsychically determined, but trusting that the interactional social reality had called out and directed the projection.

Illustration of the Method

The first step in the analysis was to see what was the preoccupation around which the respondent had built his story, for the role descriptions took on greater meaning once the basic theme, or preoccupation, was understood.

For example, a woman tells the following story:

> I think the boy is going away to the service. He's tell-
> ing the mother and father. That's his wife with him.
> The father is pretty downhearted about it. He has a

downcast look on his face. His wife doesn't feel too good about it, but she's trying to pacify the older couple. They've just been married. I can't tell how it'll end up. If he has to go overseas to fight, there's always the possibility he won't come back.

(General description of the YM) Sort of a boy who has always been close to his parents. Looks like a nice kind of boy.

(General description of the YW) Looks very sympathetic. She's a real nice girl. She's trying to sympathize with the old people.

(General description of the OM) Looks like a nice homebody. Nice fellow.

(General description of the OW) I can't see enough of her face. I couldn't say any more, because there's no face to go by. Sort of refined, from her stature.

(YM's feelings) He thinks they're all right, or he wouldn't have sat down. . . . Well, some boys wouldn't care how their folks felt, but he seems to realize that they're hurt.

(YW's feelings) She thinks her husband is a pretty fine fellow, or she wouldn't be trying to sympathize with his folks.

(OM's feelings) He's pleased with the young folks. He's interested in what his son's going to do.

(OW's feelings) She's in a bad place—can't see enough of her. I really couldn't say.

The theme which underlies this story is the theme of family dispersion, the "empty nest." The respondent tells us, in effect, that the children are leaving home and that they "won't come back."

Looking first at the description of the young man, in the story proper we are told what his action is: to leave home, presumably for some dangerous and rigorous extrafamilial environment. His action has emotional consequences for the parents, consequences which he does not seek to mitigate. His face is set beyond the boundaries of the primary group, and his only action in the group is the rather formal one of making this position clear to his parents. "He's telling the mother and father."

We are next told about the young man that he has always been close to his parents. The implication is that an earlier relationship of the son to the parents is now ending. It is of interest that the respondent speaks of the YM's affiliation to the parents only when she discusses him in the general, nonsituational context. When she is asked to consider him in relation to the immediate situation and to the actors in it, the theme of remoteness infuses the portrayal. This point is made clear when the respondent is again asked to put the young man back into the interactive context and to discuss his feelings there. Now he emerges as one who, although essentially detached, still adheres to minimal social forms. The respondent has difficulty in ascribing any but the most qualified feeling to him: "thinks they're all right," and "seems to realize that they're hurt." The YM's reaction to the parents' feelings is a relatively intellectualized one: he "realizes" or recognizes their existence, while it is his wife who "sympathizes" with them. Even this modest affective gesture on the part of the YM is doubted, for the respondent goes out of her way to assure us that the YM is not like other boys who "wouldn't care how their parents felt." In the respondent's whole recital, then, she attributes to the YM only minimal and grudging affiliation to the parents.

We can now make this general statement about the perception of the young man's familial role—his basic orientation is to rigorous and compelling nonaffective extrafamilial concerns, and intimacy for him is to be found with peers of the opposite sex. Although not too long ago (in terms of subjective time) the primary, parental group was a major focus of his interest, his present role there is governed by moral directives (superego demands) rather than by spontaneous warmth. These directives, coming into conflict with his more compelling extrafamilial interests, result in a posture of grudging punctiliousness, of bare attention to formal, socially defined demands. Himself barely participant in the family—although at the same time, a source of concern to the parents—he leaves to his wife the mediation of the emotional issues between himself and his parents. He is generally governed by outside demands, as though those demands were more congenial to his energies and motivations than are the demands made by the parental group.

Turning to the YW, we are given a different image. In the story proper she, too, appears as one whose actions are directed toward the parents, but, whereas the YM's action toward the parents— telling them that he is leaving—begins and ends his contact with them, her action—"trying to pacify them"—implies a continuing and multifaceted relationship with the older group. The young man only tells them about himself and at the most can only "recognize" the effects of his announcement on the parents. The young woman, although she "doesn't feel too good about it," does not deal with her own reaction but attempts to alleviate the parents' grief. The word "pacify" implies maternal behavior, as does the pattern of dealing with the woes of others rather than with her own.

Our interpretation of the young woman's strong, maternal concern with intimate human relations is strengthened when we look at the general description given of her. Here, the respondent persists in seeing the YW in relation to the current crisis. Again she is seen as a person whose actions are nurturant and consoling, but at this point an element of emotional distance enters into the description. The young woman is "trying" to sympathize with the older group. Here is an implication of some barrier against emotional rapport between the old group and the YW, a barrier which she feels impelled to overcome. The description of the YW's feelings give us a clue as to why she attempts to overcome the barrier. It is because of her regard for her husband that she feels a responsibility to his parents. We are told that her primary affiliation is to her husband and that responsibility to the parents is secondary, stemming from her marital tie. She takes form now as a person who must deal nurturantly with various aspects of the interpersonal universe, although institutional and generational barriers may exist between her and certain others. If formal ties exist between her and other people, she seeks to enrich the formal ties with empathic bonds.

Taking the role description as a whole and seeing it against the theme of "empty nest," we see the young woman's role as one of emotional liaison, operating in the widening breach between the parental and filial generations. Her husband moves off into what are viewed as distant and threatening events while she, though drawn after him, bridges the gap and maintains some version of the lost emotional ties between parents and children. Against the background of traumatic family dispersion, her role has a maternal quality: although her primary tie is to her husband, her immediate concern is for those who have been injured by the course of events, and she attempts in maternal fashion to compensate the injured through her nurturance. In sum, her role is complementary to her husband's in that, while he moves off to "do battle," she tarries behind to handle the human consequences of his actions and decisions.

Turning to the figure of the old man, we first see him as feeling sad at the news of his son's leaving. No actions are ascribed to him. He reacts to traumatic situations with feeling, but he is not seen as acting out his feelings or doing anything to alter the situation which made him sad.

At the level of general description, we are told that he is "a nice homebody," positively regarded. His major cathexis or emotional investment is to the family, and it is there that he is gratified. Values relevant to his role are those of comfort and ease in an affiliative setting.

Moving to the feelings ascribed to the old man, we notice a shift away from the initial description given of him. Where he was initially saddened, he is now "pleased" with the young people, and he will maintain a meaningful, although somewhat intellectualized interest in his son's future activity. There is still no intimation that he will act to change the course of his son's affairs—the son will "do," and the father will be interested—but a note of equanimity has entered the description. If we examine this shift in light of the theme of family dissolution, we conclude that it represents a concept of defensive adjustment, adjustment to the inescapable reality of the young man's maturity through defensive denial of strong personal feeling. After some initial depression, the old man resigns himself to the fact of the breach and returns to the emotional *status quo*. Although the young group, especially the YM, is no longer reciprocally affiliative, the old man's outward feelings toward them remain basically unchanged.

The old man's role, then, somewhat like the young woman's, is an adjustive one. He buffers the shocks of transition. Accepting the reality of change, he acts to minimize the consequent feelings and to find new bases for intimacy in the new situation. It is of particular interest that the old man attempts to maintain the *status quo* by changing himself and hiding his own feelings. At no point in the protocol does he act to change anything outside himself.

This interpretation of the old man's role gains support when we turn to the old woman. In the story proper we are told nothing about her; her presence is merely noted. At the general level of description, perception of her is again denied. In effect, we are told that she has no emotionally expressive surface ("there's no face to go by"). She is associated only with "refinement," a description which implies that she has no contact with a freely affective, spontaneous environment. (By contrast, the old man is the "homebody.") The word "refined" suggests the values of restraint, pride, and possibly a defensive rigidity.

As to the old woman's feelings, the respondent tells us, in effect, that she cannot imagine any feeling states which might pertain, because the OW is "in a bad place." Although there is a relative paucity of data about the OW, we nevertheless obtain the strong impression of rigidity and withdrawal in the figure. Viewed against the thematic background, this rigidity and withdrawal takes on meaning as a possible mode of coping with crisis, but a mode which is quite different from the one defined for the old man. Faced with the trauma of family breakdown, the old man's role is to adjust to the inevitable by minimizing his own reactions. The adjustive mode ascribed to the old woman seems to stress denial of the trauma and its emotional consequences, strict control, and magical defenses against her vulnerability. The old man's adjustment, although a defensive one, still is oriented toward a social universe and untroubled contact with others in future situations. The old woman's role has a more primitive, egocentric quality, as if the vulnerability of the self were the only concern and as if this concern justifies the use of archaic defenses—such as complete denial of a painful situation.

Granted that both the old man's and old woman's roles may represent possible solutions of the respondent's own problem—her defenses against the problem she has proposed—the investigators' primary interest is with the content of the roles as they emerge from the respondent's fantasy and to which figure in the picture each role is ascribed.

Treatment of the Data

Using the method illustrated above, each protocol was analyzed for role descriptions of each of the four stimulus figures. Interpretations were recorded separately for each figure. The protocols were divided according to the sex of the respondent but were analyzed without knowledge of the respondent's age or social class.

Reliability of Interpretations

The question of reliability of interpretations was dealt with at an early stage in the research. Using nine protocols selected at random, two judges rated each of the four figures on a five-point scale for each of twelve personality characteristics, and the ratings were then correlated. The average coefficients of correlation were .81 for the YM, .88 for the YW, .83 for the OM, and .88 for the OW.

This procedure proved to be a somewhat oblique test of reliability, since it was later decided not to deal with the role descriptions on the basis of such ratings, but rather to continue to draw summary descriptions of the figure and then to categorize the descriptions according to similarity. At the same time, this test of reliability was a relatively stringent one for this type of data.

Quantifying the Data

Once all the protocols had been analyzed and decoded, the data for each figure were treated separately. The procedures with reference to the data on the old man will be described here since these were the first to be dealt with and since findings regarding the OM influenced in some ways the organization of the other sets of data.

All the descriptions were grouped on the basis of similarity into mutually exclusive categories, attempting always to judge similarity in terms of the most salient features ascribed to the OM by the respondent. This was a lengthy process since the attempt was to establish categories that would produce the least distortion of the original data. At the same time, having become aware that there were age differences in the perceptions of the OM, the investigators attempted to structure the categories in such fashion as to highlight the age differences.

Six major categories were finally delineated and arranged along a continuum termed "dominance-submission." At one end were those categories in which, whatever other characteristics were ascribed to the OM, he was always a dominant figure within the family. At the other end were those categories in which he was seen as a passive or submissive figure. Dominance or submission was judged in terms of the OM's impact on the situation; the extent to which others deferred to him; the extent to which resolutions of family issues depended upon his wishes, his judgments, or his decisions.

Dealing next with one after another subsample of respondents (middle-class men, middle-class women, working-class men, working-class women), frequency distributions were made in which the role descriptions were plotted by category and by age of respondent. The distributions were then tested for statistical significance by applying the chi-square method.

For each subsample of respondents there was a shift with age in the perceptions of the OM. The role descriptions given by younger respondents (aged forty to fifty-four) more often fell in those categories in which the OM is described as dominant; the descriptions given by older respondents (aged fifty-five to seventy) most often fell in those categories in which the OM is passive. The number of cases in each subsample was too small to establish reliable chi-square values, but the trend was present in every group. Cases were then combined into larger groupings—all male, all female, all middle class, all working class. The age trends were now even more pronounced (P values were between .05 and .01). Finally, when all respondents were grouped together, the age shift was unquestionably reliable (P was .001).

At this point, whereas age of respondent consistently produced variation in the data, it was not clear which of the original variables —age, sex, or social status—was the most important in producing the over-all variation. A further step was therefore taken. Ratings on dominance-submission were assigned to each category of role description; these ratings were then submitted to an analysis of variance. It was found that of all the variables—age, sex, social status, and the interactions thereof—only age was significant (P was beyond .001). The data on the OW were also subjected to analysis of variance, with the same result emerging. Data on the YM and YW could not be treated in the same fashion, however, since the categories in these two sets of data could not justifiably be rated along a single continuum.

In the sections to follow, the data for each of the four figures are reported in turn. In moving from the role images to the implications for personality of the respondents, the investigators are aware that they move to a different area of interpretation. The statements dealing with personality are offered as speculative rather than conclusive. At the same time, the investigators believe that exploring the data in this fashion has produced hypotheses regarding adult personality that merit further research and verification.

The Young Man

Of the four figures in the picture, the YM was ascribed the least significant familial role. Almost half our respondents saw him as being oriented primarily toward the extrafamilial world and only secondarily toward the family. In the family the YM is a rather remote, detached figure. In both the family and the outside world, social forms and institutions, rather than qualities intrinsic to himself, define the YM's role and guide his actions. For instance, the YM is often seen as the suitor of the YW. He makes his request and establishes the problem, but it is then a problem that is out of his hands and depends for its resolution on the action between the OM and OW.

The YM's source of strength is that he represents the more-or-less legitimate demands of the extrafamilial social environment, and, accordingly, his claims must be treated with some respect and consideration.[2] His demands are potentially disruptive to the unity of the primary group, but they symbolize ambition, independence, and maturity and cannot be easily denied.

A frequent component of the YM's role is controlled aggression. If he is seen as an intrusive figure in the family, it is implied that, by exercising self-control, he must protect the parents from the possibly destructive consequences of his impulses. Or, if he does act assertively, he must nullify his action by propitiating the older people. Aggression in the YM can be freely expressed only when it is directed outside the family and when it takes the form of ambition or achievement drive. The YM's aggression is never antisocial. It is not only aggression that is neutralized in the family; there are also few spontaneous affiliative feelings ascribed to the YM. Only 29 per cent of respondents (in categories 3 and 5 of Table 3.2) describe an openly affective familial role for the YM, whereas 71 per cent see him primarily in terms of achievement strivings, social conformity, and impulse control.

A salient feature of the YM's role, then, is that he responds most to promptings from the outer world and least to inner prompting or impulsivity. The implication is that for the YM it is too dangerous to act directly from impulse; he must find guidance in the safe structure of environmental rules and directives.

Categories of Role Descriptions

In examining the role descriptions of the YM, it appeared that there was no single continuum by which the data could be ordered. There were at least two major dimensions of the role: one related to the YM's psychological location, whether he was seen as being oriented primarily toward the outside world or toward the family;

[2] In ninety-two stories told about the picture, the YM was seen as posing a threat to the primary group—he is asking for the daughter in marriage, or he is about to leave home, or he and his wife are thinking of moving to another city. In most of these stories, the YM's demands are being opposed by the OW (who is described in these records as giving priority to the values of intimacy and family solidarity) and are being abetted, at least tacitly, by the OM (who is seen as being more in touch with outer-world demands than is the OW).

TABLE 3.2

ROLE DESCRIPTIONS OF THE YOUNG MAN

Category		40–54		55–70	
		Men	Women	Men	Women
1. Outer-world achievement	Middle class	8	7	1	0
	Working class	7	1	2	0
	Total	23*		3	
2. Family: controlled	Middle class	3	8	0	6
	Working class	7	4	3	3
	Total	22		12	
3. Family: affiliative	Middle class	1	2	5	2
	Working class	2	2	1	1
	Total	7		9	
4. Outer-world conformity	Middle class	1	3	2	3
	Working class	2	4	5	9
	Total	10		19	
5. Family: assertive	Middle class	2	2	3	2
	Working class	3	1	4	3
	Total	8		12	

* The chi-square test was applied to these category totals. The probability that the distribution occurred by chance is less than .001.

the second related to the vitality ascribed to the YM. Five broad categories provided the best fit for the data.

1. "Outer-world achievement." Here are grouped all those role descriptions which ascribe to the YM qualities of aggressiveness or assertion directed toward the extrafamilial world and in which the YM is primarily oriented toward the outer world. Within the family, the YM is affectively remote, bland, or deferent. If self-

assertive needs within the family are recognized at all, they are seen as qualified or attenuated. If affiliative needs are recognized, there is a lack of spontaneity about them. The YM reacts to the family (especially to the parents) in moral and rational terms, rather than in affective terms.

2. "Family: controlled." Here the YM is primarily oriented toward the family and has strong needs for assertion in the intimate family group—needs which must be controlled and limited. The control resides either in parental authority or in the YM's own internalized controls. Thus the YM is seen as checking his aggressive energies and thereby protecting the older group from its consequences. If he acts assertively, he must undo his action by reverting to a supradeferent or abasive stance.

3. "Family: affiliative." The YM is seen here primarily in terms of a potent and spontaneous cathexis to the older group, with strong needs for intrafamilial affiliation. The affiliative needs are usually tempered with succorance needs. (The relative infrequency with which this category occurs is in contrast to the data on the YW.)

4. "Outer-world conformity." This category is similar to the first in that the YM is primarily oriented toward the extrafamilial world, but here he is seen not in terms of an energetic, intrinsic drive toward achievement, but rather in terms of qualities *relevant* to achievement and success. He is "intelligent," "clean-cut," "well groomed," rather than "ambitious" or "aggressive." He is trained for reliable performance, rather than driven to achievement.

Within the family, as in the first category, he is affectively bland, restrained, remote, and relates to family members in rational and moral terms rather than with spontaneous affect.

5. "Family: assertive." Central here is the perception of the YM as an assertive peer in the family. He defines his own needs, goals, purposes, and, without propitiation, he works to further them within the family. He is expressive and chooses freely the objects of affection and dislike among the older group.

Age Differences

As will be seen from Table 3.2, categories 1 and 2 occur pre-

dominantly among younger respondents (aged forty to fifty-four);
categories 4 and 5, among older respondents (aged fifty-five to
seventy). The forty-year-old tends to see the YM as energetic and
self-propelling. His aggressive, intrusive energies are funneled toward the extrafamilial environment, where he is granted the right
of self-expression and achievement; but these energies are successfully checked and controlled in the family setting.

For the sixty-year-old respondent, the outer world is still the important area for the YM (Category 4), but it is no longer an area
which passively awaits the thrust of the YM's dynamic energies. Instead, the outer world is one into which the YM fits neatly by
virtue of possessing those qualities which match the demands of a
complex environment. The older respondent is still concerned with
the YM's aggressive energies within the family (categories 2 and
5), but now there is less faith that these energies can be controlled
or profitably channeled into extrafamilial achievement.

The general age shifts, then, are from seeing the YM as energetic
in the outer world to seeing him as an intrusive figure in the family
and from seeing him as aggressive and achieving in the outer world
to seeing him as passive and conforming in the outer world.

If it is true that the stimulus figure of the YM symbolizes relatedness to the outer world, then these shifts imply personality differences in respondents at the two age levels. For younger respondents,
the individual possesses energy congruent to the opportunities in the
outer world. A certain predatory quality is present in the individual,
and the environment is seen as rewarding boldness and taking risks.

Older respondents seem more cautious. In viewing the YM as
prepared for, rather than motivated toward, achievement, there is
the implication that the outer world is large and complex. One does
not reform the world in line with one's wishes; rather, one conforms
to it. There may be some fear of the outer world among older
people—a feeling that the environment is dangerous and that it is
best approached with respectful and cautious gestures. Furthermore,
to the extent that the YM is himself a symbol of the entering wedge
of the outer world within the family, the aggression that older respondents assign to him perhaps represents their fear of a hostile
and encroaching outer world—a "young man's world."

Sex Differences

The differences between men's and women's views of the YM stem from their concerns with control versus impulsivity. Categories 1, 3, and 5 in Table 3.2 represent relatively free affective expressivity for the YM, either in the family or in the outer world, while categories 2 and 4 represent measures of conformity and restraint. Men's perceptions of the YM are clustered in the expressive categories, women's in the control categories. (The difference between the sexes in this regard is stable beyond the .005 level.)

In the family setting (categories 2 and 5), men give more stress to the YM's unhampered interpersonal assertiveness (Category 5), while women place greater stress on the note of control (Category 2). Similarly, of categories 1 and 4, men use Category 1 where the YM is achieving and self-motivated in the outer world; women use Category 4 where the YM is only functionally oriented to the outer world. Thus men see the YM in terms of intrusive, aggressive drives, while women see him in terms of plasticity and sensitivity to outer pressures. For men, the YM pushes energetically into an unstructured environment. For women, the YM is embedded in a complex, highly articulated environment—he fits neatly and without strain into an established order that has already molded him to its needs. It is as if male respondents propose that the YM is a bull, while women respondents say that he cannot be a bull because the world is a china shop.[3]

In general, then, men tend to accent the energy that the YM brings to role performance. Women recognize the energy, but obliquely, through the stress they place on controlling it.

Social-Class Differences

Although examination of the data in Table 3.2 shows certain differences between all four subsamples of respondents in the way their images of the YM are distributed, the most striking difference

---

[3] Female sexual anxieties may be involved here—the need to limit and confine the intrusive energies of the male and to make of him a "nice" person.

relates to working-class women. Of thirty-one responses from working-class women, only one falls in Category 1, while thirteen fall in Category 4. Thus the working-class women seem unable to conceive of the YM as an aggressive achiever, internally motivated; they stress, instead, the outer demands and influences which bear on him. For these women, the YM is "bleached out," affectively remote, with little strength or drive in either the intrafamilial or the extrafamilial worlds; he is related to others in terms of morality and rationality rather than through patterns of impulsivity or intimacy.

The Young Woman

The young woman, by contrast with the YM, is not only comfortably accounted for in the setting of the family, but she also seems to live only in that setting. Respondents perceive no roles for her other than familial roles.

She is seldom a sharply etched figure. "Nice" or "pleasant" are words frequently used to describe her, and she is most often seen as "waiting" for a decision to be made by the others. Few respondents attribute to her great vitality or autonomy or determination (she stands in contrast to the OW in these respects). At the same time, the YW occupies a central role in the family. Although she is not a vigorous figure who initiates or resolves family issues, she is the figure about whom issues are initiated and resolved. Typical stories are those in which the YM wants to marry her and she waits for her parents' (especially her mother's) decision; or she is already married and about to have a child, and the issue is now what her parents will think of the news; or the older couple is giving advice to the younger, and she is the one who sees both sides of the issue.

It is through the YW that the YM is usually related to the older figures; the YW who provides the tie between younger and older generations. The young man, it will be recalled, is seen as bridging the familial and the commercial worlds; in somewhat similar fashion the young woman bridges two systems of affiliation: affiliation to opposite-sex peer and affiliation to parents. Respondents seem preoccupied with the issue of the YW's affiliation. To whom does she or should she belong? How should she divide herself between the roles of woman and child? What is the nature of her affiliative bonds—are they spontaneous and affective or formal and deferent?

As regards respondents' personalities, we have suggested that the YM symbolizes the problems posed by intrusive masculine energies. The YW seems to symbolize the problems related to tenderness, intimacy, and sexuality—how much are these to be cathected to heterosexual objects, and how much to pregenital objects? For older respondents, a further problem is, given that the YW represents a libidinal fount, how much love can they expect to receive? Or what substitutes for this love can they legimately claim?

Categories of Role Descriptions

The role descriptions of the young woman can be subsumed under six broad categories, each representing a different pattern of the YW's affiliation with the other figures in the picture.

1. "Freedom from parents." Here the YW is strongly affiliated with the YM (her fiancé or husband). She strives successfully against the OW for the right to take on adult sex roles (wife, homemaker, mother), or, already filling such roles, she fights off the encroachments of the OW (usually defined as her mother-in-law).

2. "Affiliated to parents." In this category the YW is seen as related affectively only to the parents. Childlike, she has strong and spontaneous needs for affiliation only with them. Even in those stories in which the YM is seen as her husband, her relationship with him is described in formal terms only, and her primary ties remain to the parents.

3. "Complementary affiliations." Here the YW is affectively related to both the YM and the parents. She has her feet in both camps—she is a good wife and mother, she loves her husband, she loves her parents, and there is no incompatibility among these loyalties. Her affiliations are complementary and nonconflicting.

4. "Conflicted affiliations." In these stories, the YW has strong needs for autonomy, away from the parents and toward the YM, and, at the same time, strong needs for deference and succorance

toward the parents. She is seen in what might be called an adolescent role, as one who pulls forcibly away from the parents toward mature roles and heterosexual affiliation, while remaining dependent on them. She is torn between childish and mature role choices.

5. "Deference to parents." Here the YW relates to parents in terms of succorance and deference, but the relationship is formal, rational, and without warmth. She remains affectively remote from parents and her ties with them are based on superego demands rather than on libidinal demands.

6. "Controlled by parents." Here the YW appears in much the same terms as in Category 5—deference or succorance toward parents, without affective affiliation—except that here there is an added element of being controlled by the parents. These stories deal always with the situation in which the YW is considering marriage (thus at least a formal need for heterosexual affiliation away from the family is recognized) and is deferring to her parents' decision. Not bound to her parents by love, the YW nevertheless passively yields to them the disposition of her affairs.

Age Differences

As seen in Table 3.3, categories 1 and 2 represent the images of the YW held predominantly by younger respondents (aged forty–fifty-four), categories 3 and 4 occur about equally frequently in both age groups, and categories 5 and 6 are those of predominantly older respondents (aged fifty-five–seventy).

Younger respondents see the YW in polar ways. She is either pulling assertively away from the family, intent on becoming a woman and a mother in her own right, or she is freely and spontaneously relating to the parents alone, without cathexis to the YM and without desires for mature, womanly achievement. Younger respondents, as a group, are undecided about the nature of the YW's affiliation and the claims that parents can make on it. There is tension over the issue of allegiance to an extrafamilial (in this case, the YM) or to an intrafamilial identity.

On another level of interpretation, that pertaining to the person-

TABLE 3.3

ROLE DESCRIPTIONS OF THE YOUNG WOMAN

Category		40–54		55–70	
		Men	Women	Men	Women
1. Freedom from	Middle class	5	7	1	3
parents	Working class	6	2	1	1
	Total	20*		6	
2. Affiliated to	Middle class	4	3	0	1
parents	Working class	3	3	1	2
	Total	13		4	
3. Complementary	Middle class	0	3	4	1
affiliations	Working class	4	3	2	2
	Total	10		9	
4. Conflicted	Middle class	5	5	5	2
affiliations	Working class	5	2	4	3
	Total	17		14	
5. Deference to	Middle class	1	1	3	1
parents	Working class	2	1	3	3
	Total	5		10	
6. Controlled by	Middle class	1	3	1	5
parents	Working class	1	1	4	5
	Total	6		15	

* The chi-square test was applied to these category totals. The probability that the distribution occurred by chance is between .005 and .001.

alities of respondents themselves, we may infer some conflict in younger respondents between independent and dependent modes of cathexis, between sexually mature and immature tendencies.

For older respondents, the role descriptions have in common the YW's lack of affective ties with parents, but her deference toward parental authority.

Perhaps the contrast between categories 1 and 6 reveals most sharply the nature of the age shift in perceptions of the YW. Category 1 presents the YW as strongly oriented toward heterosexual affiliation and as desirous of becoming a woman in her own right. Parental controls, if they exist, are to be flouted rather than conformed to. Needs for peer affiliation and mature status are primary. Category 6, on the other hand, shows the YW as being aware of these needs, although parental controls have primacy. Rather than acting on the basis of her own motivations and her own drive toward maturity, she acts on the basis of parental needs and her own introjected controls.

Older respondents seem to have abandoned the expectation that the YW will have any strong feelings for parents. They stress the submissive rather than the libidinal qualities in the parent-child relationship (to the extent that the YW is affiliative toward the older generation, the affiliation is charged with succorance needs rather than with spontaneous warmth). Instead of love, parents will have respect. To older respondents as a group, the figure of the YW no longer presents the conflict seen by younger respondents—the conflict between heterosexual impulses that have a centrifugal effect upon the primary group and childish impulses that have a centripetal effect. Now the YW's centrifugal tendencies are seen as controlled, and the YW herself is seen as taking responsibility for maintaining some vestige of the parent-child relationship.

Turning again to questions of personality change with age, it has been suggested that the YW symbolizes the issues of intimacy and sexuality. With increased age of respondent, there is increased emphasis on the YW's dependence on parents for nurturance and control. For sixty-year-olds, then, the conflict between heterosexual and pregenital modes of cathexis appears to have been resolved in favor of the latter. Heterosexual concerns are no longer seen as compelling and are not viewed as legitimate reasons for breaking away from the home. Perhaps a further implication is that, for the older respondent, the world seems to be shrinking toward the confines of the controlling and nurturing family. Older respondents no longer strain away from the family in fantasy; instead, they seem to identify with the controls that keep them in it.

The older respondents' perceptions of the young man are also relevant here. The YM is seen as relating to the outer world as a conformist, as one who adapts himself to the demands of the extrafamilial environment. Similarly, the young woman relates as a conformist to the parents, as one who lives in a world of strictures rather than in a world of self-initiated action. (This finding, that with increasing age of respondent there is increasing conformity ascribed to the young, is statistically reliable beyond the .001 level.) The similarity in these views suggests that, to the sixty-year-old, the individual is no longer a forceful manipulator of the object world, but is instead a rather passive object manipulated by the environment. The individual can determine only partly the outcomes of such manipulations and then only by adopting attitudes of accommodation and conformity.

Sex Differences

Men and women are in general agreement in their perceptions of the YW. Table 3.3 shows that men more often than women see the YW in conflict over the question of where her primary affiliations lie (Category 4) and that women more often than men see the YW as being controlled by parents (Category 6); but the overall similarities between the sexes are perhaps more striking than the differences.

At the same time there are certain sex differences in perception of the YW that are not shown in Table 3.3. Younger men sometimes describe the YW as already established beyond the family confines, as a wife and mother in her own right, and as being affectively remote from parents (these stories form a subcategory of Category 1). This view of the YW never occurs among women respondents. Instead, throughout these data, women always demand that the YW's movement away from the family be accompanied by some compensatory gesture of affiliation or deference toward parents. Women cannot be neutral or unconcerned either about the YW's identifications nor about the more general issue of setting children free. (Something of the same tendency occurs around the figure of the young man, although to lesser extent.) Men are somewhat more willing to admit that the YW can be equally a wife and daughter; women tend to say that she is first a daughter and second a wife.

Social-Class Differences

Examination of Table 3.3 shows great similarity between middle- and working-class respondents in their perceptions of the YW. In only one segment of the data is there a significant difference: middle-class women, as compared with working-class women, more frequently see the YW in terms of Category 1—as vigorous, autonomous, sometimes rebellious, and successful in breaking her ties to parents.

It will be recalled that these women also ascribed energy and drive to the young man more frequently than did working-class women. Thus, although equally concerned with the issue of controlling the young, middle-class mothers, by ascribing greater vitality to both the YM and YW, are implying that the relationship between younger and older generations is a complex problem and that young people, by being something of a match for parents, are not easily controlled.

The Old Man

The old man is sometimes an authoritative, but more often a submissive, figure in the family. Those respondents who see him as dominant tend also to propose some hesitancies in the exercise of that role. He may act to limit the young people in some way, but, if so, he puts restrictions not on their freedom of action but on their succorant demands toward him. If he is approached for advice, he may tell children in effect to "grow up" or "use your own judgment." In short, the OM is most authoritative when he is pointing out to the others that he is not an authority.

In some instances, the OM is seen as standing between an autonomy-seeking YM and an overnurturant OW who would spoil the YM if the OM did not intervene. This issue of the YM's untrammeled achievement is one of the few about which the OM can act assertively. In most cases, however, he is overwhelmed by the complexity of an emotional situation, withdraws, and turns it over to the OW. At other times, he is isolated altogether.

On the other hand, somewhat like the YM, the OM is not altogether circumscribed in the family setting. It is recognized that he has preoccupations in other areas. Although he is seldom described as achieving or successful in the extrafamilial world (his is a custodial rather than an achieving role), still the implication is clear that to gauge his impact in the family setting is not to gauge his full worth as a person.

In comparison with the old woman, the OM has a certain blandness of affective life. He tends generally to be passive and resigned to whatever happens. The affect that he most consistently expresses is that of uncritical affiliation: "He likes them all and wants to do the right thing for everybody." The OM has, in general, less impulse life than the OW and is less often portrayed as being in conflict.

The essence of the OM's role is perhaps this: he can wrestle with the interpersonal environment when such activity has the purpose of gratifying others. If he stands opposed to others, then he must alter himself to conform to their needs, or he must withdraw to a world of inner contemplation where the actions of others do not impinge upon him.

The figure of the OM seems to symbolize for respondents the ego qualities of the personality: the rational rather than the impulsive approach to problems, concern over the needs of others, reconciliation between opposing interests, cerebral competence.

Categories of Role Descriptions

The descriptions of the OM fall into six major categories that can be ordered along a continuum from dominance to submission.

1. "Altruistic authority." In this category the OM is seen in a position of authority in the family, and he uses his authority to benefit the young people or the family as a whole. He is the benevolent monarch, the nurturant wise man, whose actions are al-

truistically motivated and lead only to benevolent outcomes. He operates effortlessly and easily in this role.

2. "Assertive, but guilty." These descriptions are those in which the OM attempts to further his own ends, but is restrained by inner reluctances, doubts, or guilt. He occupies a position of strength and asserts himself in the family, and, although he is not opposed by others, he nevertheless cannot easily and single-mindedly press for his announced goals. There is always some quality of inner doubt about the justice of his claims. He is conflicted, unsure, the insecure autocrat. "He thinks it's about time those kids left home and earned their own living—he hates to tell them, though."

3. "Formal authority." Here the father is the authority, but by default. His authority is challenged as the story progresses, or other individuals take action to decide outcomes while he acts only to approve those outcomes. He is described here not so much in terms of service to others (as in Category 1), but in terms of pliability to the wishes of others. He merely approves decisions which have already been thrashed out among more active figures.

4. "Surrendered authority." It is indicated here that the OM could be the authority if he desired—he possesses the requisite qualities—but he refuses and/or abandons the role. In some instances, he is initially described as dominant, but, as the story unfolds, he is relegated to a more submissive position. In other instances, he is ascribed the qualities associated with leadership, but these qualities are split away from action—they have no impact on the events of the story, they do not impinge on outcomes, they find no overt behavioral expression. He is inwardly "tough" but overtly passive, or he has "executive qualities" but leaves the decision up to his wife. In no instance is there an intrusion of the OM as a dominant force on the family scene.

5. "Passive, affiliative." Here the OM is described in terms of what might be called maternal qualities. He is unflaggingly and uncritically affiliative toward the others. He "loves everybody." He accepts, resignedly, outcomes which he may not approve. He is dominated by his wife, but seems to feel no discomfort or resentment in the situation. In stories where the OW is opposing some action proposed by the young people, such as marriage, the OM's attitude

is one of affiliating with both sides—of saying affectionately to the
OW, "Why fight the inevitable?"

6. "Passive, cerebral." Grouped here are those descriptions which
present the OM as passive and withdrawn. He lacks any announced
affiliative attachments to others. The issue of authority does not
even arise. His wife rules the family, and he remains remote, both
in terms of action and affect, from the family drama. As this drama
swirls about him, he "thinks." (The content of his thought or its
relevance to the situation is rarely specified.) The OM controls
events from behind the forehead, as it were, and takes a certain
satisfaction in the freedom this provides him. As one male respondent put it, "He's made up his mind about the thing. He's waiting
for the old woman to tell them what to do."

Age Differences

As shown in Table 3.4, there is a consistent shift, with increasing
age of respondent, from seeing the OM in situations of power in
the family toward seeing him as passive and submissive. (This age
shift is statistically significant beyond the .005 level.)

The stimulus figure of the OM confronts the majority of younger
respondents with the issue of familial authority. (If Category 4 is
included, then approximately 75 per cent of all younger respondents
see the OM either as an authority figure or as one who possesses the
potential for authority.)

Each of the first four categories in Table 3.4 represents a different
resolution of the issue of male dominance. The first two represent
active resolutions. If the issue is met head on—if, that is, the OM
defines self-gratifying goals and uses his position of authority to
achieve them (Category 2)—then ambivalence and guilt are the
necessary results. If, on the other hand, the OM uses his authority
nurturantly for the benefit of others, he can act easily and comfortably in his position (Category 1). The more passive solutions
involve either the OM's sanctioning of the wishes of others and attempting no intervention in the family scene (Category 3) or the
more outright abandonment of the authoritative status altogether
(Category 4).

TABLE 3.4

ROLE DESCRIPTIONS OF THE OLD MAN

Category		40–54		55–70	
		Men	Women	Men	Women
1. Altruistic authority	Middle class	5	9	2	1
	Working class	3	3	1	3
	Total	20*		7	
2. Assertive, but guilty	Middle class	2	0	2	2
	Working class	6	1	1	1
	Total	9		6	
3. Formal authority	Middle class	5	5	0	0
	Working class	2	3	1	0
	Total	15		1	
4. Surrendered authority	Middle class	2	3	4	3
	Working class	6	1	3	2
	Total	12		12	
5. Passive, affiliative	Middle class	0	4	2	6
	Working class	3	4	3	8
	Total	11		19	
6. Passive, cerebral	Middle class	4	1	4	1
	Working class	1	0	6	2
	Total	6		13	

* The chi-square test was applied to these category totals. The probability that the distribution occurred by chance is less than .001.

For our forty–fifty-four group, the issue being dealt with around the role of the OM is not only that of male dominance, however, but also that of male aggression in the family. (The latter was also one of the primary issues in the role descriptions of the YM.) The problem seems to be how the OM can be an authority without being arbitrarily, and perhaps harmfully, self-assertive. How can the cultural demand—that the father is head of the family—be met without exposing the family to male aggression? As already suggested, the solution seems to involve the stressing of the moral function of authority: the OM must be either an active force for good, or, by "letting things happen," he passively cooperates with the others in arriving at positive outcomes.

For older respondents, the OM no longer presents the issue of masculine authority. The stories are now those in which the OM has no impact upon family events, and he presents only one or another image of passivity. (Of all respondents aged fifty-five–seventy, 55 per cent are found in the last two categories. If Category 4 is included—the OM abandoning or surrendering authority—then 80 per cent of all older respondents see the OM among the categories of submission and denial of authority.)

The age shift in the image of the OM from dominance to submission is elaborated in several ways. The forty-year-old respondent sees the OM as being in doubt about his own assertive tendencies; the sixty-year-old sees him as being the passive object of others' assertion. In the forties, the OM is seen as attempting to control events. In the sixties, he attempts only to control and order the cognitive environment, the symbolic traces of objects and events. In the forties, it is proposed that the OM is aware of the pressures from an impulsive and willful woman, but that he can allow the OW full expression and still wisely control the course of events. In the sixties, it is proposed that impulse, in the form of the OW, is left in charge of the field, that the OM's wisdom can control events only behind the forehead. The OM has moved from a stance of intrafamilial autonomy to "intracranial" autonomy.

In regard to the implications for personality differences in respondents, it has been said that the figure of the OM symbolizes ego qualities of the personality. With increased age of respondent, the ego, as personified by the OM, seems to contract. On the one hand, it is no longer in contact with impulse life, controlling and channeling it (the OM no longer controls the OW's impulsivity). On the other hand, the ego is no longer in a position of mastery relative to the outer world (the OM is not successful in the extrafamilial world). Ego functions are turned inward, as it were, and, although rational thought processes are still important in the personality, thought is no longer relevant to action.

Age-Sex Differences

Although age differences in the perception of the OM along the dominance-submission axis are consistent, there are, at the same time, important differences between the sexes.

Women. Among younger respondents, it is primarily the women who see the OM in the altruistic, nurturant role (Category 1); it is the men who tend to see him in the role of insecure autocrat (Category 2).

Women see the OM as a kind of benign ego figure who exercises his authority benevolently. He allows the children to go off and get married, for instance, and he lets the OW rave about their leaving, knowing all the time that this is what reality is—children grow up, and the OW's feelings about it, no matter how stridently expressed, cannot really change anything nor hurt anyone. In allowing the OW to rant, the OM nevertheless deftly controls her, and he prevents her feelings from dominating the situation. (It is as if the women respondents who tell these stories are saying of themselves that they rely on their husbands to let them be emotional and expressive; that, as long as their husbands are present to control events, they, the women, cannot hurt themselves or others.)

Among the older respondents, it is predominantly the women who stress the OM's affective qualities, especially his "sweetness" (Category 5). There is a nurturant, almost maternal quality in the OM's passivity.

The OM appears to both younger and older women, then, as one who is identified with the needs of younger individuals. The difference between younger and older women respondents lies in the fact that, for the former, the OM is seen as enforcing his nurturant views on events, guaranteeing benevolent outcomes to the young. For the latter, the OM no longer acts effectively from his nurturant posture. The OM's role does not now have the same quality as before of a barrier interposing between an incensed OW and the vulnerable young. The OW is let loose in the situation, and the OM is no longer capable of checking her. (At the same time, it is suggested that really the young are no longer vulnerable and that they somehow operate beyond the OW's reach.) The age shift for women occurs, then, in terms of the OM's decreasing effectiveness in implementing his nurturant attitudes and in making outcomes conform to them.

With regard to personalities of respondents, women, in responding to the figure of the OM, seem to be preoccupied with concepts of altruism, nurturance, and generativity. In early middle age (forty–fifty-four), they propose that these qualities are the important ones in the disposition of affairs. Even though, in the stories told by younger women, the OW may be at odds with the OM, it is the OM who wins out. As they age, women still acknowledge the relevance of nurturance and generativity and still lodge these qualities in the figure of the OM, but they now propose that the more self-assertive, domineering OW will carry the day. Thus they imply that the soft, warm, maternal qualities are not so important on the family scene—or in their own affective repertoire—as when they were younger. Perhaps, as children become mature and less emotionally vulnerable, women can allow themselves to be more tolerant of their own needs for self-assertion and domination. Perhaps they are less frightened of the aggressive side of their personalities once they can reassure themselves that it will no longer interfere with the maternal function, will no longer have destructive consequences for the young.

Men. For male respondents, the age shift occurs along different continua than for women. Though for men, too, the OM's authority decreases with increasing age of respondent, the issues are those of competence and assertiveness. The forty-year-old male sees the OM as struggling with problems relating to assertion, guilt, nurturance, and affiliativeness—conflicts he attempts to solve in terms of complex role patterns that integrate the various elements. The sixty-year-old male tends to see the OM as one who has simplified these problems. The OM has reached a solution through relinquishing the assertive role elements and has abandoned any attempts at active manipulation of the environment. Rather than attempt to alter the environment, he adjusts to it. Rather than deal with people and events, he organizes only the conceptual traces of the environment as they intrude on his inner world of thought.

For older men, the figure of the OM is elaborated largely in terms of his continuing cerebral competence (Category 6). Rather than actively intervene in the family and take the responsibility such intervention entails, the OM restricts himself to the control of symbols. Ordering the inner cognitive world has replaced the more risk-laden transactions with the environment. For example, a man of sixty-four says of the OM: "He's easygoing. Doesn't care whether school keeps. He doesn't take care of his clothes." The theme of the story is illness, and the OM relative to this crisis is described further: "I don't know—but from his appearance he looks like a man who would like to light his pipe and get off somewhere and think about it." Here threat is met by flight and isolation; the OM's thought processes are the last remnant of competence, the surviving manipulative mode. The OM in this story has almost ceased dealing with a social environment. His only meaningful affiliation is to a non-human pacifier, a pipe. This, in rather extreme form, is the modal image of the OM given us by older men.

In relating these role descriptions with the personalities of respondents, the implication is that men, as they spell out the role of the OM, are concerned with the problems of male assertiveness. It will be recalled that somewhat the same issues are dealt with when men verbalize their fantasies around the YM. Men seem to say that, for both the YM and OM, aggression and self-assertion are inappropriate or inacceptable in the family. Young men must control themselves (or be controlled by parents). Older men, to avoid guilt, must act as altruists or conformists, or they must withdraw altogether from active participation in the family. For both the YM and OM, there is an area outside that of family interaction in which one can be competent—for the YM, the world of industry and work; for the OM, the world of thought.

With increasing age, men seem also to see a shifting pattern of interaction between YM and OM in the family scene. For the forty-year-old, a YM will direct his energies outward, and the OM will be the benevolent authority in the family. For the sixty-year-old, a YM has become a more assertive force in the family (although his assertiveness is still not harmful), and an OM has withdrawn from family interaction altogether. It is of special interest that the energies of the YM and OM do not clash; the two rarely strive for dominance in the same area at the same time.

Social-Class Differences

Table 3.4 shows great consistency between middle-class and working-class respondents of both sexes in the distribution of responses. It appears that social class is not a meaningful variable and that the same age and sex differences in perceptions of the OM occur in both social classes.

The Old Woman

The old woman, by comparison to the other figures in the picture, is the key figure in the family. The family is her arena, and within it she emerges in full scope and complexity. In stories where the solidarity of the family is stressed, the OW is the one around whom the family is centered. In stories of conflict, she is always the key protagonist. There are, for instance, a number of stories that might be labeled "Oedipal" in theme—stories in which the YW is being claimed by the YM or vice versa and in which there is conflict between the young and the old. In these stories, it is always the OW, but not the OM, who is seen as the protagonist in the struggle.

For the OW, the major issue is around retentiveness of the young —what the extent and the nature of the tie between herself and her children is to be. This issue always has strong emotional components for her.

In contrast to the young woman, the OW is seen as standing on her own feet, a person in her own right. The psychological distance between her and the old man is much greater than that between the two young figures. Whereas the YW and YM are seen in a close, collaborative relationship, the OW and OM stand separate and apart. They are often described in polar terms—if one is dominant, the other is submissive; if one is nurturant, the other is narcissistic.

Compared with the other figures, the OW is the one to whom the greatest depth and variety of feelings are assigned. In particular contrast to the YW, the OW is seldom bland and seldom neutral; she has strong feelings, both positive and negative. More often than not she is seen as acting on the basis of impulse and inner need, as the most inner-directed of the figures. Although her desires may be limited by the actions of others or she may surrender to superior forces, she never doubts the rightness of her position.

The OW is not always seen as comfortable in her role, and she is the only figure who is as often described by respondents in negative as in positive terms.

Categories of Role Descriptions

Descriptions of the old woman were grouped into six major categories. Although the categories are ordered in Table 3.5 along the general continuum from submission to dominance, there are really two major themes which, in one or another combination, form the basis for the differentiation. The first is the theme of control over others—whether the OW is seen as submissive and controlled (categories 1, 2, 3) or as dominant and the controller (categories 4, 5, 6). The second theme is that of the nature of impulsivity—whether the OW is viewed as benign and nurturant (categories 1, 4, 5) or self-assertive and aggressive (categories 2, 3, 6).

1. "Submissive, nurturant." Here the OW is viewed as passive relative to the determination of outcomes. She is affiliative, nurturant, benevolent, but never self-assertive. She takes a position of deference to a wise, authoritative old man. She is the fluttery, "little-woman" type and never intrudes on the masculine prerogatives of thought and decision. She is dependent on her husband for guidance and for control. To the extent that she takes action at all, the action is nurturant, promoting the best interests of others, especially the young.

2. "Controlled by OM." Here the OW is seen as aggressive and impulsive, but she is controlled by the OM. Although she is something of a "battle-ax," she is more the family nuisance than the

TABLE 3.5

ROLE DESCRIPTIONS OF THE OLD WOMAN

Category		40–54		55–70	
		Men	Women	Men	Women
1. Submissive, nurturant	Middle class	10	6	1	3
	Working class	4	4	2	3
	Total	24*		9	
2. Controlled by OM	Middle class	1	9	1	0
	Working class	5	5	1	2
	Total	20		4	
3. Limited by children	Middle class	2	3	1	1
	Working class	3	2	2	4
	Total	10		8	
4. The good mother	Middle class	2	0	7	2
	Working class	7	0	3	2
	Total	9		14	
5. The matriarch	Middle class	1	3	0	3
	Working class	1	0	1	1
	Total	5		5	
6. Hostile self-assertion	Middle class	2	1	4	3
	Working class	1	1	5	4
	Total	5		16	

* The chi-square test was applied to these category totals. The probability that the distribution occurred by chance is less than .001.

family menace. Her rages do not intimidate; they merely annoy. The wise and tolerant husband allows her free expression of her feelings, but deftly controls her. He determines outcomes and guar-

antees nurturant solutions to the autonomy-seeking young, often in
the face of the OW's active opposition.

3. "Limited by children." Here, as in the preceding category, an
aggressive, domineering OW tries to extend her control over a re-
sistant environment. While she now dominates her husband, she is
successfully opposed and limited by the YW and/or the YM. The
OM cannot provide a buffer between the intrusive OW and the
young, but the young take up the cudgels for themselves and win
out against the OW.

4. "The good mother." Here the issue of dominance-submission is
not specifically introduced, though the OW is implicitly given the
decisive role in the disposition of affairs. The OW is the good,
nurturant mother who guides and supports her gratified husband
and children. She is mild, benign, maternal. Though she has the
most effective role in the family, there is no tension between her
and the others. The view is rather of harmonious interaction, where
it is only right and "natural" that the mother holds the most important place in the family.

5. "The matriarch." In this category the OW is seen as a forceful
and aggressive authority. While, however, she has complete sway
over the others, this leads only to benign results. The family, rather
than opposing her, bask contentedly in their dependent and submissive positions. Everyone benefits from her rule.

6. "Hostile self-assertion." Here the OW is a stereotyped figure,
one who exercises a harsh, arbitrary, and unopposed control. Her
dominance is not tempered by any redeeming strain of affiliation or
nurturance, nor does she have any concern for others. The OW is
either pictured as the embodiment of amoral id—all impulse and
wrath—or the punitive superego who harshly judges others and
rigidly defines the moral code—a superego armed, as it were, with
the energies of the id.

Age Differences

As shown in Table 3.5, role definitions of the old woman, like
those of the other three figures, vary consistently with age of respondent. Whereas the age shift in the perception of the old man's

role is in the direction of increasing submissiveness, the OW moves from a subordinate to an authoritative family role. (The age shift is statistically stable at the .001 level.) [4]

In the first three categories, primarily those of younger respondents, the OW is seen either as "socialized"—adapting her behavior and attitudes to the needs of others (Category 1)—or as aggressive and impulsive, but being held in check by effective outer restraints (categories 2, 3). In either case, her impact on the situation is relatively unimportant. Older respondents hold that, whether "socialized" and nurturant (categories 4, 5) or punitive and narcissistic (Category 6), the OW is the dominant figure, responsible for the outcome of family affairs.

Younger respondents, then, view the OW as sensitive to, or checked by, outer demands and pressures. Older respondents propose that the OW has come to be the embodiment of controls, strictures, limits. She has taken over the moral and directive qualities which, for younger respondents, were seen as operating outside herself.

In general, with increasing age of respondent, the OW emerges more and more as the most feeling, demanding, and aggressive figure, as the other figures tend toward greater passivity, colorlessness, and conformity. In stories told by older respondents, the point at which the OW is described tends frequently to signal the breakthrough of impulsivity, as if the OW represents unchecked impulse in a scene otherwise populated by more constricted, conforming, or affiliative figures. [5]

It has already been implied that, as regards respondents themselves, the old woman symbolizes the impulsive, self-centered qualities of the personality (in contrast to the OM, who symbolizes ego qualities of the personality). The age shift in perception of the OW

---

[4] In a subsequent study of forty-seven older men in which the same TAT card was used, Margaret Thaler Singer found essentially the same perceptions of the OM and OW (Singer, 1963, pp. 230–231).

[5] Perhaps the projection of impulsive elements of personality on the figure of the OW is partially stimulated by her facelessness in the picture. If impulsivity is regarded by respondents as ego-alien, it might well be ascribed to that figure in the picture which provides fewest cues regarding social interaction.

implies, therefore, increasing pressures from the impulse life in the face of decreasing ego controls.

Age-Sex Differences

Although men and women generally agree on the broad outlines of the shift from submission to dominance in the OW's role, the shift for the two sex groups takes place along different axes and in terms of different role attributes.

Although many men view the OW as having strong aggressive and intrusive needs, still a significantly greater number see her—whether dominant or not—as benign and maternal. (Sixty per cent of all males place the OW in categories 1, 4, or 5.) The most frequent image of the OW among younger men is that of the good little woman leaning on a strong and wise husband (Category 1) or the good mother whose influence, though decisive, is only benevolent and constructive (Category 4). For older men, the most frequent image is again that of the good mother (Category 4) around whom there is no tension but only gratification. For many of the men, then, the OW remains motherly, benign, nurturant, but the implication is that these maternal, affiliative qualities come to take on greater significance in the resolution of family issues. The OW remains essentially the same person, but her impact on the family increases. She is no longer submissive or controlled by others; instead, the issue of authority disappears altogether as the OW is allowed to "come into her own."

Perhaps the implication in regard to the personalities of most older men is that they are more receptive to their own affiliative, nurturant, and sensual promptings than are younger men. In projecting these qualities on the figure of the OW and then giving the OW a central role in the determination of outcomes, these older men seem to accept "womanly" qualities in themselves and to feel little need to deny or limit these qualities.

There are, on the other hand, a sizable number of older men who see the OW as a hostile and punitive autocrat (Category 6). In these stories, the OM withdraws from the family scene (removing himself, as it were, from the fray) but creates for himself an arena in which he is not only invulnerable but also still competent—the arena of the intellect. Perhaps this group of older men, in contrast to the majority, cannot accept the new passivity in their personalities and so regress to archaic defenses against it. They project on to the old woman the responsibility for their passivity. By proposing that she is a tyrant, they justify their own submission as something imposed on them, not something inherent in their own personalities. This group of older men is perhaps saying, also, that hostile and aggressive impulses in the personality (qualities projected onto the OW) can no longer, as with younger men, be countered with more benevolent and altruistic impulses. (It is only in the younger men's fantasies that the maternal OM limits and controls the impulsive OW.) Since impulse can now be only destructive and hostile, it should be done away with altogether, and the attempt should be to lead a life of quiet reason.

Although many women recognize the OW as a nurturant figure, the majority see her in terms of assertive, intrusive qualities. (Fifty-five per cent of all female responses place the OW in categories 2, 3, or 6.) Younger women tend to see the OW's needs for dominance and aggressive self-assertion as being effectively restrained—limits are set on her by her husband or by her children. (It should be noted that, of thirty-four younger women respondents, not one sees the OW in Category 4, as merely the "good mother" untroubled by problems of narcissistic needs.) For older women, the OW is still essentially a self-assertive figure, but now the limits have become ineffectual and less charged with moral authority. Where the OW was once blocked by agents who had right on their side—an OM who had greater wisdom and nurturance than she or young people whose claims for autonomy were valid—the OW now becomes self-righteously assertive. This self-assertion may go in either direction —the narcissistic autocrat or the good mother whose benevolent sway over family affairs is unchallenged—but in either case it is the OW's domineering needs that win out.

Moving again to the area of personality, as has already been pointed out in reference to perceptions of the old man, women, as they age, seem to become more responsive toward, and less guilty about, their own aggressive, egocentric impulses. Aggression and self-assertion are, perhaps, viewed as inimical to the central functions of motherhood and can only be tolerated and acted out when the young are sufficiently independent to withstand or ignore the mother's intrusiveness. Hence it is only older women, whose children are presumably grown, who fantasy the OW's monolithic and unchecked dominance. The benign, maternal qualities meanwhile tend to become more ego-alien and are projected on to the OM, who, although seen as ineffectual, is nevertheless also regarded by women as the more lovable figure of the two.

It has been said that female respondents lay greater stress than do male respondents on the OW's aggressive needs for controlling others and on the forces which oppose these needs. These findings suggest a sex difference in regard to the more general issue of social controls. It appears that men, seeing the OW exercising a benign control over a complaisant and gratified family, are generally proposing that authority is not coercive and that self-restriction and compliance are natural and unforced. Control is essentially internalized and does not require punitive external measures for its maintenance. Authority is good, acceptable, and unquestioned. This is in contrast to the female view. Women, viewing the domineering OW as essentially in conflict with her environment—forcibly controlling it or being checked by it—suggest that for them control, submissiveness, and conformity are more difficult issues.

Social-Class Differences

Examination of Table 3.5 shows a remarkable consistency between middle-class and working-class groups in their views of the OW. As was the case with the figure of the old man, it is not social class, but age and sex, of respondent that produce the variation in the data.

Fantasy Data in Relation to Sex-Role Behavior

Since these findings have been derived from projective data, what are their implications for role behavior?

The individual, in filling real-life roles, resolves tensions between personal needs and social expectations. The task of the ego is to organize the various affective components of the personality into a personally expressive, though socially acceptable, pattern of behavior. When presented with the picture, however, a different demand is made of the respondent. He is asked not to act in the real family setting, but to breathe vitality into a representation of family life. The task of the ego is not one of integrating various aspects of the self into a coherent pattern of behavior, but the opposite—in effect, to distribute various components of the self among the various figures in the picture.

This fractionating of the components of personality makes the thematic apperception technique a valuable clinical instrument, but it also imposes qualifications on its use in the study of social roles. In the latter case, the respondent describes a living complexity (the role of YM or OW) in terms of only one or a few facets of the self. The projected aspect of the self, temporarily winnowed out of the total personality, tends to be expressed in exaggerated form. The result is a certain stereotypy and a certain overemphasis in the role descriptions. The task of the role analyst is thus made correspondingly difficult. The role patterns he wishes to describe may have been distorted into nonviable extremes as they have become the focuses for conflicting elements in the respondents' personalities. Rather than objective role descriptions, his data are the affective connotations of role behavior, those which people limit and modify in real life.

The findings presented here must be interpreted with caution, then, in applying them to actual role behavior. It should be kept in mind that, if the respondent speaks of the old man as weak and passive and the old woman as dominant and manipulative, he is describing not only two polar forms of behavior but also two aspects of himself and that both aspects will find some (though not equal) expression in his own behavior. If the respondent is an older man, he cannot be described merely on the basis of his description of the old man as passive and weak, for the respondent is a person who also has needs for strength and dominance. It is the nature of the task—responding to the picture—which allows him to describe the old man in more unitary ways than are actually true of himself.

These considerations apply equally with regard to collective role images that emerge from groups of respondents. For example, many older respondents seem to agree that older men are passive, affectless, and isolated from the stream of family events. They are described as "smoking their pipes" and "thinking." It cannot be assumed, however, that the only role of older men in the family is to stand in the corner, thinking and smoking. People who live in the family setting, young or old, do interact with others and do impinge on the environments of other family members. What can be justifiably assumed from this image is not that older men never interact or relate, but that the very activities through which they express the outward forms of intimacy also tend to highlight their desire for passivity and isolated contemplation. The image does not report the daily reality of the older man's role; rather, it is a sharply drawn, condensed expression of the affective mode which underlies his activities. The sharpness of the image is derived from the condensed expression of what is seen as being central to the figure of the old man and from the affective components of the respondents' personalities identified with this central tendency.

What we have in these data, then, is centrality rather than experienced complexity of role behavior.

To take another example, in many stories, especially in those told by men, the description of the old woman provides a point at which unchecked impulse breaks into a scene otherwise peopled by more restrained or affiliative figures. She is a figure of primal omnipotence and wrath—"a devil. Very strict. Must run everything and everybody." In one sense the description functions to bring the aggressive impulse life of the respondent into the story.[6] What emerges is not an unbiased account of the old woman, but a picture of the old woman as it is filled out by aggressive energy that has its locus in the respondent himself. (It is the respondent's own denied rage, projected on to the figure of the old woman, that he calls a

[6] In real life the respondent's wife may function so as to express elements of the respondent's impulse life that are denied expression in his own behavior. Our findings hint at the possibility that males often handle their aggression in the family by proposing that they are the passive object of attack from a woman, rather than by proposing that aggression stems from themselves.

"devil.") Women who live in a social environment cannot act purely from unmediated primitive impulse. They would soon be hospitalized, institutionalized, or dead. What we are being told in such accounts is that older women's behavior in the family expresses, for those respondents preoccupied with such issues, a central quality of free aggression.

Bearing such considerations in mind, these findings can nevertheless be related to actual role behavior. This relationship is posited on the grounds that the affective complexes energizing the perception of the stimulus figures are indeed cued by the respondents' expectations of such figures in real life. Granted that various components of the respondent's own personality migrate toward one or another stimulus figure, the impressive fact is the consistency with which the same personality components migrate to the same figure in the picture. For instance, for both men and women respondents, it is almost always the old woman, not the old man, to whom impulsivity, aggressivity, and hostile dominance are ascribed. This consistency cannot be explained by chance. The assumption seems warranted that there is something common to the actual role behaviors of older women that elicits this consistency in respondents' fantasies.

To sum up, projective data do not yield descriptions of the total and complex role of the older woman in the family as that role is expressed in everyday, overt behavior (similarly for other figures). What is obtained instead is a central aspect of the role, an aspect that, in one translated form of behavior or another, is being recognized by both men and women.

The role images of all four figures varied consistently with age and sex of respondent, but not with social class. Most striking was the fact that, with increasing age of respondents, the old man and old woman reversed roles in regard to authority in the family. For younger men and women (aged forty–fifty-four) the old man was seen as the authority figure. For older men and women (aged fifty-five–seventy) the old woman was in the dominant role, and the old man, no matter what other qualities were ascribed to him, was seen as submissive.

The different images of all four figures presented by men and women at the two age levels imply personality changes in the years from forty to seventy. For example, women, as they age, seem to become more tolerant of their own aggressive, egocentric impulses; whereas men, as they age, of their own nurturant and affiliative impulses. To take another example, with increasing age in both men and women, ego qualities in the personality seem to become more constricted—more detached from the mastery of affairs and less in control of impulse life.

4

EGO FUNCTIONS IN THE
MIDDLE AND LATER YEARS:
A THEMATIC APPERCEPTION
STUDY

Jacqueline L. Rosen

Bernice L. Neugarten

Recently advanced concepts in ego psychology have provided
a framework for integrating a variety of observations on personality
development from infancy to adulthood.[1] These concepts have not
yet, however, been systematically extended to personality changes
that occur during the middle and later years. Although there are a
number of useful references in the literature that relate to modifi-
cations in ego functions during adulthood and old age (Ames,
Learned, Métraux, & Walker, 1954; Benedek, 1957; Caldwell, 1954;
Klopfer, 1946; Prados & Fried, 1947; Weinberg, 1956), the literature is suggestive rather than definitive. Some of the references are

[1] Adapted from *J. Geront.*, 1960, **15** (1), 62-67. Reprinted with permission.

speculative or are limited to observations drawn from psychiatric practice. Among the empirical studies that are relevant, few have been conceptualized explicitly in terms of ego processes; others, based on samples of institutionalized old people, have produced findings that cannot be easily generalized. In effect, then, empirical findings are fragmentary, and there has not yet been advanced a systematic or generally accepted theory that can serve as a guide for investigations of personality change in adulthood and old age.

It appeared to the present investigators that certain of the concepts developed by ego psychologists, particularly Hartmann (1951), Rapaport (1951), and Lustman (1957), should have direct implications for personality change in the second half of life and should lead to testable hypotheses. These concepts may be paraphrased as follows. In the development of personality, the ego has from the first an energy of its own. This energy may be characterized as being highly mobile, and the amount available for coping with stimuli in the external world is highly variable. Excitations from within the organism take precedence over excitations from without, and thus, when inner stimuli demand relatively great investment of ego energy, there is less energy available for dealing with stimuli from the outer world. This situation may occur under various conditions. Rapaport (1951) has suggested, for example, several types of interference with the free flow of attention to outer events. Among these are reinforcement of repressed impulses; conditions of fatigue; and the complexity of subject matter to which attention is devoted, with more complex subject matter requiring a change from relatively effortless and involuntary response to effortful and voluntary concentration. It has also been implied (Hartmann, 1951) that available ego energy is diminished by any breakdown in the automatic nature of psychomotor acts.

Although they were not originally described as investigations of ego functions, there are a number of empirical studies that suggest a relationship between processes that accompany aging and the establishment of conditions that limit ego functioning. Birren (1955), for example, has described an increase in response latency in psychic as well as in motor acts and has attributed the time delays to processes in the central nervous system. Another example is the finding (Birren, Allen, & Landau, 1954) that certain intellectual tasks, such as simple arithmetic problems, are more difficult for older than for younger people. This suggests some breakdown in the automatic nature of the behavior elicited by such problems, with the possibility that formerly simple tasks become complex for the older person and thus require more voluntary effort.

The decrease in physical energy so often associated with aging provides a probable third condition of interference with the availability of neutralized ego energies. Other biological decrements, such as losses in visual and auditory acuity, place added burdens on the ego of the aging individual. In addition to such psychophysiological factors, Weinberg (1956) has postulated that there is a welling up of unacceptable impulses in the later years which calls upon any available energies for the process of reinforcing repression, thus suggesting another condition of interference with the outward flow of ego energy.

A constellation of such processes might well constitute inner demands upon the ego of the aging individual sufficient to render the ego less able to maintain its responsiveness to objects and events in the outer environment.

The present research was undertaken in an attempt to follow up relationships between concepts of ego function and empirical findings such as those just described and in an attempt to provide a more direct test of the hypothesis that with increased age during the middle and later years there is less energy available to the ego for maintaining involvements in the outer world. Certain dimensions of ego function were selected as the investigatory axes of the study, with the postulation that they would provide gross estimates of available ego energy. These dimensions were (1) the ability to integrate wide ranges of stimuli; (2) the readiness to perceive or to deal with complicated, challenging, or conflictful situations; (3) the tendency to perceive vigorous and assertive activity; (4) the tendency to perceive or to be concerned with the feelings and affects as these play a part in life situations. It was further postulated that these dimensions of ego function would be measurable in projective data, such as those obtained with the Thematic Apperception Test (TAT).

The research steps were, first, to develop methods for measuring these dimensions in TAT data and, second, to test the hypothesis that with increasing age there would be lower ratings on these measures.

The Sample

There was available to the present investigators a pool of 332 persons from both Sample I and Sample II (see Appendix A) who had been given an abbreviated form of the TAT. Omitting the persons of the lowest socioeconomic level, this pool of cases was distributed into eighteen cells which varied by sex, by three age categories (forty–forty-nine, fifty–fifty-nine, and sixty-four–seventy-one), and by three social-class categories (upper middle and above, lower middle, and upper lower). Eight cases were then selected at random from each cell.

The sample thus consisted of 144 cases, divided equally on the bases of age, sex, and social class into eighteen cells of eight subjects each. All persons in this sample were living in their own households and were participating in the round of activity characteristic of functioning members of the community. With a few exceptions, all were married, had raised families, and were presently living with their spouses. Of the seventy-two males, only three had retired.

Method

The Data

The data consisted of five stories from each member of the sample given in response to the following cards from the Thematic Apperception Test (Murray, 1943).

> *Card 1.* A young boy is contemplating a violin which rests on a table in front of him.
>
> *Card 2.* Country scene. In the foreground is a young woman with a book in her hand; in the background

a man is working in the fields. An older woman is looking on.

Card 6BM. A short, elderly woman stands with her back turned to a tall, young man. The latter is looking downward with a perplexed expression.

Card 7BM. A gray-haired man is looking at a younger man who is sullenly staring into space.

Card 17BM. A naked man is clinging to a rope. He is in the act of climbing up or down.

These cards were presented to the respondent at the end of an interview that covered various aspects of his present and past. All respondents were interviewed in their own homes or places of business.

The TAT Measures

Four TAT measures were delineated to reflect the personality dimensions of ego functioning stated earlier. These measures, together with the specific hypotheses to be tested, were:

1. "Introduction of nonpictured characters." The hypothesis was that older persons, less frequently than younger, will widen the range of stimuli dealt with by introducing nonpictured characters into their stories. For example, in response to Card 1, the older respondent will tell a story which deals only with the boy, whereas the younger respondent will tell a story in which the boy is interacting with a mother or with some other character not shown in the picture.

2. "Introduction of conflict." The hypothesis was that older persons, as compared with younger, would not complicate their stories by describing intra- or interpersonal situations which involve conflict, choice, or decision. The assumption here was that it requires more ego energy on the part of the respondent to produce a story

involving conflict than a story devoid of impeding or controversial elements. For example, in response to Card 1, a typical older respondent's story would be one in which the boy is concerned with his adequacy to play the violin, whereas a typical younger respondent's story would be about a boy who wishes to please an authority figure by practicing, but who, at the same time, dislikes the violin and does not want to practice.

3. "Activity-energy level ascribed to characters." The hypothesis was that older people, less often than younger, would perceive story characters as engaged in vigorous, assertive kinds of activity. This measure was derived from assumptions underlying projective theory regarding the attribution to ambiguous stimuli of one's own underlying tendencies toward movement or action. To illustrate once more from Card 1, a typical older respondent's story might be, "That boy looks like he's falling asleep," whereas a typical younger respondent's story might be one in which the boy wants to be outdoors playing baseball rather than indoors practicing the violin.

4. "Affect intensity." The hypothesis was that older persons would tell matter-of-fact stories in which little affect is described, whereas younger respondents would tell stories in which various feeling states are elaborated and in which affect plays a part in the story development. The assumption here was that the description of life situations as being affect-laden reflects a more vigorous involvement with the outer world than does the description of situations as being bland. To illustrate, an older person's story might be, "The boy is looking at the violin, wondering if he can play it." A younger person's story might be, "That boy is angry. He's so angry he'll get up and throw the violin against the wall."

The first two of these measures were rated on a simple two-point scale. A rating of 1 was assigned if nonpictured characters had been introduced into the story; 0, if not. Similarly, 1 indicated that conflict had been introduced into the story; 0, that it had not. Activity-energy level was rated on a four-point scale. Since some degree of activity was always present in the stories, the lowest rating assigned was 1. The fourth measure, affect intensity, was also rated on a 4-

point scale, but here the lowest rating was 0 because in some stories affective tone was absent altogether.

All the TAT stories were rated blind for age, sex, and social class of the respondent. To avoid halo effect or systematic set, ratings were made separately on each measure, card by card, across the sample. That is, introduced characters were rated on Card 1 for all respondents, then on Card 2, and so on. Then introduced conflict was rated on Card 1 for all respondents, then on Card 2, and so on.

Reliability of the ratings was checked by selecting at random the protocols of twenty respondents, then, dealing separately with each card and each of the four measures, computing the extent to which two independent judges agreed in rating the stories. On the first two measures there was only one instance in which agreement between the two judges fell below 90 per cent. On the second two measures, coefficients of correlation between the judges' ratings ranged from .68 to .93.

After all ratings had been made, a composite score was computed for each respondent on each measure by simply adding the ratings obtained on the five cards. Thus, the possible range of composite scores was 0 to 5 for introduced characters; 0 to 5 for introduced conflict; 5 to 20 for activity-energy level; and 0 to 15 for affect intensity.

Findings

Utilizing the composite scores, a three-way analysis of variance to include the factors of age, sex, and social class was performed for each TAT measure. As shown in Table 4.1, only the factor of age accounted for a significant portion of the variance on all four measures.

Table 4.2 shows the mean composite scores on the four TAT measures for the three age groups in the sample. It will be seen that the scores drop from age group to age group on each measure; that the difference between youngest and oldest groups is statistically significant on all four measures; and that, furthermore, in six out of eight instances the difference between adjacent age groups is also statistically significant.

TABLE 4.1

ANALYSIS OF VARIANCE OF RATINGS ON FOUR
TAT MEASURES $(N = 144)$

Source of variation	ss	df	ms	F
Introduced characters				
A	2.78	1	2.78	1.63
B	1.26	2	.63	.37
C	40.26	2	20.13	11.77*
AB	11.01	2	5.51	3.22
AC	1.01	2	.50	.29
BC	6.08	4	1.52	.89
ABC	4.57	4	1.14	.67
Withins	215.25	126	1.71	
Totals	282.22	143		
Introduced conflict				
A	1.77	1	1.77	1.40
B	3.29	2	1.65	1.31
C	13.79	2	6.90	5.48*
AB	.11	2	.06	.05
AC	1.10	2	.55	.44
BC	4.54	4	1.14	.90
ABC	5.15	4	1.29	1.02
Withins	159.25	126	1.26	
Totals	189.00	143		
Activity-energy level				
A	4.00	1	4.00	1.36
B	15.50	2	7.75	2.64
C	65.29	2	32.65	11.11*
AB	4.67	2	2.34	.80
AC	1.13	2	.57	.19

TABLE 4.1 (*Continued*)

ANALYSIS OF VARIANCE OF RATINGS ON FOUR
TAT MEASURES ($N = 144$)

Source of variation	ss	df	ms	F
BC	14.84	4	3.71	1.26
ABC	11.57	4	2.89	.98
Withins	371.00	126	2.94	
Totals	488.00	143		
Affect intensity				
A	1.77	1	1.77	.27
B	.50	2	.25	.04
C	68.66	2	34.33	5.28*
AB	22.90	2	11.45	1.76
AC	3.57	2	1.79	.28
BC	17.72	4	4.43	.68
ABC	21.63	4	5.41	.83
Withins	819.25	126	6.50	
Totals	956.00	143		

Note—A = sex; B = social class; C = age.
* Significant at or beyond the .01 level.

Discussion

It had been predicted that with increasing age people would achieve lower ratings on the four TAT measures used in this study. The results were all in the predicted direction. There was a consistent decline with age on all four measures, and the differences between age groups were statistically reliable. As shown in Table 4.2, the absolute differences between age groups were not dramatic, but, in the absence of similar data for younger people, the size of these absolute differences cannot be evaluated.

According to the theory of projective tests, the manner in which people perceive and elaborate on ambiguous stimuli reveals some-

TABLE 4.2

MEAN COMPOSITE SCORES ON TAT MEASURES FOR THREE AGE GROUPS

TAT measure	Age group		
	40–49 (N = 48)	50–59 (N = 48)	64–71 (N = 48)
Introduced characters	2.23*	1.67†	.94‡
Introduced conflict	3.02*	2.38	2.35‡
Activity-energy level	13.19*	12.27†	11.54‡
Affect intensity	5.75	5.17†	4.08‡

* Applying Tukey's test to the Studentized Range, the difference between means for the youngest and middle age groups is significant at or beyond the .05 level.

† The difference between means for the middle and oldest age groups is significant at or beyond the .05 level.

‡ The difference between means for the youngest and oldest age groups is significant at or beyond the .01 level.

thing of their underlying tendencies to act, whether or not these tendencies are manifest in overt behavior. In keeping with this theory, the age shifts on the TAT measures may be viewed in terms of the more general behavioral tendencies which the measures were designed to reflect. Thus, the findings suggest that older people, as compared with younger, are less able to integrate wide ranges of stimuli; less able to perceive and deal with complicated or conflictual situations; tend less often to perceive affect as an important part of life; and tend toward inactivity or passivity rather than toward more active, assertive forms of behavior.

Since these personality processes had been operationally defined as reflections of ego energy, the differences among the age groups lend support to the hypothesis that with increased age there is less energy available to the ego for responding to, or maintaining former levels of involvement in, the outside world. The implication is that the older person tends to respond to inner rather than to outer stimuli, to withdraw emotional investments, to give up self-assertiveness, and to avoid rather than to embrace challenge.

There are findings based upon the Rorschach technique that parallel the present findings (Chesrow, Wosika, & Reinitz, 1949; Davidson & Kruglov, 1952; Grossman, Warshawsky, & Hertz, 1951; Klopfer, 1946; Light & Amick, 1956; Prados & Fried, 1947). Although there are some inconsistencies in results among the Rorschach studies, it has been inferred from the quantitative findings that older people, as compared with younger, tend to show a decrease in productivity, an impoverishment of the creative intellectual faculties, and a diminished capacity for emotional responsiveness. Light and Amick (1956) have stated specifically on the basis of their findings that older adults are "not particularly responsive to stimuli coming from the environment"; that they show a narrowing of social and emotional contacts with others and a lack of ability to empathize. Such findings may be interpreted as supporting the present hypothesis that with increased age the ego has less energy available for maintaining former levels of responsiveness to outer events.

It is true that the use of projective techniques poses certain problems in the interpretation of age differences. Caldwell (1954), for example, has cautioned against a careless acceptance of the presumed meanings of Rorschach variables developed from investigations of other age groups when evaluating the personalities of older people. She hypothesized, "A certain limen of perceptual flexibility must be crossed before the Rorschach is a valid measure of any significant personality variable in the aged." Although similar caution must be exercised with the TAT, it is nevertheless true that the TAT differs considerably from the Rorschach in this respect. The Rorschach is first and foremost a perceptual test. Although a certain degree of perceptual flexibility is unquestionably required on the TAT, this factor is of secondary importance. The subject must be able to perceive the major elements of the stimulus presented on the TAT card, but, once this is achieved, the task becomes primarily conceptual. That all the subjects in the present study passed this necessary threshold of perceptual flexibility was evidenced by the fact that the major stimuli were always integrated into the fantasy productions.

As in other studies that deal with psychological differences between age groups, whether or not projective techniques are utilized, there is in the present study the problem of equivalence of stimuli: that is, whether or not it can be presumed that the stimuli (here, the TAT cards) have approximately the same psychological meaning and significance to subjects of various ages. Although this problem cannot be resolved in a study of this type, it is the investigators' opinion that the findings reported here depend somewhat less on such an assumption than is ordinarily the case. The present analysis rests less on the specific stimulus value of the TAT pictures than on ego processes involved in the production of the stories. The variables used here were developed according to a theory of ego functioning, and the TAT pictures were used only as a means of stimulating responses from which these functions could be assessed.

ADDENDUM TO CHAPTER 4

Marc I. Lubin

Another opportunity to investigate the hypothesis that ego energy declines with age was provided when certain sets of test-retest data became available in the course of the Kansas City Studies of Adult Life. There were fifty-one men and forty-two women in the Sample II panel, aged forty-nine to seventy-one when first contacted,[1] who had responded to five TAT pictures as part of the second round of interviewing (TAT cards 1, 2, 6BM, 7BM, 17BM) and who, by remaining in the sample some four to five years later, had responded to three of the same pictures (cards 1, 7BM, and 17BM) as part of the seventh round of interviewing. These two sets of data were analyzed for change over time.

As a first step in the analysis, eighteen cases from the Rosen-Neu-

---

[1] See Appendix A for a description of Sample II panel.

garten sample were selected from the ninety-three to represent the full range of age, sex, and socioeconomic status. Using Time I protocols on these cases and following the methods described by Rosen and Neugarten, a total score was derived for each individual, a score which was the summation of subscores on each of the four TAT measures (introduced characters, introduced conflict, activity-energy, and affect intensity). For these eighteen cases, scores based on the present investigator's ratings correlated .94 with scores based on the previous investigators' ratings.

Scores were then derived for these eighteen cases using only three of the five TAT cards, and the three-card and five-card scores were compared. The correlation between these two sets of scores was .98, indicating that a score derived from three TAT cards would be an acceptable substitute for a score derived from five and that, accordingly, a test-retest analysis of the ninety-three cases based on the three-card scores would be worthwhile. The investigator then rated all ninety-three cases at Time 1 and at Time 2, using the three-card series, cards 1, 7BM, and 17BM.

TABLE 4.3

CHANGE IN EGO ENERGY SCORES OVER A FIVE-YEAR INTERVAL

Age in 1962	N	Mean score in 1957	Mean score in 1962
55–59	24	16.5	14.6
60–64	28	16.0	14.2
65–69	16	20.0	17.1
70–76	25	14.7	15.6
Total	93	16.5	15.2*

* The difference between means for the total group is significant at the .01 level.

As shown in Table 4.3, there was a significant drop in ego energy scores for the group as a whole between Time 1 and Time 2. Because of the small numbers in each subgroup, test-retest differences for subgroups are not statistically significant. (Also, because the subgroups are not equally representative, age differences should not be read vertically from either the second or third column, but should be confined to the test-retest differences.) The decline in scores for the group as a whole represents the fact that, of the ninety-three individuals, fifty-one (twenty-nine men and twenty-two women) showed decline, whereas forty-two showed either no change or an increase in score.

These findings must be interpreted in light of the selective nature of this study population. The Sample II panel was a relatively advantaged group at the outset (see Appendix A). Of the original 144 in the Sample II panel who had taken the TAT at Time 1, only ninety-three, or 65 per cent, had survived the contingencies of aging and whatever other contingencies that had operated to produce a high rate of attrition in the sample. Of the attrition that occurred in the four to five years between the first and second interviews, 13 per cent had been due to geographical moves; 26 per cent, to deaths; and 61 per cent, to refusal or inability to be interviewed, usually because of poor health. These ninety-three people represent, therefore, a select group in terms of good health, physical vigor, and continued willingness to cooperate in the study. The mean ego-energy score (based on five TAT cards) for these ninety-three people at Time 1 was 20.7, compared to a mean score of 17.2 for the fifty-one cases who later dropped out of the study, the attrition group.

Given the fact that these ninety-three people were a select group, it might have been anticipated that measurable decline in ego energy would be relatively small in four to five years and would probably understate the amount of decline that might be found in a more representative sample. Taking into account the particular nature of this study population, these findings take on added significance in corroborating the findings of the Rosen-Neugarten study. They support the interpretation that with increased age there is less energy available to the ego for maintaining involvements in the outer world.

5

EGO FUNCTIONS IN THE
MIDDLE AND LATER YEARS:
A FURTHER EXPLORATION

Bernice L. Neugarten
David L. Miller

In the study by Rosen and Neugarten (Chapter 4), consistent and significant age differences were found in a sample of adults aged forty to seventy-one on four measures of personality based on Thematic Apperception Test data. The investigators interpreted their findings as support for the hypothesis that during the middle and later years there is a decrease in energy available to the ego for responding to outer world events. The purpose of the present study was to carry forward this line of inquiry, to verify and elaborate those findings by utilizing a different theoretical approach and a different method of scoring on the same set of TAT protocols. The method selected was one described by Dana (1959), in which TAT responses are classified according to three major dimensions: Perceptual Organization (PO), which reflects the subject's ability to produce a story, an organization of actions and characters; Perceptual Range (PR), which reflects the ability to perceive and to deal with the various stimulus properties of each card; and Perceptual Personalization (PP), which is a measure of the extent to which the subject deviates from the organized TAT story and injects personal and irrelevant comments and ideas.

Although the system of scoring had been devised to estimate degrees of psychiatric illness, Dana has referred to PO, PR, and PP as measures of the amount of psychic energy effectively operating in the individual. He has described his system of scoring as one that reflects the individual's ability to perceive reality accurately, to organize and integrate experience meaningfully, to recognize the salient features in his environment, to become involved in a task, and to be able to express himself in situations of potential emotional threat. It therefore appeared that both the Rosen-Neugarten and the Dana measures were tapping similar psychological processes which, in the main, consist of the ability to respond adequately to environmental demands; thus it would be worthwhile in this respect to explore the similarity between Rosen and Neugarten's term, "ego energy," and Dana's term, "psychic energy." It was anticipated, furthermore, that age differences would appear that would add to our understanding of personality changes with age.

The four TAT measures utilized by Rosen and Neugarten—introduction of nonpictured characters, introduction of conflict into the story, activity-energy levels ascribed to characters, and affect intensity—have been described in Chapter 3. The descriptions and scoring procedures for each of the Dana measures follow.

Perceptual Organization

Perceptual Organization (PO) reflects the individual's ability to follow the standard directions to "tell a story." Seven possible components are included:

a) "Card description" (CD) : The subject describes two or more things or persons actually present in the picture. An example is, "The man is plowing the field" (Card 2).

b) "Present behavior" (PB) : The subject describes any activity
   or behavior that is occurring in the picture, for example, "The
   man is sliding down the rope" (Card 17BM).

c) "Past events" (PE) : The subject refers to events or situations
   which have taken place before the time of the scene pictured
   on the card and described in the story. These may be in the
   immediate or remote past and must be specified and definite.

d) "Future events" (FE) : The subject refers to events or situations which will take place after the time of the scene pictured on the card and described in the story. These may be
   in the immediate or remote future and must be specific.

e) "Feeling" (F) : Any expression of feeling or emotion on the
   part of the characters present in the story. This includes affect
   (that is, "sad," "mad") and desire (that is, "wishing," "want-
   ing").

f) "Thought" (T) : Any expression of thought, memory, dream,
   or allied mental state present in the story. This includes decision, belief, realization, knowing, praying, figuring.

g) "Outcome" (O) : The inclusion of a specific statement which
   indicates the ending, finale, or conclusion of the story. This
   statement may refer to behavior, feeling, thought, or the outcome may merely be implied by reference to future events. If
   the last mentioned does occur, both outcome and future events
   are scored.

The task of perceptual organization is a complex one. To receive
a high score, the individual must synthesize a story that contains not
only the elements of thought and emotion, but that traverses three
time periods and resolves the particular issue at hand.

Scoring Procedure

Each PO component in a story is scored for presence or absence
(+ or −). No score is given if a component appears more than once
in response to an individual card. For the five cards used in the
present study, the maximum possible score was 35.

According to Dana, any response given after the test administrator asks a question is not to be counted in the final PO score. In the present study, it was felt that application of this rule to older age groups would allow much valuable data to go unused. The scoring procedure was therefore changed. Any answer by the respondent to a direct or leading question was not scored, but any pertinent datum that occurred subsequent to a direct answer was scored. To illustrate:

> Card 1: This is a little boy playing with his violin. His mother has told him to practice. (What is he thinking and feeling?) He is thinking of playing with his friends because he hates the violin. Yet he will listen to his mother and someday will be a great violinist.

In this story the T and F components are not scored because they are responses to a direct question. However, FE, "he will listen," and O, "someday will be a great violinist," are scored.

Perceptual Range

The stimulus properties in each card are those that were recognized by the majority of normal subjects. Using a criterion of 90 per cent or more inclusion and a normative group of twenty- to forty-year-old subjects, Dana had selected three sets of stimulus properties for cards 2, 3BM, 4, 6BM, and 7BM for males and for cards 2, 3GF, 4, 6GF, and 7GF for females. In the present study both sexes were given cards 1, 2, 6BM, 7BM, and 17BM. Because of this and because of the difference in the age range tested, it was necessary to establish new norms for the present sample. Using a 60 per cent criterion of inclusion, the PR stimulus properties selected for each card were:

Card 1
   a)   boy; affective state noted
   b)   attitudinal relationship
   c)   violin
   d)   success or failure

Card 2
- e) family; young girl (activity specified), older woman, man
- f) farm or fields
- g) books or school

Card 6BM
- h) male (emotion noted, activity indicated)
- i) female (emotion noted)
- j) conflict-cooperation

Card 7BM
- k) older male (activity specified, relationship specified)
- l) younger male (activity specified, emotion noted)
- m) conflict-cooperation

Card 17BM
- n) male (activity specified)
- o) rope
- p) explanation of setting (prison, circus, and so on)

Scoring Procedure

All parts of a given stimulus property must be mentioned for a score to be earned. Indefinite or ambiguous statements are not scored. For example, for Card 2, if the subject mentions the girl, the older woman, and the man but does not specify an activity for the younger girl, no score is given. The maximum possible score is 16. To score well on PR, the subject must be able to respond to and integrate both the manifest and latent stimulus properties of the various cards, thus signifying a high level of efficient ego functioning.

Perceptual Personalization

Perceptual Personalization (PP) includes statements made by the respondent that may be considered deviations from an organized, coherent TAT story. Dana states that these comments "may refer to . . . performance adequacy, parenthetical remarks, qualifications, picture criticisms, adventitious descriptions, vagueness, evasion, or direct personal reference" (1959, p. 30). Examples are: "What's that supposed to be?" "This is a silly picture." "That's what I did as a boy."

One change was made from Dana's scoring directions. When the subject used the phrase "I think" or "I believe," followed by a definite description or event, this was not included in the PP total. The comment, "I think this is a waste of time," was scored, just as were all "I don't knows."

Scoring Procedure

All phrases, words, and comments listed as PP are given one point. There is no maximum possible score. The comments included in the PP category may range from open hostility to the tester to conversational remarks about the subject's past. According to Dana, these comments reflect the subject's inability to cope satisfactorily with the task at hand. In a normal subject, PP comments should be considered primarily as defensive maneuvers, efforts to relieve the anxiety created by the perceptual task. However, such comments may also be indicative of poor intellectual organization or deviant patterns of reaction.

Procedures and Findings

The TAT protocols were the same as those used by Rosen and Neugarten. Thus the sample consisted of 144 men and women drawn from Sample I and the Sample II panel (see Appendix A) distributed over eighteen cells which varied by sex, by three age categories (forty–forty-nine, fifty–fifty-nine, and sixty-four–seventy-one), and by three social-class categories (upper-middle, lower-middle, and working class). Each cell contained eight cases.

The protocols were coded and put into random order. Each protocol was scored blind for age, sex, and social class. The reliability of the scores assigned to the PO, PR, and PP dimensions was checked by selecting at random fourteen protocols and computing the percentage of agreement between two independent judges. The percentages were 86, 88, and 90 for the three measures.

As a first step in the analysis, scores for the present sample were compared with scores reported by Dana on his samples of normal, neurotic, and psychotic subjects, all of whom were twenty to forty. For this comparison, scores on PO, PR, and PP were converted into standard Z scores. Outstanding differences were found.

Although the mean PO score of Dana's normal group was 26.9, the mean for the present sample is 17.2, a score which falls between the means for Dana's neurotic subjects (mean = 19.3) and psychotic subjects (mean = 10.8). It should be remembered that the lower mean score for the present sample was obtained in spite of the liberalized scoring procedure used in this study.

With a possible maximum score of 15, the mean PR score of Dana's normal group was 13.2. In the present study, with a possible maximum score of 16, the mean obtained was 11.0.

For the PP score, the mean score for Dana's groups were .75 for normal subjects, 5.6 for neurotic subjects, and 8.5 for psychotic subjects. The mean score for the present sample is 8.9, which slightly exceeds the mean for his psychotic group.

These large differences may be attributed to various factors, one of them differences in test administration. In Dana's studies the TAT's were obtained by a trained clinician in a clinical setting. In the Kansas City Studies the TAT's were obtained by a number of interviewers in the course of long interviews carried out in the subjects' homes. The field situations are presumably the less well-controlled situations. They might, for instance, provide atmospheres more often conducive to conversation that could increase the number of PP comments.

Another factor that merits consideration is group differences in intellectual ability. Although he does not indicate what measures were used, Dana states that all of his subjects had "average intelligence or better." Inasmuch as all the normal males in his sample were college students and all the normal females were nurses, it is probable that their level of intelligence was above the average of a more randomly selected population, such as the one used here.

For these reasons, it is possible that the differences between the present sample and Dana's samples can be attributed to extraneous factors. At the same time, the differences are so great that it seems likely that a true age difference is being reflected. It is a distinct possibility, in other words, that, even with more careful controls, fifty- and sixty-year-old men and women would still perform poorly on PR, PO, and PP, as compared with twenty- and thirty-year-olds. The issue arises, therefore, whether the Dana measures are equally appropriate for the middle-aged and for the young in reflecting the individual's ability to respond adequately to his environment. Given the fact that the present sample of middle-aged persons gave no evidence of gross pathology in their everyday lives, the question becomes: Does ego defect on the TAT have the same significance for older as for younger persons? In other words, do older men and women continue to function effectively in everyday life despite ego defects that, when they appear in a younger person, are accompanied by observable mental illness? Unfortunately, this question could not be pursued further in these data.

The investigators moved next to a comparison of the present data to those of Rosen and Neugarten. For this purpose, the raw scores for PO, PR, and PP were entered into a three-way classification table, according to age, sex, and social class of the respondent, and subjected to analysis of variance. For none of the three dimensions did age, sex, or social class account for a significant portion of the variance. Similar analyses were carried out for the seven components of the PO score and for separate TAT cards on the PR score. Only a few scattered differences appeared, a number easily attributable to chance, indicating that consistent subgroup differences did not exist in these data.

The absence of age differences was unexpected, given the fact that the same TAT protocols, when analyzed according to the Rosen and Neugarten dimensions, had shown age to be a consistent and significant source of variance. These contrary findings led to a re-examination of the two sets of dimensions and to a re-evalution of the differences between them. For instance, two of the Rosen-Neugarten measures were four-point scales (activity-energy level and affect intensity) in which intensity was rated instead of simple presence or absence of the phenomenon, as was the case with the Dana measures. This may have provided a certain refinement in the measures that is necessary if age differences are to emerge.

The more important difference, however, must lie in the nature of the dimensions themselves and in the corresponding personality processes being measured by the two systems—a difference which had appeared of much less importance at the outset of this study. It is difficult to clarify these underlying differences except by careful rereading of the definitions. It is clear, however, that the two systems which first seemed approximately the same in focus were actually quite unlike, since the Rosen and Neugarten system revealed, while the Dana system did not reveal, age differences in the same respondents. The disparity in the two systems of analysis probably reflects the different experiential backgrounds of the investigators themselves in selecting and defining their variables. In Dana's case, long familiarity with data generated in the clinical setting seems to have produced a set of personality measures that is successful in delineating clinical subgroups but not successful in delineating age differences in normally functioning adults. The same lack of suitability might be expected were the Rosen and Neugarten measures to be used for clinical purposes. The present authors may therefore have erred in anticipating that a system originally designed to detect ego pathologies would also detect differences in ego functions that are perhaps part of the normal aging process.

The two major findings in this study—that this sample scores so poorly as a group when compared to Dana's younger normal subjects and that age differences in personality processes known to exist in this sample do not appear when the Dana measures are used—raise substantive issues that must await clarification on the basis of future research. At present, however, they lend support to the view that the investigator of adult personality is likely to make faster progress in studying changes with age if he uses concepts and dimensions especially devised for his purposes than if he attempts to apply theoretical frameworks that have grown up in other areas of personality research.

6

AN EXPLORATION OF
EGO CONFIGURATIONS IN
MIDDLE AND LATER LIFE

David L. Gutmann

The formulation of psychoanalytic ego psychology permits a developmental approach to the study of personality in later life. Prior to this conceptual enlargement of psychoanalytic thought, Freudian theorists focused mainly on id aspects of personality and, accordingly, assumed that the crucial events in personality formation occurred during infancy, childhood, and adolescence—that is, during the period of physical and libidinal maturation. Once the libido settled into a final form, the personality had presumably received its life-long orientation, and later adult experience could only impart a superficial, socialized gloss to the fundamental structure. Individual destiny was coded in the instincts, and the individual's life was spent in playing out the dramas of oral deprivation, toilet training, and Oedipal rivalry. Thus viewed, the observed intellectual and attitudinal changes of later life presumably reflected cortical deficit and reduced libidinal energy, rather than intrinsic reorderings of the personality system per se.

With the growth of ego psychology, however, these views have changed. The ego is no longer regarded as a passive appendage of the id, a switchyard of the instincts on their way to gratification, but as a system of the personality that seeks its optimal maturational milieux and develops according to its own intrinsic schedules, in partial independence of the id. In this view, the ego's defensive modes determine personality as much as do the persistent strivings of the id. The epicenter of personality thus shifts from the instincts to the id-ego interface to the interplay between impulse and the ego's defensive systems. Presumably, the ego continues to revise its defenses and its controls in response to changes in both the internal and external environments, and the id-ego interface can be seen as a continually changing one (for example, see Erikson, 1959; Hartmann, 1951). Accordingly, significant changes in personality should continue to occur throughout life, thereby providing a rationale for dynamically oriented studies of personality change in adulthood and old age.

This paper reports one such study—an exploration, by means of projective techniques, of the various configurations of the ego in later life and of certain psychosexual and psychosocial issues relevant to these changing configurations.

The Sample and the Instrument

The sample consisted of 287 white urban men and women aged forty-seventy. Cases from both Sample I and Sample II were combined to maximize the age range and the total number of available protocols. Although the subjects were interviewed intensively regarding personality issues, their views of aging, and their present and past circumstances, the present study is based primarily on TAT protocols. Interview materials were later drawn on to check the TAT findings.

The TAT was administered in the usual fashion, with the respondent being instructed to provide a story with a beginning, middle, and end. The battery consisted of seven cards:

> *Card 1.* A young boy contemplating a violin which rests on a table in front of him.
>
> *Card 2.* (The farm-scene card) In the foreground a young woman with books; in the background a man working in the fields and an older woman looking on.
>
> *Card 4.* (The heterosexual card) A woman clutching the shoulders of a man whose face and body are averted as though he were trying to pull away from her.
>
> *Card 6 BM.* (The mother-son card) A short elderly woman standing with her back turned toward a tall young man, who is looking downward with a perplexed expression.
>
> *Card 7BM.* (The father-son card) A gray-haired man looking at a younger man who is sullenly staring into space.
>
> *Card 10.* A young woman's head against a man's shoulder.
>
> *Card 17 BM.* (The rope-climber card) A naked man clinging to a rope, in the act of climbing either up or down.

The investigator chose the TAT data as most suitable to his purposes not only because his clinical training had sensitized him to the mode of symbolic communication elicited by the instrument, but also because the TAT protocols, lacking specific reference to the respondent's age or to age-graded life circumstances, could be analyzed blind for age, thus avoiding self-confirming hypotheses on the relation between age and personality.

Because the TAT is an ambiguous stimulus, the respondent's particular interpretation reflects a motivated choice among a range of possibilities and serves to communicate an inner reaction to the emotional issues suggested by the pictures. The TAT, by fostering the defensive tactic of externalization, permits a personal form of communication—the individual's repertoire of fantasies, motives, and defenses can be conveniently coded in his descriptions of agents and persons perceived in the picture and perceived as being external to the self. Because the respondent is less self-conscious than he might be in a direct interview, the TAT can reveal dimensions of private personality normally masked by the respondent's adherence to social conventions.

This instrument is highly sensitive to covert differences between individuals who behave in overtly similar ways and between groups of people who adhere to the same body of social forms and conventions. By the same token, underlying trends in motivations and ego defense may be tapped as they shape private fantasy long before they openly direct public forms of thought and behavior.

Analysis of the Data

An earlier study of age changes in role perception (Chapter 3) indicated that older people were more sensitive than young people to the impulse modalities underlying behavior. It was hypothesized that aging is accompanied by increased difficulty in the management of inner life. Other investigators (Kaplan, 1956; Meerloo, 1955; Schaw & Henry, 1956), although they used different approaches, also have made much the same point. If it is generally true that normal individuals become preoccupied with inner life as aging proceeds, we would expect an accompanying redeployment of the ego, with consequent shifts in the patterning and intensity of the defenses—a change, that is, in those ego functions which maintain the psychic homeostasis. Increased impulse life is likely to pose new threats to the aging personality as the struggle against aggressive, sexual, and regressive impulses, viewed as ego-alien, must be refought by the ego.

The TAT presents metaphors of the emotional life; as such, these stimuli should call out defensive strategies similar to those devised by the ego against equivalent affects in the self. Thus, we should expect to find evidence in the TAT of age differences in the modes of ego defense—possibly along the lines of ego restriction, isolation, and repression. In instances where the inner pressures are severe, we could expect decompensation to more maladaptive and primitive defenses involving distortion of reality—namely, massive denial, blatant externalization, and projection. Under these conditions, we would expect to find some bizarre, erratic interpretations of the stimuli, reflecting either primitive defensive efforts or the subordination of the perceptual-cognitive system to unconscious demands.

Thus, given our speculations concerning the psychic stress of later life—stress perhaps related to the biological and social discontinuities of that age period—it seemed reasonable to employ a terminology and an approach which, from the standpoint of ego psychology, centered on inner stress, on conflict between impulse and ego, and on ego defense. Accordingly, each protocol was initially analyzed as to salient issues of impulse life, major defenses against impulse, and the success or failure of such coping efforts. A model of good ego functioning which may be said to be current in clinical psychology was used in assessing such success or failure. This model emphasizes smooth integration of personal strivings with social possibilities, affective richness and variety without cognitive disruption, clear self-other boundaries, and a time perspective which relates the present to the future.

Guided by this model, one looks in the TAT for interesting, lively though reasonable interpretations of the cards; for logically developed plots in which future outcomes are reasonably related to the present action; and for a sense of objectivity and distance in regard to the stimulus—that is, even as the respondent breathes life into the stimulus, he remains aware that the fantasy comes from within himself and is not the exclusive property of the picture before him. Assessed against this model, poor ego functioning would be revealed when the stimuli were either grossly misperceived or too carefully perceived, at the expense of the thematic richness and freedom. Breakdowns in the logic of the stories, absence of story outcomes, plots that bear little relation to the stimulus, and loss of distance between the respondent and the card are also relevant here.

Given our speculations about increased psychic stress in later life, evidences of poor ego functioning were expected to appear with increased frequency in the TAT protocols of successive age groups. The data were analyzed blind for age, with no information except the sex of each respondent known to the analyst. As the analysis proceeded, there developed an over-all sensitivity to thematic trends in the data, then, following the logic of projection, of the personalities that had produced the various thematic emphases. Individuals whose protocols were similar in terms of the criteria described above were grouped together. As such groupings were created and compared, newly recognized elements were often highlighted, and new groupings were established.

After a long study of the data, subgroups of persons were delineated on the basis of concepts that had become meaningful in the course of the analysis itself. The concepts of ego mastery and of ego mastery styles became particularly relevant and suggested a typology which provided a fit for all the respondents. Three major orientations, or three major styles for mastery of both intrapersonal and extrapersonal concerns, emerged. We have characterized these three as "active mastery," "passive mastery," and "magical mastery." These categories represent a continuum of ego strength wherein active mastery represents the most vigorous, effective style of ego functioning and magical mastery represents stress-laden, maladaptive ego functioning.

Although the mastery typology for both sexes is based on the same characteristics (realism and vigor of ego processes as evidenced in the TAT stories), the subgroups for men and for women differ with regard to theme and content of their stories. Accordingly, the typology is presented separately for each sex. Mastery types will be described both in terms of the protocol data and in terms of respondents' personalities as inferred from the data. Stories from individual protocols will be utilized to illustrate the types.

The Mastery Typology for Males

Active Mastery

Two subsidiary styles are included here: the "self-asserters" and the "achievement doubters."

The self-asserters tell stories in which the hero moves directly, assertively, and resourcefully toward fairly conventional goals, sometimes in the face of ineffectual opposition from parental figures. Energy is mainly located in the hero, and the wishes or opposition of others do not significantly interfere with the hero's projects. The following story, told to 17BM, the rope-climber card, is typical:

> Well, I would guess that this character is an acrobat, engaged in aerial acrobatics. I'd say he is on his way up to his performance and that he is looking out over the group of spectators gathered for the performance, and it looks as though he might be happy—he doesn't look worried—he looks as though he is equipped to get the job done, mentally and physically.

Though the respondent is somewhat defensive about the hero's adequacy, this story displays an excellent capacity for ego integration. Id elements—power, sensuality, and exhibitionism—all find modulated though recognizable expression in an appropriate social setting. Here the striving individual is the source of initiative and energy for a social world which is centered on and organized by his acts. (The spectators are gathered for the hero's performance.)

A fifty-two-year-old man from this group, in his story to Card 2 (the farm scene) implicitly accounts for all the major stimulus details, disavows a passive-receptive role, assigns a vigorous, achieving orientation to the heroine figure, and delineates her future—all in one tightly organized sentence: "That girl, I would say, is leaving the country to go to school or teach, rather than watch things grow."

The self-asserters tend to be aggressive, independent men who simplify issues through direct action, by seeking out challenge and resistance in the external world. They dissipate tension through goal-oriented action, and they translate potentially debilitating inner conflicts into struggles with external agents. They thus focus their attention on a vivid and personalized environment rather than on inner difficulties or doubts.

In many cases the rugged, masculine stance of these men seems somewhat overdone, as if they "protest too much." Theirs can be a provocative, chip-on-the-shoulder stance, as indicated by the combative emphasis in their stories. The stories often feature heroes who stubbornly resist pressures from authority figures bent on forcing them into a submissive position. Presumably, these respondents do not admit intrapyschic dependence-independence conflict; rather, they insist that pressures toward passivity originate not within themselves, but in the external world. If they submit, they do so under protest, in the face of strong odds. In their own eyes, they are not conformists but heroic rebels.

Achievement doubters also move vigorously into the world, but with inner reservations. They show notable concern over the consequence of their boldness, and alternate between doing and undoing, from focused assertion to deference and constriction. The following illustrative story was told to the rope-climber card:

> Possibly someone in a physical training class in a gym or something of that kind. Picture no doubt is of a strong, muscular type fellow and, from his expression he wants everybody to know it. It looks like he is pretty high up. (Finish?) Maybe he has too much self-assurance.

In other responses to this card, the rope climber was seen as initially triumphing against all opposition in a rope-climbing contest, but at the moment of victory the rope breaks, and the hero is crippled for life. Destruction is the punishment for competitive triumph.

Another story, told by a fifty-seven-year-old man to the boy-and-violin card, illustrates the continual vacillation between activity and passivity characteristic of this group. The hero dreams, but of the future; he cannot decide whether to rest or strive, but he finally goads himself to renewed effort:

> Poor guy's asleep. He's dreaming for the future more than anything. He can't figure out what's going to happen. He just can't make up his mind whether to go on

with it or just. . . . Finally made up his mind; he's
going to get down to business and become a good violinist.

As illustrated in the above story, many of these men are preoccupied with emergent passive-dependent wishes and regard them
as a threat to continued achievement and autonomy. Unlike the
self-asserters, these men do not externalize the conflict; they do not
make outer agents responsible for their own passive wishes. Rather,
they locate the dependence-autonomy conflict in the central figure
in the story, probably revealing their own sense of internal conflict
and indecision. These men rarely propose that the hero surrenders
to passive wishes, but at the same time they feel a strong temptation
to take life easy. When, in their fantasy, these men grudgingly move
out to strive again, they propose that they have not irrevocably
committed themselves to the battle. They reassure themselves that
their strivings for achievement and self-direction do not imply a
final breach with supportive, often maternal figures. Although it is
shameful to linger at her side, they want to keep the road back to
mother open.

Thus active mastery refers to all men who, through their fantasy
productions, gave evidence of a vigorous, alloplastic approach to the
world or of major conflict between active and passive tendencies.
That is, the men of this group are either freely assertive, defensively
extrapunitive, or uneasily shifting between assertion and deference.
All have in common the assertive orientation. For some, aggression
is easily justified and readily displayed in action; for others, the assertive stance, though maintained, is the focus of conflict.

Passive Mastery

Two subgroups are included here: "adaptive conformers" and
"depersonalized conformers."

In their TAT stories the adaptive conformers portray heroes who
are deferent, sometimes guilty, in the presence of parents and other
authority figures. Their heroes are friendly, adaptive, and even ma-

ternal in their relations to others and are careful to atone for any transgressions of others' rights.

In the fantasies of this group, aggression mainly appears as an unpleasant, even frightening quality—an attribute of criminals or punitive external institutions. Thus, in response to 7BM, the father-son card, a stimulus which often elicits themes of intergenerational strife, a respondent from this group sees the youthful hero at a moral disadvantage, passive and dependent in relation to the older figure. Here direct interpersonal conflict is minimized, replaced by the pressure of anonymous social forces: "That looks like a courtroom scene where a lawyer is asking his client certain points that he's pleading for him. It's a serious case, looks like a criminal case. I don't know if he'll get off or not."

A story told to the farm-scene card is typical for its emphasis on hard work, piety, affiliation, and submission to benign maternal authority. Some friction is hinted at, but is never integrated into the major plot:

> There are three persons—mother and daughter and father. I can't see the man's face. It looks like he's plowing the field. The older woman is just standing there smiling. The younger girl is carrying the Bible. It looks like the mother is just overseeing that the work is done. . . . (What led up to this situation?) They may have had a little fuss, and they may have come out here to discuss it. It could be that the girl is taking off to school, and she has stopped off to say good-by. The girl will be glad when she returns from school, just as much as the mother will be glad to see her back home. (What else?) The man continues to work and does a good job. The older woman is satisfied with his work, and, when he finishes, they all go home and have dinner and everybody is happy.

These men seem to be partially dominated by what might be called superego strictures. Direct expressions of anger or self-interest are probably foreign to them, and they have, perhaps, solved the aggression-deference conflict of younger men by disavowing competitiveness and by stressing instead their humility, their kindliness, and their adaptability. They do not look to the outer world for challenge; rather, they look to authoritative parental figures for control and absolution.

These intropunitive individuals do not try to reshape their surroundings; instead, they seem to turn aggression inward—they become the objects of their own disavowed drives to dominate and control—and they conscientiously reshape themselves to meet external demands. However, their aggression can emerge directly when there is a clear moral sanction for action; they can fight others' battles, though not their own.

Stories told by the depersonalized conformers are characterized by sparseness and lack of personal elaboration, as in the following example: "A boy and his violin. . . . (What's he thinking?) He's thinking something, as how is he going to play that. . . . (Outcome?) He makes a good living at it, if he studies enough."

The stimulus is correctly described by these respondents, but the plot is rarely elaborated beyond the safe stimuli provided by the card. The content and formal structure of the story quoted here are typical, since they illustrate the degree to which these respondents rely on formal, external guides—in this case those provided by the configuration of the stimulus and by the promptings of the examiner. In general, plot and syntax emphasize overt acts and external qualities rather than inner motivations, and initiative is generally ascribed not to human agents but to an impersonal environment (as in this response to the farm-scene card: "If they have good weather, the crops will be OK").

This group seems to rely mainly on isolation, intellectualization, and externalization as defensive techniques. They disengage themselves from feelings and excitement, either in the outer world or in themselves; they anxiously focus their attention on the impersonal, conventional aspects of the environment, and they project their disavowed motivations into the world beyond their immediate experience, an exotic world that they endow with undefined dangers, to be feared and avoided.

In the experience of these men, "bad" things happen to them and around them. They are overtly passive and not moved from within; they wait for outer direction, act minimally in accordance with it, and return to diffuse ruminations once the external pressures are removed.

In sum, the passive mastery group includes all men who share a major, presumably defensive proclivity to withdraw from active engagement with the external world in favor of more passive and autoplastic positions. Aggression and self-assertion are ego-alien, and, rather than reshape their environments in the pursuit of "selfish" objectives, these individuals reshape themselves in conformity either to external demands or to the external representatives of internal (superego) demands. The self rather than the world is the focus of control.

Magical Mastery

Stories produced by the magical mastery group often contain misinterpretations and distortions of the stimuli so gross and so personal as to suggest that primitive motivations and conceptions are markedly interfering with the respondent's accurate perception of the world.

The following story, told to the rope-climber card by a sixty-four-year-old respondent is an illustration. For this man, the vigorous and nude figure of the climber suggests only violence and perversion; his response to the picture reflects his fearful misinterpretation of vigorous agents in the external world or of spontaneous urgings in himself: "This looks like a 'sex.' A window peeker or somebody crazy. It looks like either one. . . . (Outcome?) He could kill somebody or some woman. It certainly wouldn't be good."

Another subject whose interpretation of the cards was otherwise accurate became disoriented when presented with the least structured card in the battery—that which depicts the head of a man and a woman in close, intimate contact. Without the support of familiar, conventional structure, the stimulus scene becomes dreamlike for him and focuses on highly personal concerns with death: "Looks like a statue or something. Don't know whether that's water or not. Looks like it could be a woman drowned and floating on water."

Other men grouped here appear to be labile, impulsive individuals whose records are notable for their childish form and language. In everyday life, these subjects are likely to express their difficulties in a fairly direct fashion, by stormy and irrational behavior. However, the majority of the respondents in this category give essentially intact records, marred by a few notable lacunae. Therefore, these individuals presumably maintain reasonable façades despite much internal stress. Few if any of these men seem to have elaborated wide-ranging delusional systems. Rather, their ego functions seem to have regressed to archaic levels of ideation and defense—especially when they are faced by unfamiliar situations—while their public manner probably remains intact.

Their distinctive mastery mode is termed "magical" because, in time of trouble, these men operate on the principle of "wishing will make it so." At such times these respondents see in the world either what they want to see or what—for internal reasons—they must see. They alter the world by perceptual fiat, not by realistic, instrumental action. For example, when they can no longer assuage guilt and relieve anxiety through the conventional repertoire of ego defenses, these men fall back on more extreme forms, such as projection, and use minimal evidence to accuse others of harboring the sexual and aggressive motivations that they fear and deny in themselves.

Essentially, then, these individuals maintain mastery through regressive behavior and/or regressive ego functioning: the world is misperceived, either to justify primitive behavior or to ratify projective forms of conflict resolution. Table 6.1 shows that, with increased age, there is an increased frequency of men in the magical mastery group, a finding which substantiates the general hypotheses of increased difficulty with inner life and changes in defensive structure in later life.

As the distribution by age and by psychological type in Table 6.1 suggests, young men differ from older men in terms of their orientation toward both the internal and the external realms. The ego state of younger men appears to be characterized by a central theme of active mastery. Their handling of the TAT suggests that the ex-

TABLE 6.1
MASTERY STYLES FOR MALES BY AGE $(N = 145)$

	40–49	50–59	60–70
Active mastery			
Self-asserters	7*	8	3
Achievement doubters	10	18	9
Total	17	26	12
Passive mastery			
Adaptive conformers	8	20	12
Depersonalized			
conformers	0	6	11
Total	8	26	23
Magical mastery			
Total	4	15	14

* By the chi-square test, this distribution is significantly different from chance at the .02 level.

ternal world is the significant realm toward which they focus their energies and attention and to which they look for justification, challenge, and stimulation. Despite some uneasy reservations, the younger men see their engagement as being with the external world, not within themselves. These men are, perhaps, struggling to make the grade before time runs out, before the future is closed. The marked extraception of the younger men is relevant here. They seem to look beyond themselves for opportunity and example, and they worriedly check the front runners in order to gauge their own positions in the race. For them, control and delay have practical justification, and their self-discipline, their efficiency, is an internal phrasing of the organization that they wish to impose on some relevant sector of the external world.

In a sense, the younger men may be fighting identity struggles. As they covertly become aware of the presence of denied, passive, succorant strivings—pressures which perhaps incline them toward more dependent contact with their wives—they may feel compelled to firm up and reintegrate their sense of masculine identity. That is, like adolescents facing the promises and dangers of sexual contact, they may find it necessary to reassure themselves of their success and maleness before they can risk the heightened contact with women and, through women, with their own denied feminine identifications.

The older men emphasize passive mastery as their major ego style. They seem to be autoplastic rather than alloplastic. The older men do not direct their efforts toward mastering and deriving fulfillment from the external world, but rather deploy their energies—in form of stringent controls—to the task of controlling and shaping themselves. In addition, they tend to withdraw from active competition, they substitute ideation for action, and they look to the external world for authoritative guidance rather than for opportunity and stimulation. In sum, the older men do not see themselves moving outward, in an assertive fashion, into a plastic, manageable environment. Seemingly mistrustful of their own aggressive motivations, they ascribe power and determination to impersonal, external forces, to whose mandate they must adapt themselves. They have not relinquished all attempts at mastery and mutual regulation of the external world, but they now achieve their ends by way of circuitous routes, perhaps by virtue of their humility and constraint. (As an example, there are those individuals so unfailingly kind—often at their own expense—that others feel guilty in their presence and become alert to their unvoiced requests. Thus, such individuals often get their way while preserving their reputation for piety.)

The relatively focused and energetic ego state of younger men appears to be dominated by ego-ideal considerations, whereas that of older men seems dominated by a more archaic, superego orientation. That is, for the younger men the sense of inner approval or self-respect gained through successful achievement may be more important than direct endowments of love or approval from authoritative and external sources. They stress aggression, disavow passivity and masochism, and strive for respect, whereas the older men stress their mildness, disown combative motivations, and look for approval from parental figures.

In a self-denying fashion, these older men tend to be kinder to others than they are to themselves. Such forced altruism and self-constraint strongly suggest an intropunitive strategy in that the self becomes subject to the coercion that was once leveled against the external world. Superego formation involves the implantation in the developing personality of such constraints, such conscientious regard for the rights and welfare of others, and such taboos against doing harm. Accordingly, the notable intropunitiveness of older men points to the increasing influence of this psychic institution in their personality.

The superego orientation projected by older individuals in the TAT is only one phrasing of a subtly pervasive regressive quality. Essentially, the depersonalized conformers and magical mastery types (those most representative of the older group) can be viewed as two facets of a single development—a regression involving both a primitivization of the impulses in their relation to the object world and an equally primitive definition of the controls against the impulse life. Thus, in the magical mastery men we see the rephrasing of the impulse life into less socialized, more archaic forms, and in the depersonalized conformers we see the concomitant focus on harsh, undeviating controls wherein the forms of control have themselves taken on the monolithic quality of the impulses that they guard against. Possibly, as infantile, oral-aggressive motivations emerge, the ego defenses against them take on a similar, harsh, biting, all-or-nothing tone. One is either good or bad, black or white, big or small, and there is little middle ground for maneuver and adaptation between these extremes.

For older men, rules may no longer serve as reasonable guides to action, to be followed, redefined, or ignored as a matter of autonomous choice. Instead, rules seem to take on a sacrosanct quality —a development perhaps related to the often described conservatism of aging individuals—and all infractions, whether great or small, are equally deplorable. Thus, parental figures and parental versions of control may acquire, for older men, the importance they have for children. (That is, when object relations regress to more oral, dependent modes, the parent-child relationships of the oral period are implicitly revived, and the aging men may begin once again to exchange compliance for parental support and affection.)

The ego defenses of the younger men, though they sometimes feature a counterphobic, denying quality, are generally consistent with the adaptive, cogitative and delaying functions of the ego. These reasonable defenses give way, in the older men, to less mature defensive modalities: stressful external reality is magically though passively altered through the use of blatant denial, and distasteful inner reality is altered in an equally magical fashion through projection and massive externalization. That is, agents in the environment are either held responsible for the individual's feelings and reactions or themselves take on the physiognomy of the denied feelings. The regressive quality characteristic of older men is here again represented in these magical defensive tactics, for, as the outer world takes on the visage of unconscious motivations, self-other distinctions (or ego boundaries) become, by definition, attenuated.

Mastery Typology for Females

Active Mastery

The two subgroups included under this heading are the "rebellious daughters" and the "moralistic matriarchs." Both groups justify effective, focused action upon the environment by finding enemies to fight and worthy causes to uphold.

For the rebellious daughters, the enemy is a restrictive (usually maternal) authority, and their identification is with young people who struggle for autonomy and self-determination against such authorities. The following story is typical:

> Well, this girl lives on a farm, and she hates it. Her mother is very defiant and wants her to stay. (Yes?) But she goes on and becomes a very good scholar and teacher. (Why does she hate the farm?) It just doesn't appeal to her. She likes books and knowledge better.

It may be that these women identify with the rebellious young— perhaps against strict teachers or interfering grandmothers—in order to disavow infantilizing, authoritarian tendencies of their own. If so, they turn what could be a disquieting inner struggle into a brisk engagement with the world.

The moralistic matriarchs give equally free-swinging, although more idiosyncratic, stories. For this group, the opponents are callow, misinformed, morally lax young people. The role of the matriarch is to guide and discipline such errant children. A typical example is this story given to the father-son card:

> This one leaves me kind of cold. . . . The young man is certainly quite sullen looking. . . . The older man is quite kindly looking, and I can't connect the two as having any relation, as this other one has such an awful sour puss, so I can't think that it is his son especially. . . . You could say that this fellow is a dope addict; that is about what he looks like, and an elderly gentleman is trying to straighten him out and make a man of him. About the future, it looks pretty black. . . . (Why?) He looks like he has such a weak character, you wouldn't expect him to come out of it.

This same respondent also perceived the young man of the mother-son card as a misguided Communist who has joined the party in defiance of his mother's teachings.

The women of this subgroup justify vigorous, intrusive action through their struggle with bad children rather than with bad authorities. They are alert to the moral deficiencies of others and, once having found such deficiencies, take direct, corrective, and retaliatory action. Essentially, as the dope-addict story suggests, they rephrase personal struggles and intergenerational friction into battles between right and wrong, with themselves on the side of the right. Thus, these women feel indignation over the moral deficiencies that they read into the stimulus figures, sometimes forgetting that it was they who put them there.

Despite their opposing identifications, these two subgroups of women are alike in their technique for maintaining inner balance and outward effectiveness—namely, they maintain active mastery by externalizing guilt. The superego is not deployed against the "bad-me" aspects of self, but against blameworthy, "not-me" aspects of the world. Thus freed from superego attrition, these women can, perhaps, act in an expansive, goal-directed fashion once they have found either a bad child or a bad parent. Although they may sometimes stretch the facts in order to find a target, we can infer from their logically developed, well-organized stories that their behavior is effective and stays within conventional bounds.

The men and women of the active mastery type are alike, as suggested earlier, in terms of the formal, structural qualities of their stories. Both sexes impart vigor and conflict to the scene in a framework of logically developed, well-organized, and reasonable stories which are generally positive in their outcomes—for example, the rope-climber succeeds in his performance, or the young woman leaves the farm to pursue an independent role. At the same time, there is a major sex difference. The men of this group tend to propose that their struggle is with an impersonal environment or task or with those passive aspects of themselves that interfere with achievement. For the women, the conflict is between people, and issues are thrashed out in terms of their interpersonal connotations and complications. For example, the man who said, to the farm scene, that the girl "is leaving . . . to go to school or teach, rather than watch things grow" did not suggest that the heroine left the farm after a successful struggle with the mother. The heroine's relation to the other figures was barely implied, and her conflict was between competing active and passive roles—to teach, to study, or to "watch things grow." For the men, the interpersonal scene tends to be muted, and the focus is on the task and the hero's capacity to deal with it. In the parallel story told by the active mastery woman, on the other hand, the interpersonal issues are the crux of the plot. The heroine's dilemma—to stay or to go—is fractionated into conflicting human protagonists, and the mother's strident objections implicitly justify the daughter's defiant departure. For women such as this respondent, decisions are fought out openly, in a vivid, sharply contrasted interpersonal arena.

Passive Mastery

In contrast to the lively, extrapunitive active mastery women, the passive mastery women are intropunitive. They solve internal or external conflict through changing themselves rather than the world. Two subgroups are included: the "maternal altruists," for whom the intropunitive style is effective, and the "passive aggressors," who seem to lack the external supports which could validate and redeem the intropunitive style and for whom, therefore, the style is ineffective.

The maternal altruists are similar to the rebellious daughters of the active mastery type by virtue of their maternal interests and their altruistic identification with children. However, while the rebellious daughters rely on externalization as a defensive technique, those grouped here rely on reaction formation. These women are not looking for a fight, nor are they seeking to dominate some aspect of the external world in order to control aspects of themselves. Rather, like the intropunitive men, they are uncomfortable with aggression, and they look for placid, predictable milieux—surroundings which support them in the denial of their aggression and in their identities as affiliative, maternal individuals.

The following story, told to the mother-son card, illustrates the self-effacing qualities of this group; here the heroine, despite her reluctance and inner despair, puts the son's career needs above her own need for companionship. Rather than involve the son in her conflict, the mother turns to busy work. This emphasis on good works suggests that the respondent handles any unvoiced anger that she might feel through imposing a penance on herself.

> The mother is sorry that the son is going away. She hates to see him leave, but she doesn't want to stand in his way. . . . (What is she thinking?) She is thinking of how lonely she will be but that she must not let him know. . . . (How does it end?) She'll get busy with club work and things and lead a happy, useful life.

The passive aggressors, the more depressed members of the female passive mastery group, are represented by constricted women who, much like the equivalent male group (the depersonalized conformers), defend themselves against both external and internal stimulation and conform in a rather apathetic manner to conventional patterns of behavior. They stress dysphoric themes, but otherwise do not go much beyond a sparse, although accurate, description of the stimuli. The following story, told to the farm-scene card, suggests the somewhat inert and self-pitying quality of this group:

> I don't know. . . . That's her daughter, isn't it?
> . . . . (Up to you.) She looks like her. Her son is plowing. She's come from school. They are sad, just like me.
> . . . (How does it end?) Sometimes things turn out good, sometimes bad. We just have to take the heartaches.

Unlike active mastery women, these women see themselves as victims, rather than as aggressive masters, of their fate. Although they may employ some of the moralistic, self-justifying tactics of the more assertive women, their capacity for externalization does not free their aggressive energies. These passive individuals cannot go into action, even when they have a worthy cause.

In some cases, the depressed mood of these women represents a socialized rephrasing of their fundamental anger. They resent very strongly the departure of their children, but they cannot implement their retentive wishes. They cannot resign themselves to their fate, nor can they fight it. Their techniques are essentially passive and autoplastic—they overconform to external control, and their obedience gives them the right to expect restitution and support or to feel aggrieved should they go unrewarded. Thus, these subjects are indirectly manipulative rather than directly intrusive. They exert influence primarily through the constraints and demands that they impose upon themselves and through the guilt that their deprived condition arouses in others.

In terms of both the structure and content of their fantasy, the passive mastery women are quite similar to their male counterparts, although the female passive aggressors are somewhat more dramatic than the male depersonalized conformers. The women announce their depression (and thus partly transcend it), while the men seem to live it—or so the burnt-out quality of their stories would suggest. Thus, however despairing they may feel, these women continue to communicate and to externalize their inner states; their depression serves as the currency of their interpersonal exchange. The men withdraw more quickly from interpersonal communication to private rumination and to internal dialogue.

Magical Mastery

The stories told by these women marked by magical mastery are notable for the open and often inappropriate display of primitive, aggresive, retentive, and sexual feelings. Such motivations are often ascribed to the stimulus figures, with little regard for objective features of the cards. These women grossly confound their reactions with their perceptions. Their ego boundaries seem unclear, and their milieux are often perceived in ways which represent or justify the personal investment they have in it. Thus, the world is an unrecognized cognate of themselves, its nature and reality defined by their own feelings.

The following story, told to the rope-climber card, illustrates how this group maintains emotional equilibrium through moralistic and zestful condemnation of their own unrecognized and projected sexuality and aggression:

> This is evolution for you—back to the cave man, back to the monkeys. I have read about Neanders man. . . . This sure looks like the cave-man age—the taming of the shrew—the men back then were small in stature. Look at his muscles. . . . (What is he thinking?) He thinks only of the carnal—kill, protect himself, get food. . . . (How does it end?) I don't believe that time will ever come again, do you? I read in *Quick Magazine* that in one thousand years there will be no race segregation. The black race will supplant the white. . . . That's what comes of Negroes and whites going to school together. When love strikes, they intermarry.

In the following story, told to the heterosexual-conflict card, the man's sinfulness and the woman's holiness are taken for granted.

Almost explicitly the woman is an agent of God, and, thus justified, the respondent's domineering tendencies clearly emerge:

> I think this little lady is trying to tell him about the Way, but he is just objecting, turning himself away. . . . (What are they thinking?) Well, I don't know if he has a need in his life and she's trying to help. He needs the Lord . . . help from his Heavenly Father. . . . (How does it end?) She'll win out. She is going to pray for him.

Thus, those in the magical mastery group grossly and often rather blandly distort and misperceive reality in order to justify impulsive and domineering behavior. They experience little internal conflict concerning their primitive needs. Their fight is with the environment, not with themselves. In a sense, these women are rather like the nearsighted Mr. Magoo—caricatures of inner direction. They see the world as they wish to see it, and they may consequently act with such self-confidence that others grudgingly confirm their egocentric versions of reality.

As Table 6.2 indicates, the proportion of women in the two nurturant subtypes (rebellious daughters and maternal altruists) drops off markedly with increasing age: 41 per cent of the forty- to forty-nine-year-old women are found under these headings, whereas only 38 per cent of women in their fifties and 18 per cent of the women in the oldest group are found here. The proportion of women in the self-centered categories (passive aggressors and magical mastery) shows a corresponding increase with age.

These results support the views on female aging set forth in the study by Neugarten and Gutmann (see Chapter 3). The younger women demonstrate a nurturant, positive attitude toward the young, including an acceptance and espousal of their autonomy. Older women display a more retentive, self-centered version of mothering; they visualize direct conflict between themselves and their children, and they delude themselves in order to justify egocentric claims.

Perhaps the attenuation of the maternal role and the growing independence of the young allow some of these older women to take

TABLE 6.2

MASTERY STYLES FOR FEMALES BY AGE $(N = 144)$

	40–49	50–59	60–70
Active mastery			
Rebellious daughters	11	16	7
Moralistic matriarchs	6	8	4
Total	17*	24	11
Passive mastery			
Maternal altruists	2	7	2
Passive aggressors	5	13	13
Total	7	20	15
Magical mastery			
Total	8	16	26

* By the chi-square test, the distribution of active, passive, and magical mastery totals by age groups is significantly different from chance at the .02 level.

a more overtly selfish and managerial position. Knowing that their children are now strong enough to stand against them, they can permit themselves a more autocratic, intrusive role in regard to the younger generation.

Along these lines, women might permit themselves, in later life, the self-indulgence that had to be denied when they were primarily concerned with the rearing of children. Just as men in later life seem to turn back upon themselves the outward-directed aggression of their youth, so older women may turn back upon themselves the nurturance which no longer finds its appropriate external object. They may become their own lost child and claim for themselves the indulgence that the younger women still claim and fight for as the right of children.

The Mastery Types and Other Measures of Male Personality

The age distributions of the mastery types showed significant age differences and were consistent with the hypothesis of increasing inner-life difficulties in the later years. However, this finding is only a partial one until it can be demonstrated, relative to some external criterion, that the mastery types thus delineated refer to real and distinctive psychic configurations and that these configurations relate to overt and observable behavior. Because the types described here have been delineated on the basis of TAT data alone, the next step was to study further the psychological meaning of these types by seeing whether the types could be differentiated in meaningful ways on other behavioral measures.

There were available a variety of judgments and ratings for these cases, based on extensive interview data gathered over time. These include judgments of the types of rewards the respondent experienced from social interaction; interviewers' ratings of the respondent's physical, affective, and intellectual functioning; and ratings of the respondent's satisfaction with life. Each of these measures will first be described in terms of its relations to the mastery types in males.

Interactional Rewards

Each respondent in Sample II had been asked to choose from the four descriptions listed below the one which he thought best characterized him. The descriptions were based on the conceptual framework of Talcott Parsons (1950) and presumably reflect the types of rewards (esteem, responsiveness, love, approval) to be gained in social interaction (Dean, 1961).

1. A person who is *esteemed* by others and takes a continual interest in human welfare in general.

2. A person who is *enjoyed* by others and takes his joys and sorrows as they come, from day to day.

3. A person who is *loved* by others and takes a continual interest in the welfare of all those who are dear to him.

4. A person who is *approved* by others and attends to his affairs consistently, from day to day.

Each respondent had also been asked, by choosing from the four descriptions the one he *wished* himself to be, to indicate his *preferred* type of interactional reward.

"Actual" versus preferred rewards. A scoring system had been constructed to compute the extent of discrepancy between actual and preferred rewards (Dean, 1961). Although the discrepancy score had been used by Dean to test hypotheses of a sociological nature, it was viewed here as a measure of externalized psychological conflict. That is, highly conflicted individuals are rarely satisfied with their current interpersonal rewards or with their social milieux, since no life situation can satisfy their full range of polarized, conflicting needs. For ambivalent, conflicted individuals, satisfaction in one sphere can only be gained at the expense of frustration in another, and the present social environment becomes the external representation of their inner frustration. Therefore, it was predicted that individuals who did not give evidence in the TAT of gross intrapsychic conflict would have lower discrepancy scores than those whose TAT's indicated conflicts so severe as to threaten ego breakdown. This prediction was borne out, as shown in Table 6.3: overall, the active mastery group received the lowest discrepancy scores; the magical mastery group received the highest.

Recognitional versus affectional rewards. Besides experiencing less discrepancy between what they want and what they get from social interaction, active mastery men should seek a different order of interpersonal rewards than do the men of other mastery styles. The active mastery men are involved in action and with future career and institutional goals. They should be oriented toward the kinds of satisfactions gleaned in an impersonal world, the rewards forthcoming from authorities and peers in recognition of worth and exploit. Accordingly, it was hypothesized that the active mastery men would tend to select, as their preferred interaction rewards, the more impersonal, public endowments of esteem and approval (self-descriptions A and D), or what could be called "recognitional rewards." The passive and the magical mastery men, on the other hand—those presumably receptive to or troubled by their oral needs—should choose items B and C, which involve the giving and receiving

TABLE 6.3

MALE MASTERY TYPES BY INTERACTIONAL REWARDS,
PERSONAL PRESENCE SCORES, AND LIFE SATISFACTION

	Active mastery	Passive mastery	Magical mastery
Mean score on discrepancy between actual and preferred rewards ($N = 50$)	1.05	1.48	2.86*
Preferred rewards ($N = 52$) Number choosing recognitional rewards	14	7	4
Number choosing affectional rewards	6	11	10†
Mean score on personal presence ($N = 59$)	81.5	75.9	72.6*
Mean rating on life satisfaction ($N = 56$)	19.9	17.7	16.9*

Note—The number of cases for whom data were available varies somewhat from measure to measure.

* By the f test, the differences between subgroup means are reliable at the .05 level.

† By the chi-square test, this distribution is reliably different from chance at the .05 level.

of the immediate, tangible rewards of love and enjoyment, or what could be called "affectional rewards."

These judgments were made by comparing the actual to the preferred style of interactional reward and assessing—without knowledge of the respondent's mastery type—the direction of the subject's interactional strivings. Four classes were established: (1) men satisfied with their present level of recognitional reward; (2) men who wished more recognitional rewards than they presently received; (3) men satisfied with their present level of affectional reward; and (4) men who yearned for more affectional rewards than they presently received. The first two classes were then combined to form a group of men oriented primarily to recognitional rewards; the last two classes were combined to form a group of men oriented primarily to affectional rewards.

Congruent with the hypothesis, the mastery types were found to differ on this basis at a statistically reliable level, as shown in Table 6.3. The active mastery men were either satisfied with a predominantly recognitional style in the present or they yearned to maximize this form of reward. The passive mastery men felt they had, and were satisfied with, a predominantly affectional pattern of reward. The magical mastery men wanted more affectional rewards than they were receiving.

Personal Presence Scores

Some measure of the general overt behavior of each respondent was desired. Since the interviewers had had sustained contact with the respondents, they were asked to rate them on intelligence, physical energy, health, intellectual energy, morale, and emotional reactions. Although the ratings of each interviewer were impressionistic and the reliability of the individual ratings have not been established, the ratings of all interviewers on an individual respondent were nevertheless combined into a mean score which is here called the "personal presence score." This score also differentiated the mastery types in the predicted direction, as shown in Table 6.3, with active mastery men receiving higher ratings; passive and magical, lower.

Life Satisfaction Ratings

Life Satisfaction ratings had been made on all respondents by an independent team of investigators. These ratings, based on four rounds of intensive interviews obtained over three years, reflect the extent to which (1) the individual takes pleasure from the round of activities that constitutes his everyday life; (2) the individual feels he has achieved his major life goals; (3) his self-concept is a positive one; (4) his mood is happy and contented versus depressed; and (5) the individual accepts responsibility for his past and looks ahead to death with relative equanimity. Ratings on these five sub-scales are combined to give a total Life Satisfaction Rating (Neugarten, Havighurst, & Tobin, 1961). When the three mastery groups of men were compared on this measure, the anticipated trends were confirmed. As shown in Table 6.3, the active mastery group was highest on Life Satisfaction; the passive and magical mastery, successively lower.

These results of comparing mastery styles and other sets of data on the same men are by no means conclusive. They are, however, sufficiently positive to justify confidence that the mastery types delineated here on the basis of TAT responses refer to distinct psychic configurations in males and that they reflect differences in personality that are measurable in both projective and overt behavior.

If this is so, the significant variation in the age distribution of the types points to the conclusion that there are consistent age differences in ego configurations and in related personality phenomena in a community sample of men aged forty to seventy. These data are cross-sectional rather than longitudinal and may therefore reflect culturally determined differences rather than positions along an age-determined continuum. That is, the older men may differ psychologically from the younger because they were raised in different cultural and familial environments, not because they are farther along a pathway which the younger men must travel in their turn. Whatever the correct interpretation, the younger men in this age range, by comparison with the older, are characterized by a vigorous and realistic approach to the external world, and their ego defenses, motivations, and thought processes are generally consistent with such effectiveness. By contrast, the older men are characterized by passivity, intropunitiveness, and by pronounced, sometimes failing, defensive efforts.

The Mastery Types and Other Measures
of Female Personality

When the mastery types for women were studied in relation to measures of interactional rewards, personal presence, and Life Satisfaction, relationships such as those found in men did not emerge. On the contrary, the magical mastery women, those who approached the TAT in arbitrary and distorting ways, often received the highest ratings on these scales. In relation to personal presence, for example, women who told rather bizarre and confabulated stories to the TAT cards were often described by interviewers as warm, friendly, intelligent, full of civic spirit and concern for their families.

The fact that the ratings which differentiated the male mastery types did not differentiate the female types suggests that the mastery typology must be differently interpreted for women than for men. A review of the data showed that psychological parameters independent of the mastery issue might account for much of the variance in the female data. Specifically, inward turned, passive mastery women seemed to receive lower Life Satisfaction ratings than the more externalizing, alloplastic, active and magical mastery women. Thus, the life satisfaction ratings (probably the most reliable of the measures used) seemed to distinguish between alloplastic and autoplastic styles in women, but not between realistic and unrealistic ego functioning.

Accordingly, the groups were reordered: the passive mastery women were called "intropunitive," and both the active and magical mastery groups were called "extrapunitive." The Life Satisfaction ratings were then distributed against these new groupings. As shown in Table 6.4, the difference between means was in the predicted direction, although it did not reach statistical significance. It is noteworthy, at the same time, that a significant number of extrapunitive women—including many of the magical mastery group— achieved Life Satisfaction scores above the median, as compared to only a few of the intropunitive women. Thus, viewed against the theoretical model of well-integrated ego functioning, the extrapunitive women were often inferior to the intropunitive, but this inferiority is not reflected in the Life Satisfaction ratings. This finding suggests that female contentment might be more related to the deployment of aggressive energies than to the formal qualities of ego functioning. A vigorous, intense engagement with the world, however arbitrarily rationalized, may ensure greater happiness for women than a self-contained position, however reasonable the latter

TABLE 6.4

EXTRAPUNITIVE AND INTROPUNITIVE WOMEN
BY LIFE SATISFACTION RATINGS

	LSR at or below the median	LSR above the median	Mean scores*
Intropunitive	12†	3	17.00
Extrapunitive	13	23	19.48

* By the T test, difference between means is not significant.
† By the chi-square test (Yate's correction), this distribution is significant at the .02 level.

may seem. For men, the sense of well-being as measured by Life Satisfaction is linked to the integrity of ego functioning and seems to decline as such integrity declines. For women, well-being seems relatively independent of the formal integrity of ego functioning. Degree of contentment may remain fairly stable while the ego functions undergo successive regressive changes in order to maintain the necessary externalized, guilt-free orientation.

Thus, the younger active mastery women fight well-rationalized battles against intrusive parents or rebellious young; they enforce discipline and demand respect or, conversely, uphold the right of the young to gain independence. The older magical mastery women seem to determinedly distort reality in order to establish grounds for what may be their continued autocratic participation in the lives of their now independent children and their somewhat emotionally withdrawn husbands. Essentially, despite important differences in reality-testing, both the older and younger extrapunitive women look for a cause and an enemy; it is the ego mechanisms involved in maintaining this orientation which change over the years. Finding external targets, these women are able to project their guilt; the outside world, rather than themselves, becomes the target of their superego reproach. Consequently, unburdened of guilt, these externalizing women, whether young or old, may experience a feeling of worth and "rightness." Because their reproaches are directed away from themselves, much affect seems to be freed, and they find it easy to like themselves, even as they vigorously like and dislike various aspects of the surrounding world. It is perhaps to this sense of affective vitality that raters respond when they assign high Life Satisfaction scores to the extrapunitive women.

Discussion

These data show, in summary, that, when mastery styles are arrayed along a continuum from realistic to regressive ego functioning, the distributions show significant age differences, differences in the direction that supports the general hypothesis that with advancing age there is increased difficulty in the management of inner life. The trends are the same for both men and women: the frequency of active mastery decreases as passive and magical mastery increases. Evaluated against a formal model of good, realistic ego-functioning, older men and women, by contrast to the middle-aged, are more frequently prone to illogical thought and to motivated misperception of stimuli.

At the same time, there are striking sex differences. Men and women of the same mastery type may be similar in terms of formal reality-testing capacities and major systems of ego defense, but the issues that concern them and the deployment of their energies become increasingly divergent with age.

Regardless of mastery type, women are more affectively labile than the men, more ready to experience internal states as external pressures. For example, although men approached the TAT cards as a task or puzzle, women tended not to maintain such distance and responded to the stimuli as vivid, exciting, or troubling events. They often forgot that life and feeling originated in themselves and not in the cards, and they would become indignant or troubled by apperceived events that had taken on a reality of their own. Thus a woman might remark at the end of a story, "I hope things will turn out well," or "A boy like that should be taught a lesson."

Generally speaking, for men there was more consistency between psychic content and psychic structure than was the case for women. Active mastery men were oriented toward achievement in the extra-familial world, the passive mastery men were preoccupied with

philosophical issues. For women, the mastery style was more independent of the issues that preoccupied them. For example, both
the moralistic matriarchs and the maternal altruists were primarily
concerned with the maternal-retentive issue, one group within the
confines of a fairly realistic and effective active mastery style, the
other in the rather placid fashion of the passive mastery style.

The distortions evidenced by older men and women seemed to
have a different meaning and function for each sex. For older men,
the distortions seemed to serve passive goals; for women, they
seemed allied to and perhaps facilitating of more vigorous, outgoing
orientations.

A sense of this disparity emerges through comparing the previously quoted stories told by a magical mastery man and a magical
mastery woman to the rope-climber card. Both stories—of the "sex"
window peeker and of the caveman—are erratic, arbitrary, dominated by the emotional implications of the climber's virile and
sensual qualities. The man's story is dominated by his fearful apperception of such sexuality. He does not like what he finds in the
card—it is dirty, bad, to be shunned and withdrawn from. The
woman's story, however, although even more distorted in formal
terms than the man's, is zestful. For all her pious horror, the respondent relishes the brute she has discovered. She goes to the card,
rather than away from it. The man terminates his story after a few
reluctant and fearful sentences; the woman rather gleefully dwells
on the hero's murderous and carnal possibilities. Thus, the male
respondent's phobic perception leads to constriction and avoidance
of further stimulation, whereas the female respondent, given license
by the card, dwells for a while in a primal world of her fantasy.

As mentioned earlier, the decline in ego integration in the oldest
men was associated with reduced estimates of self-confidence and
satisfaction with life. An equivalent lessening of ego integration was
seemingly not inimical to the well-being of the oldest women. For
men, ego functioning perhaps declines in step with a decline in active participation in the world; for women, such a decline often
accompanies a zestful, combative, though somewhat disorganized,
participation in the life around them.

Thus, as men age, they increasingly stress their self-control, their friendly adaptability, and their passivity. Action in the external world gives way to anxious, compulsive reordering of the self. For women, the converse is indicated. They are altruistic, effective in a controlled maternal fashion during the earlier years, only to become more egocentric, impulsive, and directly aggressive in later life. Where older men seek to control their spontaneous urges, older women find opportunities for vigorous action and interpersonal encounters.

In terms of the disposition and nature of the ego defenses, we can say that men defend the external world against the fantasied consequences of their impulses, while women seem to defend their personal claims against the counterpressures of the world. That is, for older men the goal of the defenses is passive mastery. The defense does not facilitate overt action, but comes to replace it. The substitution of rumination and compensatory fantasy for direct action may safeguard passivity, and the perceptual reworking of the environment through magical mastery may be a regressive equivalent for instrumental action, which has been renounced. But, for older women, magical mastery sanctions their continuing efforts at direct control of the external world. Women do not confabulate an environment in which the goals of action are magically achieved; rather, they confabulate versions of reality which permit them to act in their accustomed and preferred ways.

The explanation of the differences between the sexes can only be speculated about, given the limitations of the present data. If these differences are not due merely to sampling biases and if the data have implications with regard to age changes as well as to age differences, then the sex differences may reflect, at least in part, long-term differences in the socialization of and psychosexual development of men and women in this country. From early in life men and women are treated differently, supplied with different models, and pointed toward different versions of the future. They live out their adult lives in milieux which tend to encourage sex-appropriate ways of experiencing, conceiving, and reacting to reality.

It may be that men in later life are stymied by their allegiance to logic and controls; they fear the reactivation of infantile impulses in later life, seeing them as a threat to their long-term investment in self-control. As a result, perhaps they act out against themselves instead of against the world, funneling the energies released by regression back into the superego-based control system. A commitment to logic and to impersonal perspectives may make them vulnerable to objective definitions of their capacities and their prospects as aging men. Thus, attentive to the demands of a restrictive superego and the remorseless logic of social and biological loss, they may withdraw from the world and prepare for death. Women, who have been differently socialized and who may be more deeply wedded to an expressive and a personal world, may be less bound by logic and self-control. They may act out against the world as an appropriate way of staying affectively alive in their milieu of friends and family.

7

PERSONALITY AND
SOCIAL INTERACTION

Alexey Shukin
Bernice L. Neugarten

The purpose of the present study was to explore the relationships between certain personality attributes and the extent of social
interaction in men and women from fifty to seventy. The theoretical
issues underlying this investigation stem indirectly from the disengagement theory of aging. That theory, in part, postulates that
the crucial social-psychological differences between the middle-aged
and the old lie along a dimension of social involvement, with the
middle-aged being fully engaged with life outside of themselves and
with the old being relatively disengaged (Cumming, Dean, Newell,
& McCaffrey, 1960; Cumming & Henry, 1961). The process of disengagement is believed to be accompanied by a partial release from
the normative patterning of behavior provided by social interaction.
The decrease in normative influences is, in turn, viewed as con-

tributing to the emergence of behaviors which, if they appeared in the middle-aged, would be considered deviant, but which, if they appear in the old, are described as egocentricity, eccentricity, or idiosyncrasy.

The hypothesis was here explored that disengagement from the social network leads to idiosyncratic or eccentric behavior in the aged. This hypothesis, although not central to the disengagement theory, deals with concepts involved in that theory. A set of personality variables was delineated that presumably reflect the individual's orientation toward social norms, his readiness to meet and anticipate the needs and responses of others, and his sensitivity to the expectations of others, characteristics which are reinforced through social interaction. Among these variables, ten could be reliably assessed from the interview and projective data available in the Kansas City Studies.

1. "Tentative versus dogmatic views" estimates the extent to which the respondent is tentative rather than uncompromising in his attitudes, opinions, and preferences as expressed in response to a wide variety of interview questions. This tentativeness may be observed in opinions offered as provisional, in preferences considered temporary. Respondents who are high on this variable are also likely to show caution, reservation, an emergent quality of thought, or a suggestion of openness to experience as expressed in such comments as "the more I think, the more it seems to me that . . . ," "so it would seem," and "perhaps. . . ." In general, the implication here is that positions or viewpoints are open to continual revision. The opposite of this quality is stating one's viewpoints in final, definitive, or dogmatic form, where the respondent asserts implicitly or explicitly in a large number of areas that he knows "what's what."

2. "Supported versus unsupported views" is related to the first variable, but focuses on the respondent's tendency to support or document his generalizations and his opinions, as, for example, when he explains on what evidence an opinion is based or why a conclusion seems to him warranted. This attempt to document implies the respondent's anticipation of possible denial, objection, or dis-

belief on the part of others and his desire to justify his beliefs in the eyes of others. The opposite quality is the tendency toward unsupported statements and declarations, suggesting indifference to evidence, and little anticipation of disagreement or skepticism from others.

3. "Conventional versus idiomatic reporting" estimates the extent to which autobiographical material elicited by the interview is presented in logically controlled and conventional ways, as contrasted with idiomatic and anecdotal treatment. The latter, although it may be spontaneous, implies an egocentric mode of thought and a certain disregard for the conventional needs or expectations of a listener. Respondents who rate high on this variable adhere to typical sequences of chronology, such as "from kindergarten through college," or standard organizing themes, such as family relations or occupational history. A respondent who rates low may offer a more kaleidoscopic treatment of the past or may, for example, when asked for a summary of his life, embark on a vivid or detailed account of an inconsequential past event.

4. "Awareness of social context" represents the respondent's tendency to discuss the ways in which his self-perceived attributes have been acquired. The attributes are referred to in developmental, historical terms and are described as issuing out of one's life experiences and social circumstances as well as one's own efforts. The opposite of this tendency is indicated in self-descriptions which do not, for example, contain references to parental actions or to other formative influences and events in one's life. The implication is, for respondents who rate high, that they perceive themselves in a social context which they recognize as having been relevant in terms of the past as well as in the present.

5. "Concern with causality" estimates the extent to which the respondent thinks in terms of cause and effect relationships in describing feelings, actions, and events (Cumming & Henry, 1961). The rating is based on TAT Card 1 (the boy and the violin). The implication is that the respondent who rates high is utilizing conventional and culturally valued modes of thought. The respondent

who rates low, on the other hand, is describing feelings and events without regard for their antecedents and is thereby utilizing more idiosyncratic modes of thought.

6. "Self-improvement versus self-indulgence" estimates the extent to which the respondent's interests and efforts are directed toward self-improvement. The opposite of this quality is expressed in the preference for self-gratificatory activities, which may be centered around food, comfort, entertainment, or relaxation. The assumption is that, in maintaining the former attitude, the respondent is demonstrating his allegiance to the cultural norm in which efforts to improve the self are rewarded by others, but self-indulgence is negatively sanctioned.

7. "Future versus past orientation" estimates the degree to which the respondent is concerned with or oriented toward the future as contrasted with the present or the past. This tendency may be manifested in concern with one's own future, with the future course of events in general, or both.

8. "Concern over others' opinions" relates to expressed concern with the image other people have of oneself and with other people's approval or disapproval. The locus of self-evaluation tends to reside in the reactions of others. The opposite of this tendency is a manifest disinterest in other people's favorable or unfavorable appraisals.

9. "Concern with learning" estimates the extent to which stories told in response to TAT cards 1 and 2 show concern with didactic aspects of events and experiences. Lack of this tendency is reflected in stories which do not build plots and elaborations around the concomitants and consequences of learning and which pay little attention to possible didactic values.

10. "Optimism" estimates the respondent's general optimism about the constructive potentialities of human actions—administrative, parental, therapeutic—in the face of experienced difficulties or failures either in himself or in the environment. The opposite of this quality is an expressed or implied skepticism about human efforts and a belief in the futility of human actions.

Five-point rating scales were defined for the variables. High ratings were interpreted as indicating orientation toward socially shared conventions and expectations; low ratings were viewed as indicating idiosyncratic or eccentric behaviors—less normatively controlled behaviors. Although it was anticipated that scores on these variables would be related to age, the hypothesis underlying this study would be confirmed if the scores proved to be more closely related to social interaction than to age.

Two different measures of social interaction were available: (1) the Interaction Index, a subjective rating based on the amount of each day the respondent spends in normatively governed interaction with others, interaction in which the hints, cues, and sanctions which govern and control behavior are exchanged; and (2) the Social Lifespace, derived from a count of the number and variety of interactions the individual engages in during the period of a month with persons in various categories. In computing scores on the Social Lifespace measure, different weightings are assigned to interactions with other members of the household, with relatives, friends, fellow workers, neighbors, and with such specific people as postmen, salespeople, or bus drivers. This measure disregards the length of each interaction and tends to give high scores to people whose lives have variety.

The two measures are positively correlated, but some men and women have high scores on one and low scores on the other. For instance, a married woman who spends most of the day in the company of her retired husband but who sees few other people would be high on Interaction Index, but low on Social Lifespace. A man who lives alone but has a larger number of brief encounters with different people would be low on Interaction Index, but high on Social Lifespace. The two measures are described in detail by Cumming and Henry (1961, pp. 243–248).

Procedures

The sample consisted of 103 respondents drawn from the Sample II panel (see Appendix A) for whom the appropriate data were available. Two age groups were included, twenty-eight men and twenty-three women, aged fifty to fifty-eight, and twenty-eight men and twenty-four women, aged sixty-three to seventy-one. The two groups were approximately equally distributed over three social classes—upper-middle, lower-middle, and working class.

The data consisted of recorded interview material dealing with the individual's current and past circumstances; his attitudes toward himself, his work, his family, and his friends; his attitudes toward religion, morale, and related social-psychological material. Another part of the data consisted of stories given in response to six cards of the Thematic Apperception Test.

An attempt was made to disguise the interviews for age of respondent by removing as much as possible all information which gave direct clues regarding age. This blinding of the interviews was carried out in advance by a person other than the present investigator; and, although it was only partially successful, given the nature of the data themselves, it nevertheless provided some additional measure of objectivity. Seven of the variables (1, 2, 3, 4, 6, 7, 8) are based on interview responses; the other three (5, 9, 10), on TAT responses.

Reliability of ratings on the ten personality variables was investigated by selecting ten cases at random for rating by two independent judges and by comparing rank orders on each variable. The mean value for rho was .7. Correlations among the ten variables were low, with only two of the forty-five coefficients being above .5 (for variables 3 and 7, $r = .58$; for 6 and 7, $r = .51$). Scores on Interaction Index and Social Lifespace had been computed earlier by an independent team of investigators (Cumming & Henry, 1961).

Findings

The first question to be explored was the extent to which the variables were related to age. For this purpose, the ratings on each of the personality variables were subjected to successive two-way analyses of variance for age, sex, and social class. Results of these analyses showed that age accounted for a significant (.05) portion of variance for seven of the ten variables. (These are indicated in

Table 7.1.) As might have been anticipated, the sixty-three to seventy-one age group showed the pattern of low scores, which in this study were assumed to be indicative of idiosyncratic behavior. For four variables (1, 3, 7, 9), sex difference was also a significant source of variance in the ratings. Social class was not a significant factor.

The analyses of variance for the Social Lifespace scores showed the factors of age and sex to be significant (.05), with low scores occurring in the older group, as compared with the younger, and in women, as compared with men. The Interaction Index scores, on the other hand, did not show any significant subgroup differences.

Having established the fact that seven out of ten personality variables, as well as Social Lifespace, were closely related to age, the factor of age was controlled in exploring the hypothesized relationship between social interaction and personality. This was accomplished by separately correlating personality ratings with measures of social interaction for each of the two age groups. The obtained coefficients of correlation for the four age-sex groups were consistently very low and statistically not significant. At each age level, respondents classified as high and low on the two interaction measures were then compared on each of the personality variables. When differences between means were tested, the findings again were negative. Thus, the personality variables described here do not seem to be associated with extent of social interaction, once age is controlled, and these data therefore do not support the interpretation that disengagement from the social network leads to eccentric and egocentric behavior. The implication is, instead, that personality changes of the type measured here occur with increasing age, but not as a function of the decrease in social interaction.

The investigators do not mean to imply that personality, in old age as in any other period of life, is independent of social interaction, for in the broad sense personality always develops and changes in social-interactional settings. It is, instead, the relationships between the particular variables used in this study which are at issue. It is likely, on the one hand, that, had more refined measures of social interaction been available, different relationships would have emerged. At the same time, given the findings from

TABLE 7.1

MEAN SCORES ON PERSONALITY VARIABLES AND
SOCIAL INTERACTION $(N = 103)$*

Variable	50–58		63–71	
	Men	Women	Men	Women
Tentative versus dogmatic views	3.17	3.57	2.82	2.95
Supported versus unsupported views	3.82	3.82	3.04	3.12
Conventional versus idiomatic reporting	3.35	3.75	2.34	2.83
Awareness of social context	3.35	3.39	3.04	3.20
Concern with causality	3.94	3.85	3.10	2.89
Self-improvement versus self-indulgence	3.32	3.78	2.52	2.91
Future versus past orientation	3.64	4.03	2.34	3.16
Concern over others' opinions	3.21	3.57	2.91	3.45
Concern with learning	3.23	3.92	2.47	2.57
Optimism	2.47	2.66	2.52	2.63
Interaction Index	2.89	2.79	2.74	2.50
Social Lifespace	47.46	42.29	32.61	27.92

* Age was a significant source of variance (at the .05 level) for variables 1, 2, 3, 5, 6, 7, and 9 and for Social Lifespace. Sex was a significant source of variance for 3, 6, 7, and 9. N was 82 for variables 5, 9, and 10 because TAT data were not available for all respondents.

earlier chapters in this book that measurable personality change occurs by the mid-forties and the finding that a significant drop in these gross measures of social interaction does not occur until the mid-sixties (Cumming & Henry, 1961), the interpretation is reinforced that personality changes in middle and late life proceed in ways that are at least to some extent independent of social interaction. In somewhat overstated terms, eccentricity and egocentricity develop not merely in response to relative social isolation, but also in response to processes of change in the individual. Such changes in personality might prove, on the basis of future research, to be developmental.

8

PERSONALITY TYPES IN AN
AGED POPULATION

Bernice L. Neugarten

William J. Crotty

Sheldon S. Tobin

There have been few investigations in which a systematic set of variables has been used to study the organization of personality and the delineation of personality types among aged persons. One such study has recently appeared (Reichard, Livson, & Petersen, 1962), but the findings cannot easily be generalized since that study was based on a sample of volunteer subjects, all of them males.

In the present investigation, the variables were derived from a psychodynamic model of personality in which ego functions are viewed as central in personality structure; in which transactions with the environment are the primary focus, rather than the ego's relationships to id and to superego (as in earlier psychoanalytic models) ; and in which individuals are differentiated on the basis of coping and defense patterns rather than on the basis of different configurations of drive and impulse life (Rapaport, 1957; Rapaport, 1960; White, 1960; White, 1963a). In this model, cognitive competence and reality-testing are major dimensions. Social attitudes also become important from this viewpoint, because they signify the ways in which the ego may be said to structure the social environment.

A set of personality variables was defined that was congruent with this model and suitable to the types of data available in the Kansas City Studies of Adult Life. The investigation was intended, by methods of factor analysis, to isolate the personality types to be found in a community sample of aging men and women and, at the same time, to reduce the relatively large set of variables to a smaller number of personality dimensions and then to study the relationships between personality types, age, and adjustment.

The Sample and the Data

The population studied was a subsample of eighty-eight persons (forty-three males and forty-five females from the Sample II panel and the Sample II quasi panel who remained as participating members of the Kansas City Study of Adult Life some five years after they had been first interviewed (see Appendix A for description of the samples). This population was chosen to represent the range of the original Sample II not only with regard to sex, age, and social class, but also with regard to high, medium, and low ratings on Life Satisfaction and was available for a special round of interviewing in the summer and early autumn of 1960.

The data on which the personality ratings were based were of three general orders. First, there were six long interviews that had been obtained at intervals of six to nine months over five years. These interviews dealt with the daily round of activities; patterns of social interaction; family and other social role involvements; attitudes toward family members, friends, and neighbors; feelings about parents and other significant figures in childhood and youth; fantasies and dreams; attitude inventories; and check lists regarding values and morale. Second were projective protocols, including responses to five TAT cards and to eight especially constructed projective stories. For a majority of the subjects there were also figure drawings of a man and a woman and, for eighteen subjects, responses to the Rorschach test. Third, there was a long open-ended clinical interview, which included life history data as well as an assessment of the subject's defense-coping patterns, the congruence between his ideal and perceived self, his mood tone, and various other aspects of his life style. This interview varied in length from three to nine hours and was carried out in one to three sessions.

The Personality Variables

Forty-five personality variables were utilized, of which the majority relate primarily to ego functions, such as "intelligence" and "tolerance of ambiguity," and ego defenses, such as "projection" and "regression"; others relate primarily to drives, such as "achievement drive" and "passivity"; others, to affect states, such as "optimism-pessimism"; and still others to major personal and ideational cathexes, such as attitudes toward members of the opposite sex, younger persons, or religious values.

In delineating the ego variables, the definitions provided by Kroeber and Haan in their study of middle-aged adults (Kroeber, 1963) were particularly useful. In that study, a series of ego variables was conceptualized as having both a coping or conflict-free modality and a defensive modality. For instance, "detachment," defined as "the ability to let the mind roam freely, to speculate, analyze, create without restriction from inside or out," has a coping modality entitled "intellectuality" and a defensive modality entitled "intellectualization."

The variables that relate to drive, affect, and cathexes were selected primarily from those used by Reichard and associates, but reduced in number in the light of Reichard's own findings. The forty-five variables are defined in Appendix B. Their meanings in terms of overt behavior can be implied from the descriptions of personality types that follow in a subsequent section of this report.

Reliability of Ratings

Each of the forty-five variables was converted into a five-point rating scale. As far as possible, each scale point was described in advance, in terms of behavior that could be observed or inferred from interview and projective data. To establish reliability of ratings, three raters who had had extensive clinical experience and training in psychoanalytic and ego theory worked together for several months in refining the variables, delineating the scale points, and testing the scales against sample cases. A preliminary reliability was then undertaken on ten cases, followed by a careful analysis of the points of agreement and disagreement. Forty new cases were finally drawn, and rotating pairs of judges made independent ratings. Product-moment correlations for the forty-five scales on the forty cases ranged from .73 on the variable "religiosity" to .93 on the variable "intelligence."

Personality Factors and Personality Types

The ratings for men and women subjects were separately inter-correlated, and the two matrices then submitted to a principal-component factor analysis and Varimax rotation on the IBM 7090 computer. Ten meaningful factors were extracted for men; ten, for women.

At the same time, obverse factor analyses were carried out in which ratings on the forty-five personality variables for each male subject were correlated against the forty-five ratings for every other male subject and in which each female subject was correlated against every other female. These two matrices were also analyzed by the principal-component method and Varimax rotation. The "factors" extracted in the latter operations may be thought of as representing abstract or ideal persons. The subjects who load high on such a "factor" may be grouped as a cluster of persons who resemble one another more than they resemble other subjects in the sample. Each cluster may then be further analyzed as constituting a "type." Just as in a traditional factor analysis, each factor is interpreted and named by studying the variables which load highest on that factor, so, in this obverse factor analysis, each "type" was interpreted and named by studying the individuals who load highest on that "factor."

In this instance, clusters of persons were studied in terms of the forty-five personality variables (ratings were expressed as standardized scores), then in terms of scores on the ten personality factors that had been derived in the preceding factor analyses. (Factor scores were computed by weighting the variables according to their loadings on the respective factor and computing a subject's scores on this basis, then converting the distribution of factor scores into Z scores.) Following this method, six personality types emerged for males; six, for females. The twelve types accounted for thirty-three of the forty-three males and for thirty-seven of the forty-five females —a total of seventy of the original eighty-eight persons in the sample.

The personality types for males and for females are shown in tables 8.1 and 8.2 in terms of mean scores on the ten personality factors. Although the types were obtained directly from the forty-five personality variables, the tables show that they are clearly differentiated in terms of the ten personality factors as well. The data which underlie tables 8.1 and 8.2 are given in Appendix B, where tables B.1 and B.2 show the results of the factor analyses that produced the personality factors and where tables B.3 and B.4 show the results of the obverse factor analyses that produced the personality types.

Although the steps taken in studying the relationships between the types and the factors cannot be spelled out here in detail, the investigators found they could move with relative ease between the two orders of abstraction provided by the statistical analyses: that is, the personality types were meaningful in terms of the ten factors, and the factors were meaningful in terms of the twelve types of persons when, in both instances, interpretations were repeatedly checked against the original observations. In somewhat different terms, the three orders of data—the original observations of behavior as recorded in the interviews, the ten factors of personality, and

TABLE 8.1

MALE PERSONALITY TYPES BY FACTOR SCORES, LIFE SATISFACTION,
AND AGE $(N = 33)$

Mean Z score on personality factors	Personality type					
	Integrated $(N = 9)$	Introspective $(N = 3)$	Defended $(N = 7)$	Passive dependent $(N = 4)$	Constricted $(N = 3)$	Unintegrated $(N = 7)$
Integrity	1.16	.62	.14	.27	−.93	−1.40
Ego energy	.99	−.37	.62	.47	−.33	−1.41
Cognitive competence	.67	.30	.51	−.57	−.90	−1.32
Differentiated social perceptions	1.24	−.11	.52	−.05	−.51	−1.02
Aggressivity	.80	−.25	.94	−.09	−.43	−.93
Passive dependency	.37	.39	−.17	.80	−1.63	−.26
Superego control	.07	1.30	−.15	.05	.06	−.47
Sex-role identification	.84	−.43	−.38	.11	−.44	−.69
Intimacy	1.01	.33	−.64	.73	−.55	−1.03
Internalization of institutionalized values	.95	−.60	.55	−.29	−.47	−1.08
Mean rating on Life Satisfaction*	20.60	18.60	18.30	17.00	13.00	9.40
Age range	56–90	61–73	54–72	53–64	62	58–76

* Mean LSR for the thirty-three males is 15.3.

the twelve personality types—seemed to fit together and to provide no major problems in translation from one to the other.

To lend meaning to tables 8.1 and 8.2, brief descriptions of the personality factors are given first. (The statistical composition of each factor can be seen in tables B.1 and B.2 in Appendix B.) Although none of the factors represent identical patterns of high loadings for both sexes, it will be seen from the descriptions to follow

TABLE 8.2

FEMALE PERSONALITY TYPES BY FACTOR SCORES, LIFE
SATISFACTION, AND AGE ($N = 37$)

Mean Z score on personality factors	Personality type					
	Integrated ($N=14$)	Passive dependent ($N=7$)	Defended constricted ($N=5$)	Self-doubting ($N=3$)	Competitive ($N=4$)	Unintegrated ($N=4$)
Integrity	1.10	.21	−1.10	−.30	−.39	−1.67
Ego energy	.90	−.50	−1.07	.34	.75	−1.41
Cognitive competence	1.00	−.44	−.88	−.10	.18	−1.30
Differentiated social perceptions	.84	−.13	−1.40	−.20	−.80	−.40
Aggressivity	.72	−.06	−1.27	−1.21	.51	.59
Passive dependency	−.03	.81	−.68	.04	−.35	−.85
Superego controls	.22	.06	.91	−.48	.13	−1.01
Sex-role identification	.71	.47	−.95	−.21	.01	−1.61
Intimacy	.41	.90	−.70	.49	−.99	−1.20
Outer-world involvement	.30	−1.11	.43	−.09	.27	.43
Mean rating on Life Satisfaction*	20.30	17.40	15.40	14.30	13.30	10.80
Age range	57–85	60–83	61–79	53–54	53–59	61–79

* Mean LSR for the thirty-seven females is 15.3.

that nine of the factors are similar for both men and women. At the same time it is clear that the personality variables are differently related in the two sexes.

1. "Integrity" represents a continuum in which, at one end, coping mechanisms are those which facilitate a mellow, nondefensive, and flexible capacity to adapt to stresses of aging; an identity which represents successful integration of past identifications; a sense of continuity with the past; competence; optimism; sensitivity to

emotional cues as well as to ideation. At the other end of this continuum are affective states which reflect anxiety, despair, and depression. For men, this end of the continuum also involves a rigidity of defenses and overcontrol of impulse life; for women, a high reactivity and undercontrol of impulse. This factor accounts for a large proportion of the total variance in the data (50 per cent for males; 47 per cent for females) and may well be an over-all adjustment or "maturity" dimension that influences a large number of the ratings.

2. "Ego energy" is the dimension which represents the ability to focus on and to integrate stimuli that arise both from within and from without and to maintain a certain detachment and objectivity; the capacity to analyze thoughtfully the bases for decision-making and to invest energy in achievement and planning. The obverse traits are perceptual and intellectual impairment and listlessness in cognitive and rational functioning. For women, but not for men, ego energy includes also an affective component which is directed toward nurturant activities.

3. "Cognitive competence" represents the purposeful use of thought processes: interest in ideas and ideation, in thoughts and feelings, as they relate to personal goals. For men, these processes seem to be directed outward, in support of various forms of environmental manipulations, especially those which have to do with achievement and competence. For women, this dimension also includes an affective quality and a dependence on fantasy, not necessarily in the interest of action or competence. Thus this dimension, although common to both sexes, has a greater component of instrumentality in males and a greater component of expressivity in females. For both sexes, the obverse of this dimension suggests anticognitive defenses: for males, a rigid reliance on outer events and an exclusion of inner stimuli; for women, a rigid separation of cognitive from affective components in thinking and perception.

4. "Differentiated social perceptions," a dimension that is difficult to interpret and to name, involves capacities to perceive differences and to make differentiated judgments about other people—for men,

judgments about members of the opposite sex and younger persons of both sexes. In men, the factor includes the investment of energy and affect in social institutions and thus suggests an outer-world orientation. For women, this factor relates primarily to perceptions and judgments of males and includes affective qualities—fondness and capacity for close relationships with members of the opposite sex.

5. "Aggressivity," although a meaningful dimension in the personalities of both men and women, encompasses different sets of variables for each sex. In males, this dimension reflects modulated aggression and drive that is guided by cognitive processes into means-ends and goal-oriented behavior. The obverse is inertia, apathy, and retreat into ideational behavior. Withdrawal is the defense against aggressive impulses. In women, aggressivity is composed of those variables which reflect manipulation of the environment (as in forceful, matriarchal relations to the young) and/or in displacement onto the external world by projection. The obverse represents intropunitive and masochistic reactions along with armored and rigid controls. There is no suggestion that, in females, control is reinforced by seclusive tendencies.

6. "Passive dependency" represents a dimension of personality in which passive and dependent drives and impulses are successfully integrated and there is an accompanying acceptance of aging. The obverse represents the rejection or repression of these drives and impulses. For males, the integration of passive-dependent impulses is apparently related to a successful identification with the mother, a relationship which does not appear in the females. This suggests that, for women in this age range, as compared to men, passive dependency is a dimension relatively independent of early patterns of identification.

7. "Superego control" represents, for both sexes, the internalized conscience or superego controls, but there are important sex differences in the variables which load heavily on this factor. For men, the dimension represents intropunitive, repressive-regulative, and moral traits, where guilt and anxiety are overt referents. The rigidity

of the controls is, however, modified by rational and affective differentiations. For women, the dimension represents a strong cathexis toward religious and ethical percepts and toward other institutionalized values. The intropunitive quality does not occur. For both sexes, the obverse of this dimension is the externalization and acting out of tension rather than an internalized control of impulse life.

8. "Sex-role identification" for males reflects, at the one end of the continuum, acceptance and appreciation of the father's values and identification with the father; complex, integrated affect life; and, at the other end, covert identification with the mother, anxiety, and counterphobic investments in work and work routines. For females, it represents acceptance and appreciation of the mother's values and identification with mother; warmth, candor, and an equalitarian interpersonal style; complex, integrated affect life; and, at the opposite pole, rejection of the mother and her values; undifferentiated and judgmental reactions to persons; intense status needs; and defenses that suggest brittle and sterile abstractions.

9. "Intimacy" is a dimension of relational style which involves, for men, friendly and equalitarian relationships with other men; close, intimate relationships with women; and a warm, nurturant interest in children. The obverse is a formal, sometimes hostile and suspicious, sometimes authoritarian, distancing from other persons. For women, there are relatively few of the forty-five variables which showed high loadings on this factor, but those few reflect some of the same qualities as in males—capacities for close, intimate relations with the opposite sex and a nurturant warmth for children. The obverse of this dimension for women is involvement in achievement and work goals.

10 M. "Internalization of institutionalized values" emerged as a dimension for males, but not for females. This dimension reflects an internalization of and subscription to social values which are used as a basis for action and which form the core of the man's identity; for example, the competent worker, the responsible citizen, the churchgoer. In many ways this dimension in males is comparable to

superego control in females in that in both instances the internalization of socially delineated values is salient. In the male dimension, however, the superego variables do not appear.

10 F. "Outer-world involvement" emerged as a dimension for women, but not for men. It reflects investment in social activities and social roles outside the home; in status aspirations; and in the ability to substitute new activities for earlier ones. A related variable is optimism. The obverse includes an intense interest in children and a withdrawal of cathexis from outer-world activities.

The Male Types

In the anticipation that the personality types will be most meaningful to the reader if described in terms that remain close to observable behavior, the descriptions to follow have been written in such terms, with the view of highlighting only the most salient differences between the types. Tables 8.1 and 8.2 should be consulted in relation to these descriptions.

The Integrated Men

The "integrated" represents a cluster of nine men, four of whom were retired and five of whom were still working at a variety of occupations—a university professor, a building superintendent, a railroad engineer, a small business owner. Eight were married, and the ninth had been recently widowed. All but two were grandfathers. This group, representing the full age range in the sample—from fifty-six to ninety—was distinguished from the other five patterns by the capacity to integrate aggressive as well as passive-dependent drives. They were self-assertive men who sublimated aggression into goal-directed activities which required sustained effort, energy, and initiative. For example, one said, "Well, of course . . . you have to meet a challenge. . . . You have to plan. . . . You must create something out of your own thoughts and efforts. . . . You must assert yourself."

These men steered a middle course with regard to passivity. When faced with retirement, they managed to view their extra time as a means of doing the things they wanted to do. One, an eighty-one-year-old former cabinetmaker, earned money between trips and was still traveling about the world, gathering archaeological specimens for his collection. He said, however, "I'm getting a little old for this now; I still take care of myself, but it's time that I learned to turn to my children. . . ."

Most of these men were insightful and objective about themselves. Part of the objectivity rested on an internalized conscience, neither excessively severe nor inconsistent, which might best be described at this point in their lives as a relevant set of values and principles providing a perspective for evaluating their behavior and a basis for their sense of personal worth. These men frequently spoke with a candor which reflected their ease in handling impulses and in controlling affect. For example, the ninety-year-old druggist said, "What's wrong with sexual feelings and desires even at ninety? Of course [with a smile], you can't have quite the same enjoyment as you used to."

All these men communicated a firm sense of identity. They could assert themselves in defense of their values; some of their deepest gratifications came from finding an outlet, within their definition of appropriate male behavior, for manipulating their environments in ways that showed a sense of mastery and control. One of the oldest men was a church member who quietly assumed responsibility for the upkeep of church fixtures: "No one wants to do these things. . . . They're not only glad that I do them, but they know that I'm still here."

The integrated males are probably best characterized by their excellent adjustment to aging and their clear sense of what Erikson (1959) calls "integrity": some see themselves as unchanged in their essential characteristics and still capable of perfecting themselves further; others have come to know themselves well enough to enjoy their lives without sensing, as they did at earlier ages, a nagging doubt about their basic worth.

There is in this group an almost complete absence of conscious anxiety about death. Some men had resolved the issue by a deep faith in the continuity of self after death; others took a less religious view, as the railroad engineer who said, "When one reaches seventy, the best part of life is gone. . . . One accepts death as one accepts life. . . . Most of the good things must be in the past, and this, of course, hurts a little. Still, most of these things seem, with age, transitory. The most important things are really family, self-respect, honesty, and a reputation for fairness; and even some of these seem less significant as time passes. . . ."

The Introspective Men

The "introspective" type was a small cluster of three men—a seventy-three-year-old music teacher, a sixty-one-year-old bus driver, and a seventy-year-old man who worked as an usher at various sports arenas. All had married; two had grandchildren who appeared to be a major source of satisfaction in their lives.

These men were differentiated from the integrated men by a more rigid internalized conscience and by a highly developed capacity to resolve conflicts and tensions by fantasy and by sublimation, rather than by achievement. In interpersonal style, these men were nurturant with their children, yet emotionally removed from most adults. For instance, their relationships with their wives seemed to have been one of distance and manipulation. One of these men commented, after musing about his inability to discuss important issues with his wife:

> Don't get me wrong; my wife is a wonderful woman, but. . . . You know, I was reading one of those psychological articles. They say you got to get a woman thinking that something is her own idea. . . . I've thought about this a lot. Do you really think this is the way to deal with women?

The central issue for each of these men was the need to establish for themselves further evidence of competence. The music teacher had struggled for years to overcome the timidity which he still felt when he moved outside the universe of music; the bus driver was still struggling to disprove his father's predictions that he could not succeed; the usher was busy devising new and efficient procedures for ushering. At the same time these men were coping relatively effectively with their conflicts and were adjusting reasonably well to aging. None could be described as dysphoric or depressed, and each had his own style of compensating for what he felt were his deficiencies. The bus driver said: "I'm an ordinary guy, but I pay my bills. . . . I've got something in the bank, and maybe, later, there will be a trailer business. . . ." One of the music teacher's comments was representative of the intense feelings and the high investment in the power of thought all these men have. In the interviewer's words: "He spoke excitedly about science; he is intrigued by the future and by the tremendous strides which science has made. It is so tremendous to be alive at a time like this; so much is to be discovered. These times are so wonderful!"

The Defended Men

The "defended" men were an ambitious, striving, and achievement-oriented group, one of whom said, "I thrive on competition," and another of whom said, "I've had a life-long perspective of hard work, self-assertion, and seriousness. You take chances, because nobody really wants to be a small frog in a big pond. . . ."

All these men, who ranged widely in occupation and educational levels from a foreman for a utility company to a corporation lawyer, were highly dependent on work for maintaining ego integrity and self-esteem. None considered retirement desirable; one, a federal employee who had been automatically retired, was busy keeping busy. The minister in this group described retirement as "being put out to pasture . . . as synonymous with death. . . ." The contractor said, "I'll work as long as I can; my life is my work."

These men are characterized by a combination of successful defenses against anxiety and successful control of passive-dependent needs. They assume social responsibilities; they remain intellectually energetic; their activities are not disrupted by conflict. The defended men's interpersonal relations are formal, at times, authoritarian. With their children, they stress accomplishment. They seem cautious about exploring early memories, especially of their parents. They often express mild depreciation of their fathers for "weakness" or for lack of ambition, saying, at the same time, that they once were frequently mildly anxious. They appeared to have many reservations about themselves, a sense of inferiority or deficiency. (One spoke of his life-long struggle to get ahead because of his poor eyesight; another, because of insufficient intellectual ability. At least three others mentioned concerns over lack of masculinity). At the same time, they maintain a good adjustment to aging by remaining active, involved, and productive. The primary issue for these men is that their identity, built around competence and mastery of the environment, must also be an assurance that they are capable of control over feelings and impulses.

Most of these men avoided the subject of death, preferring to focus on the present. They stressed their strength, success, and optimism and preferred to see themselves as unchanging and unchangeable. Their comments suggested over and over the need to prove to themselves that they were completely capable of remaining in control of their impulses as well as their destinies.

The Passive-Dependent Men

The "passive-dependent" group included only four men, aged fifty-three to sixty-four, all of them blue-collar workers—a railroad engineer, a foreman in an optical laboratory, a skilled machine repairman, and a truck mechanic. Only one had a high-school education.

All four could be described as becoming increasingly passive with age, of welcoming opportunities for relaxation and a reduced work load. The interviewer commented about the truck mechanic, for instance:

> His big investments are not in his work, he tells me. He used to prefer the big cities, night life, and driving a truck. Now the important part of life is the here and now; the simple pleasures of home. Even fishing and hunting do not hold the attraction they once did. He can't get excited over baseball; even his new TV set

> doesn't interest him too much. He's more interested in relaxing over a can of beer and puttering about the house.

And about the optical foreman:

> He had a worn-out quality as he told about the struggle connected with raising a large family on a small income. He has worked hard. . . . Seems to see retirement as synonymous with sitting in a rocking chair. This does not seem to be a depressive trend, but a reflection of his values and perspectives. . . .

This group tended to repress hostile impulses and to lead quiet, peaceful, and subdued lives. Three of the four complained of illnesses such as rheumatoid arthritis, and two had had severe ulcers.

Strong passive-dependent needs were the outstanding characteristic. Three of the four men had married late in life, after maintaining close dependent relationships with their mothers. They now saw their wives as their main source of emotional support, although they were not incapable of reciprocating in these relationships.

These men depend mainly on their past identities as competent and hard-working men and on a simplification of present life as a means of maintaining ego integration. At the same time, there is a basic ego strength, and the superego appears to be well-integrated and adaptive. There are no indications of guilt or neurotic preoccupations.

Three of the four men gave a clue to their basic self-concepts when they proudly referred to themselves as "one of the common men." The term seemed to communicate a sense of identity as competent people who had worked hard, met their obligations, and could now look forward to rest and relaxation because they had earned it.

The Constricted Men

A cluster of three men, who all happened to be sixty-two, constituted the "constricted" type. One was an insurance salesman; one, a manufacturer's representative; and the third, a skilled tradesman. All three had been divorced and were now remarried.

These men were much like the defended in their preoccupation with work and in their avoidance of affect. They differed, however, from any of the well-adjusted types along most of the other important personality variables. Ego integration was maintained by rigid and inflexible defenses directed against aggression and hostility, but particularly against passive and dependent needs.

Although these men were intensely ambitious, they seemed less capable of achievement, and their feelings of failure and self-derogation took various forms, among them, a depletion of intellectual resources and obsessive preoccupations and rumination. Interpersonal relations were difficult. The tradesman complained bitterly, "People are less interested in being friendly as they grow older. . . . I can't face people. . . . Younger men in my trade don't represent my values. . . . The union is no longer interested in older members . . ." The salesman complained about unfair competitors. The manufacturer's representative said, "The influx of foreigners will depreciate property values. . . . So far we've been able to keep them out of this neighborhood. . . ."

Many of the preoccupations of these men involved fears about aging, loss of strength, and decreased virility. One of these men, reported the interviewer, "talked for a half-hour without interruption about the most important aspect of aging for men. . . . He poured out his fears and disappointments about the loss of sexual capacities. . . ." Another said, "I've run out of steam. . . . Well, you know, wine, women, and song. I've run down in all areas."

The emotional tone vividly communicated by the constricted men suggested covert depression. They were pessimistic about the future and, at times, bitter and extrapunitive. Although they were not willing to give up their struggles to succeed, they were also beginning to despair over chances of reaching their goals.

The Unintegrated Men

The "unintegrated" represent nine men who range in age from fifty-eight to seventy-six, six of whom are retired and one of whom works only part time. They represent a variety of occupations, mostly in blue-collar or lower-level white-collar jobs. Only two owned small businesses, and none were professionals. As a group, they were least prepared financially for retirement. Of the six already retired, four had only small Social Security checks to cover their living expenses. Although no physicians' diagnoses were available, these men seemed in poorer health as a group than the other five groups. Three had serious heart conditions, one had had an operation for carcinoma of the throat, one was badly crippled by arthritis, one seemed clearly paranoid, one was in acute depression.

In addition to the few whose psychological disturbances were so immediately apparent, the group as a whole showed gross defects in ego functions. There were examples of acting out of impulses, such as the retired freight handler: "He subscribed to the ideas of the nudists . . . often wandered about the house naked. . . ." More frequent were the examples of tight control over impulses, especially over all forms of aggression. Reaction formations are sustained by grandiose ideas and elaborate rationalizations, as in the case of one man in this group:

> He sees fear all about him. . . . It has complex origins. . . . For one thing, there is a division of power in Congress; the Supreme Court is ruining the country; we lack a strong president. There is danger all over. . . . A person, but especially a woman or a child, doesn't dare go out into the street. He traces the beginning of his insights to the year his wife died. . . .

Projections like these were apparent, and the acute anxiety and tension which accompanied these behaviors were readily discernible, as in the case of a retired mechanic:

> His only mission in life, he says, is to convince others that their way of life is wrong. . . . He says he can understand all that goes on about him. . . . By this, he means he knows what is going on in other people's minds. He would like to save people, to show them a

more magnificent life, . . . but he is becoming discouraged and feels he will soon not worry about people any more. . . .

All nine of these men were preoccupied with their conflicts, their fears, their deprivations; all had dysphoric mood tone; a number were openly depressed. Aging was an especially upsetting experience to them. Physical and intellectual losses, as well as retirement, were interpreted as narcissistic blows. Two men talked of their acute consciousness of the nearness of death; others were more inclined to focus on their losses or their illnesses: "This man, a retired janitor, made frequent moves as rooms closer to his doctor's office became available." "This retired foreman was tremendously preoccupied with his health . . . and with the fact that he's slowing down, mentally and physically. He is trying a number of bizarre remedies for his alleged illnesses, none of which have been diagnosed by a doctor."

The unintegrated men, as a group, are enduring old age with great anxiety, and they are characterized by despair.

The Female Types

The Integrated Women

Fourteen women compose the cluster called the "integrated." They range in age from fifty-seven to eighty-five and come from all socioeconomic levels in the sample. Ten had been married; eight were now widowed; eight had children and numerous grandchildren.

There were no serious economic problems for any of this subgroup. Some lived on savings; three supplemented their income by part-time work; and four of the younger were still employed full time. Their educational level was superior to the other female groups—five, for instance, were college graduates. Ten had worked outside the home at some time; five were teachers; one was a university professor; one was a semiretired bank executive. Two others worked part time as a cafeteria helper and a switchboard operator. Eight of these women were apparently in good to excellent health, but six had recovered or adjusted to such serious illnesses as cardiac attacks, carcinoma, and cerebrovascular strokes.

In personality, these women were affectively complex—mellow, unanxious, untroubled by ambivalence; usually forceful and goal-directed, but not without passive and dependent strivings. Essentially there was a balance between active strivings and passive-receptive qualities. Inner controls were built around a firm identity of self as a competent person. Impressions of other people were empathic; intellectual strivings were usually integrated into role activities which had a distinctly feminine-expressive quality. For example, when these women were workers, they stressed the more nurturant and insightful requirements of their jobs.

Of the ten who had married, they described their marriages, their husbands, and their children in ways that reflected their identification with them and their support of their ambitions. A seventy-five-year-old widow said of her husband's terminal illness: "One of the saddest things I've ever done was to close his office for him. . . . It was like striking him in the face to bring home his things." She did her part to help him reclaim his life: "The biggest problem was convincing him that she didn't mind the change. She gave up her own activities and sensed when he could not stand inactivity any more. . . . Then she would help him find some diversion. . . ."

Although these women were maternal, they had evidently had long-standing identities more inclusive than the roles of wife and mother. Widowhood for these women was a crisis which, after periods of mourning, was gradually resolved by shifts to club activities, social activities, intellectual interests, and friendship patterns. These women were not now overly dependent on children or grandchildren.

Certain of these women seemed invested in roles which required an overtly competitive effort, yet even with this small group the emphasis was more on achievement than on competitive, aggressive feelings. One said: "No promotion comes without hard work. . . . In business, I guess a woman has to work harder because of her sex, so I merely worked harder to convince my customers. . . ." This woman has now shifted to a schedule that allows her to travel, to be a consultant.

The Passive-Dependent Women

The "passive-dependent" type represented seven women who ranged widely in age, family patterns, and educational and socio-economic levels. One of this group had never married; two were now widowed. Only two of these seven had worked throughout their adult life—one as a nurse, the other as a restaurant cook. The others had never worked outside the home or had worked only before marriage. The most salient characteristic of this group was a self-definition structured around the roles of homemaker and mother. One, for instance, said: "I've built my life around my family. My husband is my most important thing. . . . He works very hard during the day, so we just relax in the evening. . . . Aside from my husband, it's my grandchildren. I love every inch of their bodies. . . ."

Although these women had strong feelings about their families and could be demanding or angry about issues which affected their homes or their children, they were generally unassertive, dependent on their husbands (earlier, on their mothers), and showed bland and relatively undifferentiated affect concerning issues outside the home. They were directly invested in nurturant activities and in passive-narcissistic or erotic gratifications. For one woman, for example, to age successfully meant to become "nicer and sweeter."

Although they were not opinionated, these women were satisfied with their patterns of life and saw little reason for change. They depended on the habits and orientations which had previously served them well. They had neither the rich ideational processes of the integrated nor the complexity of roles, but, like the integrated women, these women had a clear sense of identity and were adjusting well to aging. Although they showed limited capacity to re-evaluate and reintegrate around new investments and new self-definitions, their relatively good adjustments rested on the availability of opportunities to continue their roles as homemaker, mother, and grandmother.

One of these women illustrates a number of salient points about this type: "I always went running to my mother when something went wrong. . . . My mother was a serious person; so am I. My mother had set ideas about children; so do I. . . ." Earlier in life this woman had a number of phobic fears, but, as she has grown older, these have left her, and in their place is a perception of herself as a senior member of the family. Now she sees herself as insisting on certain standards, even for her grown children. She traces these changes to the death of her mother, when she herself was forty-seven, and, shortly after, to an operation (a hysterectomy). She can now see life slipping away and that soon she, too, will be dead and her children middle-aged. With this acceptance has come a feeling of competence. She is sure of herself, and she is not afraid to act, as she once was.

The Defended-Constricted Women

The "defended-constricted" women, like the male defended, were uncomfortable with issues or impulses having to do with love, tenderness, or sexuality and protected themselves from anxiety by activity and outer-world involvement. Like the male constricted group, they maintained ego integration by rigid and inflexible defenses.

These women, five in number, ranged in age from sixty-one to seventy-nine and varied in marital status, education, and socioeconomic status. One had never married; two were married; and two were widowed. All five were very active women whose activity did not entirely mask their chronic anxiety. Four had worked most of their adult lives—one was a successful businesswoman; one, a nurse; one, a teacher; and one, an office worker. Their work activities were ordinarily perceived as representing a lifetime of sacrifice and dedication, and now, with retirement and aging, as they received fewer satisfactions from work, their anxiety centered around the control of both passive-sexual and/or hostile, competitive impulses.

These women insisted that their values and life patterns were of their own choosing, yet their involvement with work, religion, social organizations, or other projects was defined as a search for a more complete feeling of fulfillment. Still, given the rigidities and the underlying anxieties, these women were preserving minimal ego integrity and moderately good morale. Their satisfactions with life seemed to continue well into old age so long as they were able to keep their lives maximally active and compulsively compartmentalized. For example, Mrs. C, the retired nurse, after being widowed many years earlier, had given more and more of herself to her work. The interviewer says:

> Nursing became not just a way of life, but something of a crusade. She went into public health nursing, then into private duty, giving her services to poor families. . . . She tried to give affection to the children and at the same time to instill into these families the fundamentals of good hygiene. . . . Since her retirement, she has tried to become a guardian of the neighborhood. . . . She feels decidedly responsible for maintaining law and order on her corner—to keep the children from playing on the street, for instance.
>
> Her devotion to duty is not entirely an expression of nurturant characteristics, for she began a long tirade about the youngsters in the neighborhood. . . . The younger generation is going straight to hell. . . . Still, she isn't as grouchy as this might lead one to expect; eccentric is perhaps the better word. Since her retirement from nursing, she has built herself a new routine which is actually a schedule that completely fills her waking hours.

The Self-Doubting Women

Three of the youngest women in the sample (aged fifty-three and fifty-four) constituted the "self-doubting" type. All had married, and one was now widowed, but none had borne a child. One was now working as a hotel manager; one, a teacher; and one, a nurse. All three appeared mildly depressed, depression which seemed to stem from the need to overcontrol aggressive and hostile impulses. They all referred explicitly to the fact that the menopause had been particularly stressful, and they spoke of sex-role dissatisfactions and conflicts. These conflicts seemed, however, to have characterized them all their adult lives. One of this group was described by the interviewer in the following terms: "A woman of medium height— very pretty grey hair and a very feminine quality about her. . . . She was dressed fashionably with carefully chosen accessories. . . ." She said about herself, however, "I don't know if you could guess. . . . Maybe it's stupid, but I have the feeling that I'm not attractive. . . . I've always had this feeling. . . ."

All three of these women described having been hurt by other people when they were younger. They gave evidence of having maintained psychological distance from others, including their husbands; of equating self-assertion with hostility; and of sacrificing initiative and autonomy for the sake of security. They seemed now to be undergoing an identity crisis—a painful self-awareness that earlier emotional gratifications were no longer functional and an acute concern about finding some new self-definition.

There were signs that at least two of these women were tending gradually toward a new emotional equilibrium where they were feeling less guilty and fearful, were able to be more self-assertive, and were beginning to feel more competent. For instance, one woman, in describing an argument with a sister-in-law, said: "I said what I had to say. . . . I would not have done that before. . . . I would not have answered her back . . . I'd have kept my peace. I'm a little more sure now."

The Competitive Women

The "competitive" women were another group of four younger women (aged fifty-three, fifty-four, fifty-six, and fifty-nine) who, like the self-doubting, seemed involved in identity crisis, but who were oriented toward achievement, upward mobility, and competitive striving. All of these women had married, and one was now divorced. Three had raised families of three to five children. All four were working—one as a private secretary, one as a retail clerk, one as a skilled machine operator, and the fourth as the proprietor of a small business.

These were active women whose roles as wives and mothers were characterized by an efficient, matriarchal, subtly aggressive style. Of relatively low morale, they were emotionally complex women, suffering from dissatisfaction, anger, and self-doubt—feelings that had been precipitated by menopausal changes, by loss of children from the home, and by marital tensions generated, in part, by their reactions to what they regarded as a decrease in their husbands' emotional and physical capacities. These women seemed to identify with masculine and active qualities; they had been deeply invested in their husbands' careers, which they had sought to shape, and had intense investments in their children's, especially their sons', growth and development.

These women were now attempting to cope with shifts and changes in their lives by undertaking a variety of activities. These activities involved striving for competence and independence and, at times, hostile and competitive attitudes toward men, co-workers, and friends. At the same time, these women were endowing their work, hobbies, and social activities with their capacities to plan, to manage, to learn, and to administer. The likelihood is that these women, although presently troubled, would, by their high intelligence and their capacity to invest themselves in new undertakings, show better adjustment in the near future as they developed new interests and found new sources of gratification. One of these women, for example, is described in the following terms:

> Her children are all successful, productive people. Her son is on his way to the top, and her daughters, all college graduates, are helping their husbands to obtain graduate degrees. She has good insight into her need to control and manage her children. Although she loves them and seems to live for their visits, she would not think of living near them and sees their futures as quite separate from hers. . . .
> Since her divorce, she has tried to build a new life

around activities where she can find a sense of purpose. . . . Although she began as a steno-pool secretary, on her own initiative, she added duties and tasks until now, she says, they find her indispensable. . . .

Her biggest interest in her job is not in the work itself, but in the role she plays. She takes a lively interest in the men in her department, men "on the way up." Her ambition is to work out interpersonal problems, to be the peacemaker of the department.

The Unintegrated Women

The "unintegrated" were four women ranging in age from sixty-one to seventy-nine, of varied family patterns, educational levels, and physical health. In terms of mental status, however, they were comparable: two had earlier had what they called "nervous break-downs" (descriptions of their symptoms suggested cyclical depressions) ; three appeared to have paranoid traits and characteristics; and the fourth, although quite elderly and perhaps presenile, was also a suspicious and hostile person.

Aggressive drives and aggressive traits were the most singular characteristics of these four women. Unlike the integrated women, who were also moderately aggressive, the unintegrated women did not sublimate these drives into flexible, adaptive behaviors, nor were they softened by empathy for others. Their histories suggested that these women had earlier acquired a measure of control over these impulses. (Two of the women had been very authoritarian, matriarchal mothers who identified with their sons and had pushed and prodded their families along to success; another had invested her energies in competitive hobbies.) At this point in their lives, however, their behavior suggested a minimal control and an almost explosive reactivity. For instance, Mrs. A had at first tried to retain her composure during an interview:

One immediately noted a compulsive need to talk. . . . She finally brought herself to her key question, "What were we trying to do, analyze her and find out

her problems?" When reassured, she seemingly felt free
to be more directly hostile. At this point I noticed for the
first time her habit of gritting her teeth when she talked
about emotionally charged topics. . . .

    She described herself as a clubwoman. . . . She con-
sidered her memberships in clubs and her social involvement as essential for a person in her position in society.
. . . Her lack of friends was her most trying problem.
. . . She has been told she has a sharp tongue, but she
cannot tolerate stupidity in people.

Another of these women was described as follows:

    Her stern front dropped away as she talked, and her
anger became apparent. She says she is not going to let
anyone push her around or relegate her into a niche
which she doesn't choose to accept for herself. . . .
Later she said she is terrified of growing old, of losing
her strength and her vitality, but she cannot find a way
out of this dilemma.

The Personality Types, Adjustment, and Age

From the preceding descriptions of the personality types and as
summarized in tables 8.1 and 8.2, it can be seen that the types are
clearly distinguishable in terms of what might be called efficiency
of ego functions: the coping and adaptational qualities reflected in
the integrity factor, as well as the factors that have been called ego
energy, cognitive competence, and differentiated social perceptions.
For both men and women, the integrated and the unintegrated types
are contrasting groups in terms of these cognitive components of
personality, with the other four types falling between these two
extremes.

    In part, the finding that the personality types are easily differ-
entiated in terms of these ego components is circular and is only a
reflection of the fact that the investigators chose, at the outset, to
use ego variables in making assessments of individuals. From this

point of view, the statistical analyses can be said merely to have produced order in those data which constituted the original input. On the other hand, it could not have been taken for granted that the cognitive factors in personality would have been equally salient in differentiating between types of men and types of women nor, as seen in the tables, that they would have been even more differentiating than the drive and control components of personality, such as those reflected in the factors called "passive dependency," "aggressivity," or "superego control."

It is not inaccurate to interpret the typologies for both men and women as producing, first, three main groups of persons along a major axis of ego competence: the high, the medium, and the low. In the high and low groups (the integrated and the unintegrated), the ego dimensions are of paramount importance and overshadow other segments of the personality in producing clear-cut types. In the medium group, four discernible types emerge, defined mainly in terms of affect and drive. Among the latter, there are the passive-dependent men and the passive-dependent women, personalities in which, as the name itself conveys, the passive, oral, dependent, expressive components are most salient. The defended males, the constricted males, the defended-constricted females, and the competitive females represent configurations in which the elements of control, autonomy, and achievement are most salient.

The extent to which the types described here account for the major variations of personality to be found in aged men and women is a question which can be answered only in future studies in which these or similar methods are used. It seems likely that these types will appear again in other samples, but whether new types can be delineated will depend not only on the scope of the personality variables used as measures, but primarily on the degree to which samples are more heterogeneous than the one studied here.

Adjustment

The six personality types for men and the six for women have been arrayed in tables 8.1 and 8.2 from high to low on a measure of adjustment called the Life Satisfaction Rating (LSR). The derivation and validation of this measure have been described else-where (Neugarten, Havighurst, & Tobin, 1961), but, in brief, the LSR consists of five-point ratings on each of five components: the extent to which the respondent (1) takes pleasure from the round of activities that constitute his everyday life; (2) regards his life as meaningful and accepts resolutely that which life has been; (3) feels he has succeeded in achieving his major goals; (4) holds a positive self-image; and (5) maintains happy and optimistic atti-tudes and mood. The ratings are summed to obtain an over-all rating with a possible range from 5 to 25.

The LSR ratings on the present eighty-eight respondents had been made some two to three years earlier by a different team of in-vestigators, when the first four rounds of interview data had been gathered. The fact that these ratings were based on a portion of the same data that were used here to make the personality ratings means that there is a lack of independence in the two sets of measures, but the fact that the LSR ratings were made by different judges and at a different time offsets that disadvantage to some extent.

The differences on Life Satisfaction help to delineate the person-ality types and highlight the fact that, for both sexes, the integrated personalities, those high on ego qualities, are high on the measure of adjustment; the unintegrated, those low on ego qualities, are low on adjustment. The implication is that those in whom the cognitive abilities have remained intact, or, more accurately, those whose cognitive abilities are at the high end of the continuum, are those who find satisfaction with life.

Age

An important finding is that the personality types described here are not, on the whole, related to age. As shown in the tables, four of the six male types and four of the six female types are distributed over wide age ranges from the early fifties to the late eighties. It is true that males of the passive-dependent and the constricted types did not occur after age sixty-five and that self-doubting and com-petitive women were even more clearly distinguishable on the basis of relative youth (six of these seven women were in their early fifties). For the large majority of the cases, however, personality type was independent of age.

All the types are based on cross-sectional data and should be interpreted cautiously with regard to processes of change. The implication, nevertheless, is that personalities maintain their characteristic patterns of organization as individuals move from middle into old age. The fact that some of the oldest members of this sample were found among the integrated and some of the younger members among the unintegrated suggests that it is not the factor of increasing age, but other factors, that leads to personality disintegration. Such factors might be closely related to health and biological loss, on the one hand, or to social and psychological losses, on the other. In either case, these findings are consistent with those of other recent studies (Birren, Greenhouse, Sokoloff, & Yarrow, 1963; Kleemeier, 1963), in which the effects of health losses, social losses, and age have been disentangled and in which psychological changes usually attributed to age have been found more properly to be attributable to the first and second of these factors.

9

SUMMARY AND
IMPLICATIONS

Bernice L. Neugarten

In all the studies reported in this book, a central problem under investigation has been to delineate changes in personality that are associated with chronological age and thus to contribute to a developmental view of adult personality. In some of these studies age has been shown to be a consistent and significant source of variation from forty on (chapters 3, 4, 6, 7). In others, age has not appeared to be an important variable (chapters 1, 2, 8).

On first examination, these differences in findings seem to reflect differences in the degree to which the expressions of personality under observation have been relatively overt or relatively covert. There is one exception (Chapter 5), to which we shall return presently, but, in general, significant and consistent age differences emerged in those studies where the investigator's attention was on such issues as the perception of the self vis-à-vis the external environment and the coping with impulse life and where the respondent's statement and resolution of such issues were assessed on the basis of projective data. To recapitulate some of these findings, forty-year-olds seem to see the environment as one that rewards boldness and risk-taking and to see themselves possessing energy congruent with the opportunities presented in the outer world. Sixty-year-olds seem to see the environment as complex and dangerous, no longer to be reformed in line with one's own wishes, and to see the self as conforming and accommodating to outer-world demands. This change has been described by one of the present investigators as a movement from active to passive mastery (Chapter 6).

Different modes of dealing with impulse life seem to become salient with increasing age. Preoccupation with the inner life becomes greater; emotional cathexes toward persons and objects in the outer world seem to decrease; the readiness to attribute activity and affect to persons in the environment is reduced; there is a movement away from outer-world to inner-world orientations (Chapter 3).

There is a constriction in the ability to integrate wide ranges of stimuli and in the willingness to deal with complicated and challenging situations. Certain types of rational thought processes, although they remain important, become separated from affective processes in motivating social behavior (chapters 3, 4).

Differences with age appeared not only in TAT responses, but also in interview data when the investigator's attention was on relatively latent, rather than manifest, content and when inner modes of thought and feeling states were inferred from indirect evidence. Thus older men and women, in verbalizing their opinions in more dogmatic terms than younger persons, in failing to clarify past-present or cause-effect relationships, in using idiosyncratic and eccentric methods of communication, gave evidence of lessened sensitivity to the reactions of others and a lessened sense of relatedness to others (Chapter 7).

Important differences in intrapsychic processes are discernible between men and women as they age. Older men seem to be more receptive than younger men of their affiliative, nurturant, and sensual promptings; older women, more receptive than younger women of their aggressive and egocentric impulses. Men appear to cope with the environment in increasingly abstract and cognitive terms; women, in increasingly affective and expressive terms. In both sexes, however, older people seem to move toward more eccentric, self-preoccupied positions and to attend increasingly to the control and the satisfaction of personal needs (chapters 3, 6).

On the other hand, age did not emerge as a significant source of variation when the assessments were based primarily on interview data alone (Chapter 1) or on both interview and projective data (chapters 2 and 8) and when the investigator's attention was at the same time primarily on socioadaptational patterns rather than on intrapsychic processes themselves. Thus in Chapter 1, where the variables were based on Erikson's concepts of ego development, and in Chapter 2, where the variables were based on Peck's concepts of psychological crises, the phenomena under observation were certain broadly defined adaptive qualities of personality. The same is true in Chapter 8, where the focus was on over-all personality structure and organization. Such generalized variables as "integrity" in Chapter 1, "adjustment" in Chapter 2, and "cognitive competence" in Chapter 8 were not related to age, and both the middle-aged and old were to be found among the integrated, the defended, and the unintegrated personality types described in Chapter 8.

The contrast in findings between the two sets of studies may reflect to some degree a difference in research method. When analyses rested primarily on projective data that had been blinded in advance for age of the respondent (chapters 3, 4, and 6), age differences emerged as a significant finding, but, when the analyses rested primarily on unblinded interviews (chapters 1, 2, 8), age differences did not emerge. This point about method is not merely that projective data and interview data may yield different information about the same personality nor that research of this kind is always improved to the extent that the investigator's biases can be controlled, as when data are blinded for age. The point is, rather, that the investigator's biases are particularly difficult to control in studying the relatively unfamiliar area of age differences in adulthood, as compared, for example, to studying age differences in child-hood or adolescence, and that the bias may operate in indirect fashion not so much to distort as to obscure the very phenomena the investigator seeks to illuminate.

The researcher operates under special difficulties in making judgments that relate even indirectly to adjustment and to adaptational patterns, judgments which tend to be heavily value-laden no matter how much the investigator strives for objectivity. Not only is the adult subject more practiced than the child in controlling the information he reveals in an interview, but it is also difficult for the investigator to avoid a shifting frame of reference as he makes his assessments. The same datum of behavior is often evaluated quite differently when it appears in an individual known to be forty and when it appears in an individual known to be seventy, a fact that can be easily witnessed in any attempt to establish interjudge agreements on data obtained from adults of widely differing ages.

This point is illustrated in the study reported in Chapter 7, where a systematic attempt was made to blind the interviews in advance by having deleted from the transcripts all of the direct and as many as possible of the indirect references to age. Such blinding can, of necessity, be only partial, since the approximate age of a respondent is revealed in the very recital of life sequences and in the description of everyday behavior. Nevertheless, even the partial blinding of the interviews had a certain freeing effect and enabled the investigator to focus attention on the more covert phenomena in the interviews rather than on the otherwise compelling phenomena related to the respondent's adaptational pattern. The fact, then, that in Chapter 7 significant age differences appeared when interview data alone were used may be owing in some part to an improvement in method whereby a greater measure of objectivity was provided here than in those other studies in the series in which interview data were used.

Differences in method are not unimportant, and the freedom from age bias on the part of the investigator who uses projective data has been an important asset in discovering age-related phenomena. The more essential difference between the two sets of studies, however, lies not in method but in the areas of personality under investigation. Whether in TAT or in interview data, it is when the investigator's attention was on the adaptive, goal-directed, and purposive qualities of personality that the differences between individuals have been relatively independent of age. This interpretation is not contradicted by the findings in chapters 5 and 7. In Chapter 5 the absence of age differences—even though the data were TAT responses—seemed to stem from the fact that the dimensions being measured were ones which originally had been validated against mental health classifications and which, accordingly, reflected adaptive processes of personality. In Chapter 7, the presence of age differences—even though the data were interview responses—seems due to the fact that the personality processes being measured were nonpurposive.

When all the studies in this book are considered together, then, it appears that they form two groups. Those in which chronological age provides order in the data are those where the focus was on the intrapsychic, the processes of the personality that are not readily available to awareness or to conscious control and which do not have direct expression in overt patterns of social behavior. The second group, those in which individual differences are relatively independent of age, are those where the focus was on more purposive processes in the personality, processes in which attempted control of the self and of the life situation are conspicuous elements. For purposes of the discussion to follow and with the recognition that the terms are to some extent arbitrary, we shall call the first of these two orders of personality phenomena the intrapsychic; the second, the socioadaptational. Although both are congruent with a transactional view of behavior, the second order of phenomena takes into account the intrapsychic attitudes and reaction modes as well as the overt and regulated responses to environmental press.

In demonstrating significant age differences with regard to the intrapsychic aspects of personality—in perceptions of the environment and in modes of dealing with impulse life—the findings presented in this volume are congruent with the findings of other investigators who have reported increased introversion, reduction in measurable interests and social interactions, and decline in intellectual functioning in old age. They are also consistent with other reports on the aged which note increased eccentricity, stereotyped attitudes, flattened affect, conservation of energy, avoidance of stimuli—in general, a shrinkage in the psychological life space.

At the same time, the fact that in these studies socioadaptive qualities of personality were not related to age is consonant with the findings of other investigations in which attention has been more directly on personal-social adjustment or psychological well-being. No relation to age was found, for example, in a study of these Kansas City men and women carried out by a different team of investigators who used a measure called Life Satisfaction (Neugarten, Havighurst, & Tobin, 1961). The same is also true of other populations of older persons in which various measures of adjustment were either unrelated to age (as in Birren, Butler, Greenhouse, Sokoloff, & Yarrow, 1963) or show positive correlations with age (as in Kutner, Fanshel, Togo, & Langner, 1956, where the seventy-year-old males had higher morale than the sixty-year-olds, and Reichard, Livson, & Petersen, 1962). The implication is that such factors as work status, health, financial resources, and marital status are more decisive than chronological age in influencing degrees of adjustment in people who are fifty and over.

Not only is there a difference between the intrapsychic and the socioadaptational qualities of the personality, but there are also, in turn, two sets of processes involved in the intrapsychic: first, the increased saliency of the inner life, or what may be called the increased interiority of personality with age; second, the decreased efficiency of certain cognitive processes.

With regard to the first process, the studies reported in chapters 3, 4, and 6 have contributed to the theory of disengagement, in which aging is perceived as an inevitable and mutual withdrawal resulting in decreased interaction between the aging person and others in the social systems to which he belongs. (The theory was set forth by Cumming and Henry [1961], then somewhat modified by Havighurst, Neugarten, and Tobin [1953], by Cumming [1963], and by Henry [1963]). In demonstrating increased preoccupation with the self and decreased emotional investment in persons and objects in the environment as the individual ages, the contribution of the present studies has been to recognize the psychological components of disengagement and the view that these components are in part intrinsic as well as responsive.

Although personality processes are to be seen as transactional throughout life and the personality is seen as developing only through interactions between the individual and his environment, the increase in interiority has the characteristics of developmental change in much the same sense as do changes in earlier periods of life—that, as the result of the life history with its accumulating record of adaptations to both biological and social events, there is a continually changing basis within the individual for perceiving and responding to new events in the outer world. In this sense the age-related differences that have emerged in these studies are based in the personality rather than in the social environment. Psychological components of disengagement seem to precede the social components, since the increased inward orientation is measurable by the mid-forties in this sample of well-functioning adults, well before the social losses of aging have occurred and well before the decrease in social interaction described by Cumming and Henry (1961) or in competency of performance in adult social roles described by Havighurst (1957). These findings, furthermore, argue against the implication that increased interiority and increased eccentricity of behavior in the aged follow a thinning of social interaction and a lessening of normative controls over behavior. In Chapter 7, eccentric and idiosyncratic behavior was found to be more related to age than to extent of present social interaction. Although there is undoubtedly a circular process between psychological and social elements of disengagement, the implication is that the psychological changes described here as increased inward orientation and decreased cathexes for outer-world events seem to precede, rather than follow, measurable changes in extent of social interaction.

Moving now to the second set of intrapsychic processes, there is the implication in these data that certain of the changes associated with age are deteriorative. There are losses of efficiency in cognitive processes—certain breakdowns of control over impulses observable in TAT protocols, certain perceptual impairments, certain inabilities to deal with wide ranges of stimuli. In Chapter 6 such phenomena are reflected in the magical mastery style of both men and women.

In this connection, the issue of autonomy between intrapsychic and adaptational qualities of personality again arises. It was shown in Chapter 5 that as a group this sample of middle-aged and elderly people fell outside the "normal" range when their responses to the TAT were scored by a method known to be successful in delineating normal, neurotic, and psychotic subjects among younger adults aged twenty to forty. Since the present study population as a group could hardly be regarded as mentally ill, the question was posed: To what extent are diagnostic signs of pathology different for different age groups of adults?

Not only did this question arise in regard to group averages, but, as implied in Chapter 5 and as corroborated by others of the present group of investigators, it was not uncommon to find a TAT protocol which gave evidence of grossly ineffective thought process in an individual in whom there was no discernible pathology in everyday behavior. Unfortunately, because of differences in samples, systematic analysis of the data could not be undertaken on this point, as, for instance, by comparing the TAT mastery styles of Chapter 6 for those individuals who were designated as integrated or unintegrated personalities in Chapter 8. In individual cases where comparison was possible, however, there were found instances of magical mastery as well as instances of active mastery among integrated persons.

The fact that pathologies of thought and affect are to be found in aged persons who are getting along well in their communities and who rate high on adaptation is a finding that has been also reported by other investigators. In one recent study of healthy aged men, for instance, there was autonomy between psychological test performance, including projective tests, and evaluations of purposive-adaptational behavior (Singer, 1963). Even more interesting is the fact that in the same study, when both sets of judgments were based on psychiatric interviews, there was relatively little relation between psychiatrists' judgments of pathology in cognitive and affective processes and in their judgments of the subjects' success in meeting the expectations of everyday life (Perlin & Butler, 1963). Functional psychopathologies were diagnosed with relative frequency, but, when the same psychiatrists made evaluations of over-all adaptational patterns in these subjects and when they estimated the morale of the men themselves, there were few relationships between the presence of functional psychopathology and the latter two measures. Thus it is not only on tests as such that signs of pathology are discernible in otherwise well-functioning older people.

The delineation of diagnostic signs, the relations between projective test performance and other aspects of behavior, and definitions of mental health and mental illness are all thorny problems which arise in studying other age groups as well as in studying older persons. The question being raised here, however, is whether the relationships between various orders of psychological phenomena can be expected to be the same for young adults and older adults. We have already raised something of a parallel question in suggesting earlier in this book that constructs suitable for describing personality at earlier age periods may not be suitable for describing personality in older persons. Here the question takes a somewhat different form: To what extent are the signs of mental illness and the underlying dynamics the same for different age groups?

Questions of autonomy and interrelatedness between personality processes and the ways in which the organization of personality may vary through adult life have their parallels in a set of similar questions raised by psychologists who have studied intellectual functions and intelligence. There has been the issue of the adequacy of test intelligence in evaluating the adjustment of adults to their occupational and social tasks. Just as different factorial structures of intelligence have been found to characterize adolescents, young adults, and old adults, so different factorial structures of personality may, perhaps, also be found in these varying age groups.

To return to the distinction between the intrapsychic and the socioadaptational, the former may lie closer to biological than to social determinants of behavior. This is a complex problem beyond the scope of the present investigations, but the point made earlier is also relevant here: that measurable changes in the intrapsychic processes appear in these data in the forties and fifties, at a time when biological changes are occurring, but when measurable changes in the competence of social role performance or in the range of social interaction have not yet appeared.

The relationship between intrapsychic personality processes and biological processes postulated here is not to imply necessarily that change along either of these dimensions reflects an inherent aging process. It has been suggested by other investigators that changes observable in a large number of biological functions as well as in cognitive and affective functions may be more related to health and disease than to increasing age (Birren, Butler, Greenhouse, Sokoloff, & Yarrow, 1963; Kleemeier, 1963). This point is a reminder that chronological age has no meaning in and of itself, but is used only as a convenient index for representing the events that occur with the passage of time. Which biological events represent an inherent process of senescence and which represent the accumulated effects of illness and injury remains unclear, but it seems increasingly likely that many of the accompaniments of biological change attributed to the first should more properly be attributed to the second.

Returning once more to our findings, the question arises: How is it that individuals, as they age, continue to function effectively in their social environments despite not only increased interiority but also decreased efficiency in certain cognitive processes? How do those men and women who give evidence of ineffective thought processes continue to appear integrated? Although these questions did not fall within the direct line of inquiry in these studies, the implication is that there are coping and synthesizing processes which mediate between the two orders of personality investigated here and which presumably provide continuity. Analysis of individual case materials leads to the conclusion that there is no sharp discontinuity with age in regard to adaptational qualities or in personality organization in the typical men or women in the Kansas City sample, a conclusion also reached by others for other samples (for example, Reichard, Livson, & Petersen, 1961). Coping patterns therefore seem to become stable over time, and the individual comes to deal with his environment in well-established and habitual ways. Perhaps the most striking personality phenomena to be seen in these cases are the abilities to synthesize, to rationalize, and to reorganize experience. Much in the way that individuals substitute for biological losses as they move from middle into old age, as they learn to conserve physical energy and to compensate for lessened acuity of the senses, so do they also seem to make adjustments for losses of cognitive processes—for the slippage of memory, for example.

In a sense, the self becomes institutionalized with the passage of time. Not only do certain personality processes become stabilized and provide continuity, but the individual builds around him a network of social relationships which he comes to depend on for emotional support and responsiveness and which maintain him in many subtle ways. It is from this point of view that the typical aging person may be said to become, with the passage of years, a socioemotional institution with an individuated structure of supports and interactional channels and with patterns which transcend many of the intrapsychic changes and losses that appear.

Along with increased interiority there seems to go a certain reduction in the complexity of the personality. With the shrinkage in psychological life space and with decreased ego energy, an increasing dedication to a central core of values and to a set of habit patterns and a sloughing off of earlier cathexes which lose saliency for the individual seem to occur. It is probably this quality which has led to frequent observations, on the one hand, that behavior in a normal old person is more consistent and more predictable than in a younger one—that, as individuals age, they become increasingly like themselves—and, on the other hand, that the personality structure stands more clearly revealed in an old than in a younger person.

Withdrawal of cathectic attachments from the outer world and a heightened sensitivity to the inner life do not necessarily imply a greater yielding to impulsivity or to hedonistic self-indulgence, although the latter elements appear in some of the Kansas City cases. Superego qualities may also become more prominent with increased age, as the values and moral standards which have been so long internalized become focal. Among these cases were some old people who were stridently moralistic, even punitive—the self-appointed defenders of public morality.

The direction of personality change, then, from middle to old age seems to be one of increased inner orientation; increased separation from the environment; a certain centripetal movement which leads to increased consistency and decreased complexity and in which the synthesizing and executive qualities, in maintaining their centrality, maintain also the continuity of the personality.

This description of personality change is based only in part on the quantitative findings described in preceding chapters and in part on implications drawn from case analyses that stand in need of more systematic substantiation. As implied in foregoing comments, the next set of studies in this field are likely to be most fruitful if they are focused on what might be called a middle ground between the two orders of phenomena that were investigated here; if they focus on the executive qualities of personality and the relatively discrete areas of behavior rather than on over-all adaptational styles. Especially needed are investigations in which small samples of adults at two or more age levels are studied in detail and in which, in delineating the salient dimensions of personality, attention is centered on intimate social networks and subtle aspects of social interaction. Given the fact that the studies in this book in which age differences were clearest are those in which the dimensions of personality have been inductively derived (chapters 3, 4, 6), the most useful studies in the immediate future are also likely to be those that depend on inductive approaches and methods of naturalistic observation rather than on the deductive and experimental. Particularly valuable would be studies in which the subjects are trained to give introspective accounts of the cognitive strategies they employ in dealing with the exigencies of inner- and outer-life events.

In future studies, furthermore, the constructs provided by ego psychologists should be further operationalized—constructs of competence, mastery, manipulation of outcomes, self-awareness, constructs that Rapaport (1957) had in mind when he spoke of Hartmann's "self" and Erikson's "identity" as concepts which could account for the continuity of the personality and which White (1963a) speaks of as "effectance motivation." Three recent studies, one by Murphy (1962), who described a variety of coping patterns in boys and girls as they moved from infancy through childhood; one by Coelho, Hamburg, and Murphey (1963), who focused on a group of college freshmen; and one by White (1963b), who analyzed the case studies of two young men along dimensions of competence and effectance motivation, illustrate research approaches that are relevant. In adapting such approaches to older subjects, however, a point made earlier should be repeated: age-related phenomena will be better understood only as investigators isolate variables that they have reason to believe have particular relevance for a developmental psychology of adulthood. It cannot be taken for granted because there are certain consistencies in personality—a point which is not likely to be challenged even though it has most often eluded demonstration (Neugarten, 1964)—that constructs useful in describing personality in the child, the adolescent, or the young adult will therefore be useful in describing personality in the older adult.

A developmental theory of adult personality is likely to emerge only after more such studies are available and only after more of the relevant dimensions have become measurable. In the meantime, the investigator will proceed patiently with the descriptive studies that must first be carried out, in the confidence that both his theories and his more rigorous research designs must grow from, rather than precede, systematic observations on normal adults.

A

THE SAMPLES

All of the studies reported in this volume were based on study populations of persons aged forty through ninety who were residing in the metropolitan area of Kansas City in the mid-1950's. The inhabitants of this area were predominantly native-born, the proportion of foreign-born being approximately half that of Chicago and a third that of New York City. On the other hand, Kansas City had a relatively high proportion of people originally from rural areas in Missouri and Kansas. There had been a rapid influx of Negroes, so that the nonwhite population amounted to about 12 per cent of the total. The area was overwhelmingly Protestant, with only 20 per cent Catholic and 3 per cent Jewish.

In connection with the Kansas City Studies of Adult Life, two community samples had been drawn from this area, the first in 1953, the second in 1954. Combined, the two constituted a pool of cases from which the various study populations described in this book were drawn.

Sample I

The first sample was designed so that, as far as possible, it would be representative of the noninstitutionalized people between the ages of forty and seventy who resided in the metropolitan area of Kansas City. A two-stage, stratified, systematic probability sample was drawn, with the field work carried out by Community Studies, Inc., a nonprofit research agency which had been conducting research in Kansas City for civic and welfare agencies for some ten years.

About two thousand households were included in the first stage of the sampling procedure. Excluded were people living in institutions and in such quasi households as dormitories, hotels, rooming houses, and convents, but not people living in rented rooms in ordinary family dwellings.

First, a representative sample of blocks containing dwelling units (DU's) was chosen. The address or description of each dwelling unit in each of these blocks was then noted on a form, and every nth dwelling unit was drawn. The intervals used to draw the sample blocks and, later, to draw the DU's within blocks were derived from the ratio of the number of DU's in the total area to the number desired in the sample. This over-all ratio was 126 to 1, with certain variations so that the larger blocks would not be disproportionately represented.

Interviewers were then sent to each of the selected DU's. From the preliminary round of interviews, information on age, sex, color, occupation, income, and number of persons per room in the household was obtained for 1,889 persons aged forty through sixty-nine. With this information, the sample was divided into socioeconomic groups on the basis of occupation of the head of the household, number of persons per room, amount of income per family, and residential area. (Ratings on residential area were made on the basis of census data and the judgments of real-estate salesmen and others who knew property values and neighborhood prestige factors. The

occupational ratings were based on those made earlier by Warner, Meeker, and Eells [1960, p. 140], but with the list of occupations enlarged to suit the complexity of occupations in a metropolitan area.) A derived score, known as the Index of Economic Status (IES), ranged from 4 to 28 (a score of 1 to 7 on each of the four subscales). This range was broken into four segments roughly corresponding to the social class divisions made by Warner: upper middle and above, lower middle, upper lower, and lower lower. Each of these four groups was then broken down further by sex and by five-year age groups.

At the second stage, this sample was stratified—that is, approximately equal numbers of men and women were randomly selected from the various socioeconomic levels, but with different proportions at each age, so that the age distribution would reflect that of the total population in the Kansas City area. Thus, larger numbers were drawn at ages forty–forty-four and forty-five–forty-nine, with successively smaller numbers at fifty–fifty-four, fifty-five–fifty-nine, sixty-sixty-four, and sixty-five–sixty-nine.

Intensive efforts were made to secure interviews from those persons whose names had been drawn. Interviewers were trained by the professional staff members in charge of the studies, and interviews were conducted in the homes of respondents (in some instances, in a man's office). In the case of upper-status respondents, letters were first sent out explaining the nature of the research and asking for an appointment. Negro interviewers were used in interviewing Negro respondents.

Of nearly thirteen hundred names assigned to interviewers, some 6 per cent had moved and could not be traced, 2 per cent had moved out of the city, 7 per cent could not be contacted for other reasons, and 1 per cent had died in the year that intervened between the time the sample was drawn and the interviewing was completed. Another 22 per cent refused to be interviewed, and 4 per cent began but did not complete the interview for various reasons. Of the total assignments, then, 58 per cent completions were obtained, giving a total of 751 persons interviewed. Some of the people who refused undoubtedly did not have time to spare, but others may have had personality characteristics which made them significantly different from those who cooperated. The personality factors that determine which subjects will and which will not cooperate in such a study are unknown. Generally speaking, the higher-status groups gave more refusals than other groups (although special efforts were made to keep these people in the sample), and women refused more often than men. The percentage of refusals was greater among younger persons than among older.

Because several parallel studies were being carried out simultaneously, the content of the interviews varied from one subsample to another. Psychological data of the type required for the personality studies reported in this book were obtained from 420 of the 751 persons interviewed. It is this pool of 420 cases which constitute Sample I.

Sample II

In the second phase of the Kansas City Studies, two groups of people were interviewed successively over several years: one group of persons between fifty and seventy years of age, called the panel; and one group aged seventy to ninety, called the quasi panel.

The Panel

The universe from which the panel was drawn was a random selection of 8,300 dwelling units and 400 persons living in quasi households in the metropolitan Kansas City area in 1954. This sample had originally been drawn by Community Studies, Inc., for a study of chronic illness and rehabilitation, and all persons in the sample (except 3 per cent who could not be reached for various reasons and 2 per cent who refused) had been given a health questionnaire. The names of persons who were found to be in good health and who did not, therefore, qualify as respondents for the study of chronic illness were made available to the field director of the Kansas City Study of Adult Life. It was this group of persons from which the panel was selected.

Persons living in rural parts of the area, Negroes, and those over sixty-eight and under forty-eight years of age were first eliminated.

The remaining people were each assigned a score on the Index of Status Characteristics (ISC) based on level of education, area of residence, and occupation. Persons of highest and lowest status were then eliminated. From the remaining group, which was about half working class and half middle class, a panel of 216 names was drawn, half men, half women; one-third in each of three age groups forty-eight–fifty-four, fifty-five–sixty-one, and sixty-two–sixty-eight.

Of the 216 persons chosen, 174 agreed to join the panel and to be interviewed at regular intervals; thirty-seven refused; and twenty-five could not be reached because of change of address, death, or error in the original interview with regard to the criteria for inclusion.

The initial refusal rate was high (17 per cent), but, because it was necessary to secure continuing cooperation, the interviewers were instructed to avoid high-pressure techniques.

As interviewing proceeded, more losses were sustained. At the end of the seventh round of interviewing, when the study ended, 62 per cent of the original panel remained. Of the losses, 13 per cent were because of geographical moves; 26 per cent, deaths; and the rest, refusals to be interviewed at some time during the series of interviews, usually because of reportedly poor health.

The Quasi Panel

After the first two rounds of interviews with panel members, it became evident that a wider age range was desirable in order to follow up certain initial findings. It was not then possible to secure a random stratified sample of healthy old people that would be continuous with the panel. A group of old people was therefore secured through "chain sampling." Three staff interviewers—an upper-middle-class professional, a lower-middle-class grade-school teacher, and a working-class clerk—were asked to secure from among their acquaintances and from persons residing in their neighborhoods a group of respondents between seventy and ninety years of age who were ambulatory and not obviously ill. These old people, in turn, were asked for the names of their acquaintances who would qualify for inclusion in the quasi panel and who they felt would be willing to cooperate in the study. One hundred and seven persons (fifty men and fifty-seven women) were contacted in this fashion and constituted the quasi panel.

The old people in the quasi panel cannot be strictly compared with the panel members, since they were not randomly selected and were not given the preliminary health interview. From their responses to questions concerning recent illness and general health, however, it was concluded that they did not differ a great deal in health status from the panel, although, as was to be anticipated, there were more cases of impairment (such as blindness, deafness, arthritic crippling, and heart trouble) among the oldest age group. On the quasi panel, however, fewer people than in the panel group complained about their health—a finding which may reflect decreased preoccupation with matters of health among the very old or which may reflect the often superior state of health of those who live to advanced ages.

There is also some evidence that the panel had a greater middle-class bias than the quasi panel. On the whole, the respondents in the quasi panel lived in less prosperous residential areas than the panel. Because, however, old people are often attached to their homes and remain in them in spite of deteriorating neighborhoods, it is difficult to evaluate area of residence as a measure of socio-economic status.

In both the panel and the quasi panel, there was a greater proportion of men than in the population at large.

As the study progressed, the quasi panel suffered marked attrition. Originally interviewed when the panel was being interviewed for the third time, the quasi panel decreased in number from 107 to fifty-one in the four years that intervened between the third and the seventh rounds of interviewing. Of the losses, 11 per cent were because of geographical moves; 28 per cent, deaths; and 61 per cent, refusal or inability to be interviewed because of poor health.

The Combined Pool of Cases

In sum, then, Sample I, the Sample II panel, and the Sample II quasi panel were, to varying degrees, representative of the population of Kansas City residents aged forty to ninety in the mid-1950's. Altogether, they constitute a pool of 701 men and women on whom psychological data of various types were available to the investigators who contributed to this volume. In each of the chapters of this book, there is a brief description of the particular study population drawn from this pool of cases. The studies reported in chapters 1, 2, and 3 used only Sample I cases; the studies reported in chapters 4 and 5, both Sample I and II cases; and the studies reported in chapters 6, 7, and 8, only Sample II cases.

B

THE PERSONALITY VARIABLES

1. "Intelligence": the capacity to act purposefully, to think rationally, and to deal effectively with the environment.

2. "Perceptual impairment": impairment of perceptual processes indicated by concrete thought and confusion and distortion of frames of reference; perceptions that are confused, tangential, or grossly inaccurate.

3. "Ideational output": rate and fluidity of words and thoughts.

4. "Affective complexity": sensitivity toward emotional nuances in the self and in others.

5. "Overt anxiety": conscious experience of physical as well as mental powerlessness; presentiment of impending danger; alertness as if facing an emergency.

6. "Optimism versus depression"

7. "Intropunitive versus extrapunitive feelings"

8. "Passivity": the tendency to adopt a style of adjustment to old age characterized by reduced activities and involvements.

9. "Aggression": open, assertive expression versus repression of aggressivity.

10. "Dependence": reliance on significant others for emotional support and decision-making.

11. "Intellectualization": the tendency to retreat from affect and impulse to a world of words and abstractions.

12. "Intellectuality": intellectual investments, interests, and orientations which are not defensive in nature; the capacity for detachment; cognitive complexity; richness of ideation.

13. "Isolation of affect": excessive separation of affect from idea; inappropriate affect which interferes with efforts at abstraction.

14. "Rationalization": tendency to offer apparently plausible casual contexts to explain behavior which allows justification or *sub rosa* gratification of impulse or affect.

15. "Logical analysis": interest in carefully analyzing the casual aspects of situations.

16. "Doubt": defensive behavior by which subjects seem to doubt the validity of their perceptions or judgments, are unable to make up their minds, and are unable to commit themselves to a course of action.

17. "Tolerance of ambiguity": ability to cope with cognitive and affective complexity or dissonance.

18. "Denial": a cognitive defense characterized by unrealistic attitudes toward important areas of life; magical thought.

19. "Concentration": ability to set aside recognizably disturbing or distracting feelings or thoughts to focus on the task at hand.

20. "Projection": a defensive process by which an objectionable internal tendency is unrealistically attributed to another person in the environment instead of being recognized as part of the self.

21. "Empathy": ability to put oneself in the other person's place and to imagine how he feels.

22. "Regression": behaviors, defenses, and tactics suggestive of earlier stages of development.

23. "Regression in the service of the ego": a cognitive style in which the subject is open about the past and experimental with ideas, thoughts, and feelings in reference to the past.

24. "Displacement": tendency temporarily and unsuccessfully to repress unacceptable impulses, then to allow expression in a situation of greater internal or external tolerance.

25. "Sublimation": ability to express primitive impulses in ways which are socially accepted, tempered, and satisfying.

26. "Reaction formation": permanent alterations of personality structure characterized by their symbolic meaning and by rigid and compulsive quality.

27. "Sex-role identity"

28. "Suppression of affect"

29. "Counterphobic activity": emphasis upon keeping busy as a defense against anxiety stemming from repudiated passive-dependent needs.

30. "Seclusiveness": withdrawal from social participation.

31. "Congruence between perceptions of self and ideal self"

32. "Equalitarianism versus authoritarianism": social and personal relations are conceived in terms of mutuality and permissiveness; democratic versus social relationships seen in terms of status, position, dominance, and submission.

33. "Intraception": interest and preoccupation with ideas and feelings (in contrast with a rigid orientation toward external and physical events).

34. "Religiosity": involvement in religious rituals and activities; personal goals which are carefully equated with the teachings of the church and dependence upon religion for *raison d'être*.

35. "Achievement drive": orientation toward meeting internal standards of excellence rather than toward external rewards and recognition.

36. "Status drive": preoccupation with status needs and characteristics and with social-status characteristics; behaviors carefully controlled to reflect understanding of reference group expectation.

37. "Participation": membership and involvement in civic, fraternal, and/or social groups outside work and family; sense of engagement with community activities and values.

38. "Positive attitudes toward the young": attitudes toward younger people and their behavior are accepting, nurturant, admiring.

39. "Differentiations perceived in the young": tendency to individualize younger people, to recognize variability, and to avoid categorical judgments.

40. "Acceptance of same sex parent": awareness of relatedness between own and parent's values, attitudes, and characteristics.

41. "Acceptance of opposite sex parent": attitudes toward this parent are accepting or admiring.

42. "Attitude toward opposite sex" (accepting, intimate versus hostile, competitive): attitudes characterized as fond, admiring, not typically colored by covert patterns of hostility or competitiveness.

43. "Differentiations perceived in opposite sex": ability to make differentiated descriptions of opposite sex; recognition of variability in behavior and in personal characteristics in the opposite sex.

44. "Concern over morality": involved and concerned about moral issues; speaks out clearly about the good versus the bad, the right or the wrong, in reference to various areas of human behavior.

45. "Acceptance of aging": an attitude of calm recognition of growing old without experiencing either depression or need for defensive tactics in relation to aging.

Derivation of Personality Types

The obverse factor analysis shown in tables B.3 and B.4 might have been carried out on the basis of the subjects' scores on the ten factors rather than the subjects' ratings on the forty-five variables. To have done so, however, would have meant the unnecessary sacrifice of much of the complexity of the data.

Once the obverse analyses were completed, the determination of the types involved several steps. First, groups of persons were isolated by examining the loadings on each factor in tables B.3 and B.4. Second, each factor was plotted against each other factor, and these plots were examined to see whether the groups of cases did, indeed, remain clustered on the successive plots. Each group of

TABLE B.1
FACTOR ANALYSIS FOR MALES ($N = 43$)

Variable					Factor					
	1	2	3	4	5	6	7	8	9	10
1. Intelligence	.26	−.37	.03	−.11	−.71	.08	−.04	.11	.20	−.09
2. Impairment	−.05	.85	.04	−.01	.15	−.03	−.08	.09	.16	.20
3. Ideation	.09	.22	.31	.06	−.40	.63	.10	−.19	−.07	−.17
4. Aff. complexity	.59	−.19	−.30	.12	−.30	.31	.19	.06	−.11	−.06
5. Anxiety	−.37	.80	.12	−.13	−.09	.16	.04	−.16	−.01	.07
6. Optimism	.60	−.54	−.15	.28	−.11	.07	.08	−.09	.12	−.25
7. Punitiveness	−.16	.02	−.01	.21	.11	.74	.20	−.02	.07	.23
8. Passivity	.13	.03	−.25	.80	−.02	.05	.03	.07	−.01	.29
9. Aggression	.18	−.29	−.01	−.09	−.07	−.02	.11	−.03	.24	−.81
10. Dependence	.03	.15	−.05	.86	.12	.07	.09	.08	.10	−.27
11. Intellectualization	−.51	.17	−.08	−.24	−.20	.22	.03	−.17	.10	.45
12. Intellectuality	.21	−.69	−.04	−.05	−.46	−.08	.09	.06	.23	−.30
13. Isolated affect	−.77	.28	−.06	.02	.14	.11	−.07	−.17	.10	.06
14. Rationalization	−.58	.58	.08	−.04	.09	.17	−.05	−.24	−.19	.07
15. Logic	.22	−.76	−.04	−.04	−.37	−.02	.17	.02	.17	−.10
16. Doubt	−.50	.48	.28	−.02	.15	.14	.03	−.12	−.33	.07
17. Ambiguity	.54	−.61	.05	.16	−.11	−.06	.26	.16	.26	−.12
18. Denial	−.30	.74	.09	.28	−.01	−.08	−.25	.05	.01	−.07
19. Concentration	.25	−.82	−.07	−.05	−.36	−.12	.08	.03	.10	−.06
20. Projection	−.28	.46	.18	−.21	.19	.07	−.25	−.44	−.26	.13
21. Empathy	.73	−.27	−.11	.01	−.01	.07	.25	.22	.18	−.21
22. Regression	−.28	.84	.12	.01	−.04	−.12	−.19	−.07	−.04	.11
23. Regression: ego	.59	−.49	.02	.05	−.26	.10	.18	−.01	−.06	.05

212

TABLE B.1 (*continued*)

Variable					Factor					
	1	2	3	4	5	6	7	8	9	10
24. Displacement	−.43	.40	−.19	−.25	.22	−.30	−.07	−.19	−.49	.08
25. Sublimation	.66	−.27	−.08	−.01	.41	−.05	.26	−.11	.19	.02
26. Reaction	−.75	.26	−.21	−.07	.14	−.21	−.23	−.03	−.17	.01
27. Sex role	.53	−.51	−.26	−.01	.01	.05	.12	−.15	.31	−.28
28. Suppression	.80	−.29	−.01	.23	−.21	.15	.01	.11	−.01	−.01
29. Counterphobia	−.43	.23	.37	−.49	.22	−.02	−.22	−.04	.19	−.06
30. Seclusiveness	−.46	.44	.03	.08	−.02	−.06	−.15	.14	−.24	.54
31. Self/ideal	.74	−.32	−.26	.01	−.01	.15	−.18	.11	.21	−.15
32. Equalitarian	.44	−.40	.06	.12	−.07	.08	−.04	.68	.07	−.11
33. Intraception	.23	−.10	−.15	.05	−.81	−.05	.09	−.04	.06	.14
34. Religiosity	.09	−.05	−.02	−.03	−.14	.15	.17	.01	.83	−.17
35. Achievement	−.28	−.30	.05	−.25	−.56	.25	.28	−.08	−.03	−.31
36. Status	−.35	−.24	.11	−.09	−.15	.10	−.17	−.68	.07	−.26
37. Participation	.44	−.26	−.12	.19	−.05	−.11	.42	−.20	−.33	−.18
38. The young	.81	.08	.10	−.05	.01	.04	.18	.31	.09	.02
39. Diff'n: young	.29	−.23	.02	.04	−.14	.12	.74	.16	.05	−.12
40. Same parent	.14	−.21	−.87	.15	−.07	.04	.02	.04	.05	.01
41. Opposite parent	.36	−.07	.34	.63	.09	.09	−.21	.03	.20	.16
42. Opposite sex	.61	−.19	−.10	.20	−.03	−.07	.13	.36	.06	−.24
43. Diff'n: opp. sex	.26	−.42	−.07	−.01	−.11	−.04	.67	.07	.20	−.02
44. Morality	.83	−.31	.01	.32	−.07	−.02	.06	.06	.08	−.08
45. Aging	.17	−.03	−.26	−.10	−.02	.71	−.25	.10	.35	−.12
Per cent of total variance	50.1	12.0	7.5	5.8	5.8	5.6	4.0	3.8	3.5	2.5

213

TABLE B.2

FACTOR ANALYSIS FOR FEMALES $(N = 45)$

Variable	Factor									
	1	2	3	4	5	6	7	8	9	10
1. Intelligence	-.25	.18	.52	-.04	.13	-.54	.08	-.23	.04	-.19
2. Impairment	.02	.04	-.88	-.04	.10	.03	.02	.12	.01	-.04
3. Ideation	.52	.66	-.17	.09	.03	-.18	-.07	-.25	.01	.04
4. Aff. complexity	-.29	.06	.58	.04	.02	-.39	-.13	.01	.43	.11
5. Anxiety	.79	-.04	-.22	.10	-.11	.27	.10	.23	-.04	.04
6. Optimism	-.68	.33	.15	-.18	.19	-.28	-.03	-.01	.25	.01
7. Punitiveness	.01	-.04	.09	-.03	-.27	-.20	-.83	.01	-.04	.10
8. Passivity	-.05	-.22	.05	.10	-.85	-.01	-.22	-.07	.11	.22
9. Aggression	-.03	.43	.06	.09	.08	-.11	.75	-.05	-.24	.01
10. Dependence	-.03	.07	-.03	.02	-.92	.01	-.10	-.05	-.01	-.11
11. Intellectualization	.40	.27	-.26	-.27	.12	.22	.11	-.37	-.42	.01
12. Intellectuality	-.44	.05	.65	.17	-.05	-.44	.03	-.14	.02	-.06
13. Isolated affect	.59	.12	-.04	-.06	.21	.47	-.11	.14	-.15	-.04
14. Rationalization	.57	.27	-.32	.01	.20	-.02	.20	.01	-.51	-.13
15. Logic	-.32	.21	.76	.10	.14	-.18	-.07	-.04	.09	-.04
16. Doubt	.81	-.14	-.35	-.09	-.20	-.05	.02	.10	-.13	-.08
17. Ambiguity	-.44	.01	.59	.17	-.13	-.12	-.10	.01	.41	.08
18. Denial	.46	-.13	-.67	.04	-.11	.09	.04	.01	.11	-.04
19. Concentration	-.27	-.03	.87	-.05	.01	-.17	.01	-.04	-.01	-.03
20. Projection	.75	.15	-.39	.01	.16	-.09	.12	-.02	-.25	-.05
21. Empathy	-.64	-.02	.49	.09	-.02	-.10	.01	-.20	.30	.09
22. Regression	.32	-.17	-.83	.10	.10	-.01	.05	.07	-.09	-.05
23. Regression: ego	-.45	.01	.52	.16	.02	-.48	-.04	-.06	.23	.03

214

TABLE B.2 (continued)

Variable					Factor					
	1	2	3	4	5	6	7	8	9	10
24. Displacement	.71	.22	−.21	.32	−.01	.06	.30	−.06	.09	−.12
25. Sublimation	−.64	−.07	.47	.01	−.09	−.34	−.02	.07	.19	.11
26. Reaction	.71	−.07	−.09	−.02	.22	.23	−.28	.32	−.10	−.28
27. Sex role	−.65	.12	.37	−.05	−.28	−.15	.05	−.15	.20	.23
28. Suppression	−.64	−.05	.24	.11	−.11	−.33	.02	−.24	.35	.12
29. Counterphobia	.22	.43	−.03	−.06	.24	.01	−.17	.62	.06	−.27
30. Seclusiveness	.16	−.49	−.56	.06	−.06	−.13	−.15	−.23	−.18	.06
31. Self/ideal	−.80	−.16	.19	−.04	.06	.05	.12	.23	.13	.20
32. Equalitarian	−.41	−.23	.50	−.09	−.08	−.25	−.01	.03	.55	.05
33. Intraception	−.17	−.06	.38	.01	−.01	−.81	−.17	.15	.02	−.06
34. Religiosity	−.04	.20	−.05	−.85	−.06	.23	−.01	.09	.01	−.06
35. Achievement	−.02	.24	.48	−.32	.04	−.29	−.08	.04	−.03	−.44
36. Status	.09	.67	.22	−.23	−.10	.03	.18	.12	−.33	.08
37. Participation	−.12	.75	.15	−.18	.11	.04	.17	−.02	.12	−.10
38. The young	−.32	−.31	.47	.01	−.06	−.10	.27	.27	.22	.42
39. Diff'n: young	−.20	−.25	.62	−.13	−.01	−.17	.35	−.11	.18	.11
40. Same parent	−.23	.10	.02	−.30	−.02	−.01	.01	−.06	.75	.01
41. Opposite parent	−.39	−.07	.01	−.16	−.03	.03	−.08	−.05	−.09	.80
42. Opposite sex	−.37	.17	.06	.01	−.02	.05	−.19	−.32	.26	.54
43. Diff'n: opp. sex	−.24	.07	.26	.14	−.04	−.01	−.02	−.78	.08	.02
44. Morality	−.87	−.01	.22	.08	−.08	−.06	.05	−.18	.03	.12
45. Aging	.02	.05	.05	−.82	.20	−.21	−.10	.07	.24	.18
Per cent of total variance	46.8	12.2	8.4	6.9	5.9	5.0	4.0	3.8	3.6	2.9

215

TABLE B.3

OBVERSE FACTOR ANALYSIS FOR MALES ($N = 43$)

Subject	*Factor 1	2	3	4	5	6	7	8	9	10
1	.48	−.18	.73†	.02	−.11	.03	.01	−.06	.12	.08
2	.84†	.06	.36	−.03	−.02	.03	−.15	.02	−.03	−.01
3	−.57†	.11	.34	−.22	−.08	−.29	−.24	−.20	.37	−.06
4	−.20	−.26	.15	−.05	.08	−.13	−.12	.08	.82†	−.03
5	.66†	.09	.24	.06	−.43	−.01	−.04	−.18	.08	.10
6	−.23	−.12	.15	−.03	.07	−.20	.01	−.07	.31†	−.07
7	−.23	−.25	.65†	−.24	−.16	.26	−.12	.16	.27	−.27
8	−.04	.14	.84†	−.04	.08	−.03	.10	−.03	−.03	−.08
9	.33†	.25	.12	−.04	−.72	.03	−.24	.27	−.03	−.01
10	.36	.32	.26	−.05	.16	.52	−.14	−.39	−.18	−.13
11	−.83†	.07	.15	.06	.08	.03	−.14	−.13	.13	.02
12	−.12	.13	.01	−.02	−.03	.81	−.23	−.04	−.03	−.01
13	.87†	.18	.17	.12	.04	.11	.02	.01	−.27	−.12
14	.33	.17	.59†	−.01	−.40	.16	−.07	.01	−.14	.08
15	.13	.20	.55†	.34	.09	−.08	.12	.32	.25	−.10
16	.86†	.13	.19	.18	−.02	.16	.01	−.12	.01	−.04
17	−.73†	−.03	.15	−.14	.14	.09	.01	−.05	.14	.13
18	.89†	.04	.23	.03	−.13	.03	−.10	.07	−.15	−.07
19	.22	.02	.75†	.16	−.14	−.16	.22	−.18	.18	.13
20	.40	.66†	−.07	.28	−.19	.06	−.03	.03	.08	−.08
21	.39	.01	.02	.57†	−.09	.16	.08	−.07	−.13	−.43
22	−.27	−.06	.27	−.03	−.29	−.58	−.39	−.02	.27	−.12
23	.41	.39	.18	.20	−.10	.48	−.04	−.18	−.12	−.22
24	.60†	.33	−.17	.33	.03	−.01	.21	.01	−.22	−.28

TABLE B.3 (continued)

Subject	Factor*									
	1	2	3	4	5	6	7	8	9	10
25	−.85†	−.02	−.03	.13	−.01	.17	−.11	−.02	−.05	.22
26	.15	.25	.13	.66†	−.01	.04	−.37	.23	.05	.06
27	−.03	.16	.05	.87†	−.01	.01	.06	−.01	−.06	.05
28	.25	.26	.37	.46†	−.40	−.04	−.12	−.29	.12	−.03
29	.20	−.11	.65†	.30	.10	−.17	−.07	.13	−.26	−.34
30	−.83†	.12	−.17	−.16	.15	−.09	.08	.01	.04	−.70
31	−.42†	.06	−.20	−.01	−.19	−.10	−.70	−.19	.08	.14
32	−.65	.16	−.03	.03	−.01	.08	−.06	−.28	.55†	−.03
33	−.42	.76†	.02	.12	−.04	.17	.04	.05	−.04	.16
34	−.07	.81†	.10	.13	−.19	.02	−.25	−.01	−.24	−.15
35	−.72†	.27	−.17	−.09	.16	−.05	.21	−.14	.24	−.13
36	−.74†	−.08	−.36	.36	−.09	−.07	−.17	.05	−.06	.11
37	.21	.33	.06	.30	−.26	.01	.04	.57	−.14	−.16
38	−.80	.06	.05	−.06	−.11	.03	−.10	−.22	−.13	−.12
39	−.46	.26	.08	.23	.01	.21	−.07	−.51	−.15	−.23
40	.29	.27	−.06	.08	−.02	.19	.05	.06	−.35	−.67
41	.45†	.33	.09	.12	−.35	.38	−.03	−.15	−.26	−.30
42	−.47	.26	−.36	.28	−.50	−.07	.02	−.04	−.22	.01
43	.32	.26	.18	−.33	−.09	.12	−.34	.18	.15	−.47

* Both the integrated and the unintegrated types have been derived from Factor 1, the first representing those individuals with high positive loadings; the second, those with high negative loadings. The introspective were derived from Factor 2; the defended, from Factor 3; the passive dependent, from Factor 4; and the constricted, from Factor 9.

† These cases were identified as representing the respective type.

217

TABLE B.4
OBVERSE FACTOR ANALYSIS FOR FEMALES $(N = 45)$

Subject	Factor*									
	1	2	3	4	5	6	7	8	9	10
1	.90†	−.02	−.06	−.05	−.01	.02	−.17	−.23	.07	.11
2	.24	.24	−.21	−.23	−.20	.16	−.11	.14	.08	.14
3	.75†	−.05	−.06	−.17	−.02	−.05	.17	−.32	.03	−.05
4	−.06	−.11	−.07	−.09	−.01	.90†	−.08	.12	.14	−.05
5	−.29	−.11	−.85†	−.11	−.10	.06	−.04	.05	.05	−.13
6	.73†	.28	−.13	−.03	.18	.26	.09	−.22	.04	.01
7	−.25	.43†	.34	.08	−.05	−.33	−.10	.08	−.07	.36
8	−.62†	−.06	.04	−.08	−.10	.19	.04	.25	−.48	−.16
9	−.60†	−.36	−.14	.17	.04	.18	.08	.13	.03	−.40
10	.03	−.19	−.20	.53	.05	.08	.28	.36	.02	−.38
11	.87†	−.14	.01	−.01	.01	−.01	.07	.01	.15	−.11
12	.50†	.08	−.08	.14	.10	.02	.17	−.02	−.09	−.70
13	.24	.06	−.27	−.16	.03	.24	−.60	.25	.05	−.01
14	−.68†	−.02	−.03	.17	.28	.04	−.05	.19	−.51	.08
15	−.21	.36	−.06	.07	.29	.36	−.08	.46†	−.02	−.42
16	.15	.02	−.27	−.68	.10	.45†	−.09	−.26	.16	.18
17	−.46	−.22	−.16	.21	−.17	.45†	.36	.21	−.12	−.14
18	−.51	.01	−.21	.34	.11	.26	.06	.58†	−.07	−.12
19	−.34	.05	−.05	.08	−.17	−.32	−.19	−.03	−.73	−.09
20	.28	.05	−.17	.13	−.06	−.01	.76	.02	.27	−.13
21	−.26	.72†	−.05	.13	−.08	.09	−.28	.07	.01	.29
22	.71†	.05	.17	−.52	.02	.01	.06	−.15	−.06	.12
23	.77†	−.02	.02	−.12	−.26	.08	.16	.01	−.01	.01
24	.76†	.19	.21	−.19	−.05	−.18	.15	.21	−.09	−.19

TABLE B.4 (*continued*)

Subject	Factor*									
	1	2	3	4	5	6	7	8	9	10
25	.40	.20	−.51†	−.34	.14	.29	−.12	−.01	−.03	.19
26	.49	.64†	.09	−.26	−.09	.14	.18	−.24	−.14	.14
27	.40	−.01	−.03	−.18	.19	.44†	−.07	−.07	.13	.05
28	.10	.15	.69†	.03	.01	.10	.39	.16	−.23	.06
29	−.31	.05	−.27	.08	.05	−.08	.01	.60†	−.18	−.21
30	.74†	.41	−.06	−.02	.14	.01	.16	−.20	−.04	.05
31	.15	.74†	−.11	−.20	−.25	.05	−.03	.09	−.06	−.02
32	−.38	.26	−.22	.15	.31	−.27	−.32	.01	.54	.03
33	.09	.18	−.13	.84	.14	.01	−.10	.25	.01	−.01
34	−.22	.69†	−.14	.15	.23	−.28	.32	.24	.11	−.01
35	.75†	−.29	.11	−.22	−.03	.10	−.12	−.01	.21	−.14
36	.02	−.10	.06	−.21	.84	.03	−.05	.11	.01	−.09
37	−.39	.19	−.33	−.09	.11	.06	.12	.57†	−.38	.09
38	−.70†	.04	−.07	.04	.17	.29	.03	.16	−.37	−.31
39	.78†	.18	.17	−.07	.08	.05	−.19	−.15	.13	−.25
40	.52†	.03	.04	−.51	.18	.02	.05	−.09	.13	−.31
41	−.21	.02	−.02	−.02	.03	.04	−.07	.90†	.01	−.01
42	.47	.62†	.23	−.14	.10	−.15	−.05	.11	−.12	−.22
43	.77†	.01	.03	.12	.03	.01	.06	−.02	.24	−.15
44	.60†	.33	.02	−.01	.19	.10	.02	.27	.15	.18
45	.10	.85†	−.03	−.16	.01	−.11	.01	−.06	−.02	−.14

* Both the integrated and the unintegrated types have been derived from Factor 1, the first representing those individuals with high positive loadings; the second, those with high negative loadings. The passive dependent were derived from Factor 2; the self-doubting from Factor 3; the competitive from Factor 6; and the defended constricted from Factor 8.

† These cases were identified as representing the respective type.

219

persons was then further examined to determine which of the forty-five variables covaried for each group. The last process was followed in order to isolate the salient variables which characterized each of the groups. The variables so isolated were then examined in relation to the factor scores obtained for each group of persons. Only after all these steps had been completed were the final assignments made of cases to types and were the types named.

REFERENCES

Ames, L. B., Learned, J., Métraux, R. W., & Walker, R. N. *Rorschach responses in old age.* New York: Hoeber-Harper, 1954.

Benedek, Therese. Personality development. In F. Alexander & H. Ross (Eds.), *Dynamic psychiatry.* Chicago: Univer. Chicago Press, 1952.

Birren, J. E. Age changes in speed of simple responses and perception and their significance for complex behavior. In *Old age in the modern world.* (International Association of Gerontology, Third Congress.) London: Livingstone, 1955.

Birren, J. E., Allen, W. R., & Landau, H. G. The relation of problem length in simple addition to time required, probability of success, and age. *J. Geront.,* 1954, 9, 150–161.

Birren, J. E., Butler, R. N., Greenhouse, S. W., Sokoloff, L., & Yarrow, Marian R. (Eds.) *Human aging.* (Publ. Hlth Serv. Publ. No. 986.) Washington, D.C.: U.S. Government Printing Office, 1963.

Bruner, J. S. The course of cognitive growth. *Amer. Psychologist,* 1964, **19**, 1–15.

Caldwell, Bettye M. The use of the Rorschach in personality research with the aged. *J. Geront.,* 1954, **9**, 316–323.

Chesrow, E. J., Wosika, P. H., & Reinitz, A. H. A psychometric evaluation of aged white males. *Geriatrics,* 1949, **4**, 169–177.

Coelho, G. V., Hamburg, D. A., & Murphey, Elizabeth. Coping strategies in a new learning environment. *Arch. gen. Psychiat.,* 1963, **9**, 433–443.

Cumming, Elaine. Further thoughts on the theory of disengagement. *UNESCO int. soc. Sci. J.,* 1963, **15**, 377–393.

Cumming, Elaine, Dean, Lois R., Newell, D. S., & McCaffrey, Isabel. Disengagement—a tentative theory of aging. *Sociometry,* 1960, **23**, 23–35.

Cumming, Elaine, & Henry, W. E. *Growing old.* New York: Basic Books, 1961.

Dana, R. H. Proposal for objective scoring of the TAT. *Percept. mot. Skills,* 1959, **9**, 27–43.

Davidson, H. H., & Kruglov, L. Personality characteristics of the institutionalized aged. *J. consult. Psychol.,* 1952, **16**, 5–12.

Dean, Lois R. The pattern variables: some empirical operations. *Amer. sociol. Rev.,* 1961, **26**, 80–90.

Erikson, E. H. *Childhood and society.* New York: Norton, 1950.

Erikson, E. H. Growth and crisis of the "healthy personality." In C. Kluckhohn, H. A. Murray, and D. M. Schneider (Eds.), *Personality in nature, society and culture.* New York: Knopf, 1953. Pp. 185–225.

Erikson, E. H. The problem of ego identity. *J. Amer. psychoanal. Ass.,* 1956, **4**, 56–121.

Erikson, E. H. Identity and the life cycle: selected papers. *Psych. Issues,* 1959, **1** (1).

Freud, S. *The problem of anxiety.* New York: Norton, 1936. (First published 1926.)

Fromm, E. *Escape from freedom.* New York: Rinehart, 1941.

Grossman, C., Warshawsky, F., & Hertz, M. Rorschach studies of personality characteristics of a group of institutionalized old people. *J. Geront.*, 1951, 6 (Supplement to No. 3), 97. (Abstract)

Haggard, E. A. *Intraclass correlation and the analysis of variance.* New York: Dryden, 1958.

Hartmann, H. Ego psychology and the problem of adaptation. In D. Rapaport (Ed.), *Organization and pathology of thought.* New York: Columbia Univer. Press, 1951.

Havighurst, R. J. The social competence of middle-aged people. *Genet. Psychol. Monogr.*, 1957, 56, 297–375.

Havighurst, R. J., Neugarten, Bernice L., & Tobin, S. S. Disengagement and patterns of aging. Paper read at the International Research Seminar on Social and Psychological Aspects of Aging, Markaryd, Sweden, August, 1963.

Henry, W. E. The thematic apperception technique in the study of culture-personality relations. *Genet. Psychol. Monogr.*, 1947, 35, 3–315.

Henry, W. E. The theory of intrinsic disengagement. Paper read at the International Research Seminar on Social and Psychological Aspects of Aging, Markaryd, Sweden, August, 1963.

Hollingshead, A. B., & Redlich, F. C. *Social class and mental illness: a community study.* New York: Wiley & Sons, 1958.

Jung, C. G. *Modern man in search of a soul.* New York: Harcourt, 1933.

Kaplan, O. J. *Mental disorders in later life.* (2nd ed.) Stanford, Calif.: Stanford Univer. Press, 1956.

Kleemeier, R. W. Intellectual changes in the senium, or death and the IQ. Paper read at the annual meeting of the American Psychological Association, St. Louis, September, 1961.

Kleemeier, R. W. The interaction of aging and illness as a psychological problem. Paper read at the International Research Seminar on Social and Psychological Aspects of Aging, Markaryd, Sweden, August, 1963.

Klopfer, W. G. Personality patterns of old age. *Rorschach Res. Exch.*, 1946, 10, 145–166.

Kroeber, T. C. The coping functions of the ego mechanisms. In R. W. White (Ed.), *The study of lives*. New York: Atherton Press, 1963. Pp. 178–198.

Kuhlen, R. G. Age and intelligence: the significance of cultural change in longitudinal vs. cross-sectional findings. *Vita humana*, 1963, 6, 113–124.

Kutner, B., Fanshel, D., Togo, Alice M., & Langner, T. S. *Five hundred over sixty*. New York: Russell Sage Foundation, 1956.

Light, B. H., & Amick, J. H. Rorschach responses of normal aged. *J. proj. Tech.*, 1956, 20, 185–195.

Lustman, S. Psychic energy and mechanisms of defense. In *The psychoanalytic study of the child*. Vol. 12. New York: International Universities Press, 1957. Pp. 151–165.

Maslow, A. H. *Motivation and personality*. New York: Harper, 1954.

Meerloo, J. A. Transference and ·resistance in geriatric psychotherapy. *Psychoanal. Rev.*, 1955, 42.

Murphy, Lois. *The widening world of childhood*. New York: Basic Books, 1962.

Murray, H. A. *Thematic apperception test: pictures and manual*. Cambridge: Harvard Univer. Press, 1943.

Neugarten, Bernice L. A developmental view of adult personality. In J. E. Birren (Ed.), *Relations of development and aging*. Springfield, Ill.: Charles C Thomas, 1964.

Neugarten, Bernice L., Havighurst, R. J., & Tobin, S. S. The measurement of life satisfaction. *J. Geront.*, 1961, 16, 134–143.

Parsons, T. *The social system*. Glencoe, Ill.: Free Press, 1950.

Peck, R. F. Psychological developments in the second half of life. In J. E. Anderson (Ed.), *Psychological aspects of aging*. Washington, D.C.: American Psychological Association, 1956. Pp. 42–53.

Peck, R. F. Measuring the mental health of normal adults. *Genet. Psychol. Monogr.*, 1959, 60, 197–255.

Perlin, S., & Butler, R. N. Psychiatric aspects of adaptation to the aging experience. In J. E. Birren, R. N. Butler, S. W. Greenhouse, L. Sokoloff, & Marian R. Yarrow (Eds.), *Human aging.* Washington, D.C.: U.S. Government Printing Office, 1963. Pp. 159–191.

Prados, M., & Fried, E. G. Personality structure in the older age groups. *J. clin. Psychol.,* 1947, **3,** 113–120.

Rapaport, D. Toward a theory of thinking. In D. Rapaport (Ed.), *Organization and pathology of thought.* New York: Columbia Univer. Press, 1951.

Rapaport, D. Cognitive structures. In *Contemporary approaches to cognition.* Cambridge, Mass.: Harvard Univer. Press, 1957. Pp. 157–200.

Rapaport, D. Historical survey of psychoanalytic ego psychology. *Psychol. Issues,* 1959, **1** (1), 5–17.

Rapaport, D. *The structure of psychoanalytic theory.* New York: International Universities Press, 1960.

Reichard, Suzanne, Livson, Florine, & Petersen, P. G. *Aging and personality.* New York: Wiley, 1962.

Schaw, L. C., & Henry, W. E. A method for the comparison of groups: a study in thematic apperception. *Genet. Psychol. Monogr.,* 1956, **54,** 207–253.

Singer, Margaret T. Personality measurements in the aged. In J. E. Birren, R. N. Butler, S. W. Greenhouse, L. Sokoloff, & Marian R. Yarrow (Eds.), *Human aging.* Washington, D.C.: U.S. Government Printing Office, 1963. Pp. 259–279.

Warner, W. L., Meeker, Marchia, & Eells, K. *Social class in America.* New York: Harper Torchbooks, 1960.

Weinberg, J. Personal and social adjustment. In J. E. Anderson (Ed.), *Psychological aspects of aging.* Washington, D.C.: American Psychological Association, 1956. Pp. 17–29.

White, R. W. Competence and the psychosexual stages of development. In M. R. Jones (Ed.), *Nebraska Symposium on Motivation: 1960.* Lincoln: Univer. Nebraska Press, 1960. Pp. 97–143.

White, R. W. Ego and reality in psychoanalytic theory. *Psychol. Issues,* 1963, **3** (3). (a)

White, R. W. Sense of interpersonal competence: two case studies and some reflections on origins. In R. W. White (Ed.), *The study of lives.* New York: Atherton Press, 1963. Pp. 72–93. (b)

INDEX

GROWING OLD

An Arno Press Collection

Birren, James E., et al., editors. **Human Aging**. 1963

Birren, James E., editor. **Relations of Development and Aging**. 1964

Breckinridge, Elizabeth L. **Effective Use of Older Workers**. 1953

Brennan, Michael J., Philip Taft, and Mark Schupack. **The Economics of Age**. 1967

Cabot, Natalie H. **You Can't Count On Dying**. 1961

Clark, F. Le Gros. **Growing Old in a Mechanized World**. 1960

Clark, Margaret and Barbara G. Anderson. **Culture and Aging**. 1967

Crook, G[uy] H[amilton] and Martin Heinstein. **The Older Worker in Industry**. 1958

Derber, Milton, editor. **Aged and Society**. 1950

Donahue, Wilma, et al., editors. **Free Time**. 1958

Donahue, Wilma and Clark Tibbitts, editors. **New Frontiers of Aging**. 1957

Havighurst, Robert J. and Ruth Albrecht. **Older People**. 1953

International Association of Gerontology. **Old Age in the Modern World**. 1955

Kaplan, Oscar J., editor. **Mental Disorders in Later Life**. 1956

Kutner, Bernard, et al. **Five Hundred Over Sixty**. 1956

Lowenthal, Marjorie F. **Lives in Distress**. 1964

Munnichs, J.M.A. **Old Age and Finitude**. 1966

Nassau, Mabel L. **Old Age Poverty in Greenwich Village**. 1915

National Association of Social Workers. **Social Group Work with Older People**. 1963

Neugarten, Bernice L., et al. **Personality in Middle and Late Life**. 1964

Orton, Job. **Discourses to the Aged**. 1801

Pinner, Frank A., Paul Jacobs, and Philip Selznick. **Old Age and Political Behavior**. 1959

Reichard, Suzanne, Florine Livson and Paul G. Peterson. **Aging and Personality**. 1962

Rowntree, B. Seebohm. **Old People**. 1947

Rubinow, I[saac] M[ax]., editor. **Care of the Aged**. 1931

Shanas, Ethel. **The Health of Older People**. 1962

Shanas, Ethel, et al. **Old People in Three Industrial Societies**. 1968

Sheldon, J[oseph] H. **The Social Medicine of Old Age**. 1948

Shock, N[athan] W., editor. **Perspectives in Experimental Gerontology**. 1966

Tibbitts, Clark, editor. **Social Contribution by the Aging**. 1952

Tibbitts, Clark and Wilma Donahue, editors. **Social and Psychological Aspects of Aging**. 1962

U.S. Dept. of Health, Education, and Welfare. **Working With Older People**. 1970

Vischer, A[dolf] L[ucas]. **Old Age**. 1947

Welford, A[lan] T[raviss], and James E. Birren, editors. **Decision Making and Age**. 1969

Williams, Richard H., Clark Tibbitts, and Wilma Donahue, editors. **Processes of Aging**. 1963